Information Technology for Pharmacists

Information Technology for Pharmacists

Richard Fisher

BSc, MRPharmS

Consultant
Synapse Consulting Limited
Wigan, UK

London • Chicago **Pharmaceutical Press**

Published by the Pharmaceutical Press
Publications division of the Royal Pharmaceutical Society of Great Britain

1 Lambeth High Street, London SE1 7JN, UK
100 South Atkinson Road, Suite 206, Grayslake, IL 60030-7820, USA

© Pharmaceutical Press 2006

 is a trademark of Pharmaceutical Press

First published 2006
Typeset by MCS Publishing Services Ltd, Salisbury, Wiltshire
Printed in Great Britain by TJ International, Padstow, Cornwall

ISBN 0 85369 577 6

A catalogue record for this book is available from the British Library.

Contents

Preface

There is no shortage of books on the different aspects of computing and information technology (IT). However, many of them are specific to a particular topic and assume that the reader has an overall understanding of IT in general. One of the main reasons for writing this book, as with any subject, is to explain the basics so that the reader can build on their basic understanding. Thus the purpose of this book is to give the reader the necessary information to make informed decisions relating to all aspects of information technology. What is information technology? It is the term used to describe all the products and activities related to the computer and telecommunications industry. One of the main aims of this book is to explain the terminology and jargon used in relation to IT. Wherever possible new terms or jargon will be explained in the text, but because there are so many acronyms used in IT a glossary has been included as a quick reference. Although this is comprehensive in the context of this book, it cannot cover every aspect of IT. Thus, the reader is encouraged to purchase additional IT-related books, such as the *New Penguin Dictionary of Computing*, if the contents of this book and the glossary do not provide an explanation of the term used. The early chapters explain the fundamental components and tasks of computer systems and how they are used. The later chapters deal with all the issues relating to the procurement, implementation, training and support of computer systems.

One of the most important facts to grasp about computers is that they are merely tools that are used to help perform a particular function in a bigger overall system. Take, for example, the computer labelling systems used in a dispensary. The labelling system is a tool – albeit a very important one – that is used in the overall process of dispensing drugs to patients. One of the requirements of the labelling tool is that it produces labels with the relevant information both quickly and efficiently. If it does not, then the whole system – i.e. the dispensing process – grinds to a halt, with the obvious consequences. The labelling system is a specialised tool that consists of both hardware and software, which are totally dependent on each other. The software has been designed to meet the specific labelling requirements of the dispensing process in mind, and in common with all tools it must be designed around the function it is seeking to enhance, thereby making it more efficient. All too often business processes are designed around computer systems, and as a result fail to deliver any benefit. Even if the tool has been well designed to fit in with the overall process, it is still possible that it will not provide the desired benefits. For example, the labelling system is itself composed of many different elements, and if any part of it fails, such as the hardware or the software, then the system as a whole fails. Often it is the issues surrounding the use and management of the computer system that result in its failing or not providing the required benefits. Many of these issues revolve around the staff who use the IT systems, such as education and training, which are all too often not properly or adequately covered. It is very common when buying or procuring IT systems to only take into account the cost of the hardware and software, when in fact the majority of the costs relate to the implementation and the training of staff. It is essential, therefore, that when computer systems are introduced their implementation should be planned and the appropriate resources identified and allocated to cover all aspects of its installation. With the changing role of pharmacists many of the computer systems in place will have to be modified and upgraded to cope with the new practices. This will require modifications to software, which can take months or even years, as detailed systems analysis needs to be carried out if the final software and system are to meet the end requirements of the ultimate system. It is very important for pharmacists to understand the impact of computer systems on the overall processes they will use to fulfil their new roles.

The rate at which IT has progressed and is still progressing means that the majority of people use and rely on technology to carry out many aspects of their life, both at work and at home. Training and education on how IT can be used to enhance their role should be seen as an essential part of a pharmacist's continuing professional development. In the final analysis, it is the people who use IT systems who will determine their success or failure. Hopefully this book can explain and educate the reader on some of the basics of IT and remove some of the mystique that surrounds it.

Richard Fisher
August 2005

About the author

After studying pharmacy at Manchester University the author completed his preregistration year in 1975 at Preston Royal Infirmary, and decided to get experience of the three major sectors of pharmacy at the time, namely hospital, industry and community. During his time in industry the author received his first exposure to computers, and after moving to community pharmacy, which was at the time when personal computers such as the BBC Micro were being used to generate dispensary labels, realised the potential for computers and their ability to manipulate and disseminate information. He left retail and studied systems analysis and design for 6 months, and since that time has been employed in the healthcare IT industry, working for various companies supplying IT solutions to healthcare-related organisations. Latterly he has worked as an independent IT consultant for the RPSGB and other healthcare-related organisations. During his 21 years in the IT industry he has performed regular locums in community pharmacy to keep in touch with the 'coal face', and has recently taken up part-time employment as a primary care pharmacist.

1

Fundamentals

PC terminology

One of the problems with information technology (IT) is the terminology and jargon used. As with any subject, it is essential to understand the basics. This section will help the reader to understand the fundamental components of a PC, and their function. Before the components are described one of the most fundamental and important aspects, which has a major bearing on the operation of the computer, needs to be explained: memory. Computers operate by manipulating and moving data stored in memory. Memory is the term used to describe devices that store information, and its size is measured in bytes. There are two main types of memory: volatile and permanent. A PC will have a certain amount of volatile memory, the contents of which are lost when the power is switched off. In a PC this memory is supplied as a separate module, known as memory module, and is plugged into the memory slot of the main PC circuit board. There are different types of memory module, depending on how the memory is arranged on the module (Figure 1.1).

It will also have a much larger amount of permanent memory which is not lost when the power is switched off. The hard disk and CD-ROMs are examples of devices that have permanent memory. Volatile memory is more expensive than permanent memory. It is also much faster to manipulate the contents of volatile memory than those of permanent memory. Permanent memory is analogous to a person's memories, which can be recalled when required. Volatile memory is analogous to the brain's ability to take in new information and recall events from permanent memory, manipulate the information and then store it in permanent memory for later use.

Bits, bytes and kilobytes

Why is it important to understand what bits and bytes are? Memory size is measured in bytes and multiples of bytes. Computers move and store information as a series of bits and use binary numbering to operate.

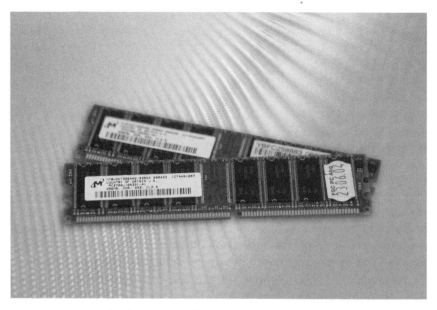

Figure 1.1 Example of memory modules.
[Courtesy of Chris Elmes]

Therefore, in terms of computing, the lowest level of information is a bit. Think of it as a switch that can be on or off, i.e. 'on' is represented by 1 and 'off' by 0. The bit is the fundamental unit of information in computing.

As a bit can only store 1 or 0, eight bits (a byte) are grouped together to represent the binary numbers 0000000–11111111, or decimal 0–255 (Table 1.1).

Therefore, the binary number 10101010 would represent the decimal number 170:

```
Byte (8 bits)    1    0    1    0    1    0    1    0
Decimal        128   +0  +32   +0   +8   +0   +2   +0   =   170.
```

Think of a byte as being able to represent one letter of the alphabet or a numerical character. When text is stored on a computer one byte is used

Table 1.1 Binary-based number system

Position	8	7	6	5	4	3	2	1
Binary	1	1	1	1	1	1	1	1
Decimal equivalent	128	64	32	16	8	4	2	1
Sum = 255								

Table 1.2 Conversions between different units of memory

Unit	Equivalence	Notes
8 bits	1 byte	1 byte can represent the decimal numbers from 0 to 255
1024 bytes	1 kilobyte	Normally referred to as 1 k or 1 kb
1024 kilobytes	1 megabyte	$1024 \times 1024 = 1\,048\,576$ bytes, normally referred to as 1 megabyte or Mb
1024 megabytes	1 gigabyte	Referred to as Gb

to store one character of text (the standard normally used to define the sequence of binary digits or its decimal equivalent is the American Standard Code for Information Interchange – ASCII).

Since the early days of computing, the byte has become the fundamental unit of measurement. Table 1.2 gives the conversions between the different memory units.

Note: Normally the word kilo refers to 1000, but in computing it refers to 1024, which is the nearest number to 1000 based on the binary numbers.

Files

Files – the basic 'containers' in which the computer stores data – are measured by the number of bytes each contains. When a computer connects to the internet, for example, data is moved from one computer to another. The speed at which this data is moved is measured in bytes per second. The larger the size of the file being manipulated or moved, the longer it will take to get the data from one computer to the other. For example, whenever a computer is connected to the internet using a web browser, data is moved from the website computer to the local computer. The rate at which it can be moved will be determined by the amount to be moved and the speed of the link. The speed is measured in bytes per second.

It is not uncommon for picture files to be 3 or 4 megabytes (Mb) in size. This means that approximately 3 million bytes of information need to be manipulated or moved. These files are often sent as attachments to emails. If the size of the attachment is relatively small, e.g. 50 kb (the size of a four-page Word document without graphics embedded), the download will take a few seconds. If the file is 5 Mb it will take 1024 times as long. Therefore, if it takes 10 seconds to transfer 50 kb of data, it will take 17 minutes to transfer 5 Mb.

All PCs store data in files, and the operating system is responsible for ensuring that each one has a unique name. Storing information in files is fundamental to the way the computer operates, therefore there are facilities that allow the user to view, copy, delete and move files. In Windows this facility is known as Windows Explorer, which can be configured to display the size of each of the files. There are many thousands of files on a typical PC. Files are stored in folders, which are analogous to the drawers of a filing cabinet. The folders can have additional folders placed within them, and these are known as subfolders. Subfolders are analogous to the dividers within the drawer of a filing cabinet. Subfolders can then be further subdivided ad infinitum. This makes files far easier to organise and locate.

Windows Explorer (Figure 1.2) displays a window which is split into two. The left-hand window displays devices such as the hard disk drives and CD-ROM and the folder structure. Folders are shown by displaying a 'folder icon'. Clicking a 'Folder Icon' in the left-hand window will show all the subfolders and files in the right-hand window.

Data transfer over a network

The impact of moving large files can be seen when connecting to the internet using the telephone line. Transfer of data when connecting using a normal modem at maximum transfer rates of 56 kb per second (kbps) will take a relatively long time. If connected via ADSL or cable the speeds will be much quicker (download speed of 512 kbps; see Telephones lines and modems).

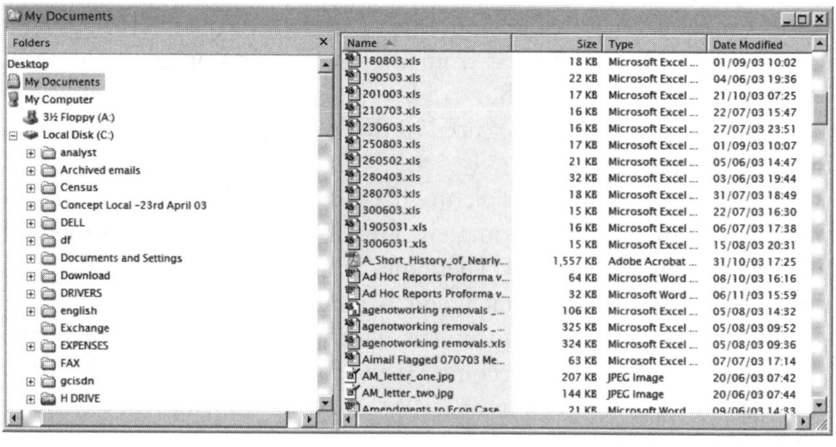

Figure 1.2 Windows Explorer.

Note: Sometimes the speed at which data is moved can be quoted in bytes and sometimes in bits. Be careful not to confuse the two. Figures quoted in bytes are approximately eight times faster than speeds quoted in bits (or kilobits, i.e. 1024 bits).

The data transfer occurs in the background and the user sometimes has no visual indication that it is taking place, giving the perception that the computer has crashed or is not working. This is one of the reasons why it is important to have some awareness of the amount of data being manipulated by the computer (Figure 1.3).

Data transfer within a computer

All computers work by moving data stored in memory to the central processing unit (CPU). This is why the memory size of a computer, quoted in megabytes (Mb), combined with the speed of the processor determines the performance of the PC. In general the more volatile memory installed in a PC and the faster the central processor, the faster a task can be undertaken.

Before the CPU of a computer can manipulate the data it fetches that data from permanent memory and loads it into volatile memory. It is then manipulated according to the instructions (programs), which have also been loaded from permanent memory. If the program then needs to save data it will transfer it from volatile to permanent memory.

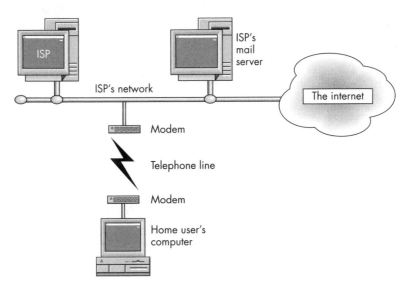

Figure 1.3 Email user requests email with attachments.

If a computer crashes or the power fails, all the data in volatile memory is immediately lost as it has not been saved to permanent memory by the operating system (Figure 1.4).

Having explained how a computer stores data, the function of the different parts and devices that make up a computer can be described. Personal computers (PCs) will be described separately from personal digital assistants (PDAs), as the hardware components are very different even though, fundamentally, PCs and PDAs work in exactly the same way.

Personal computer (PC)

Most personal computers consist of a monitor, base unit, keyboard and mouse. The base unit (or case) contains all the major components that make up the computer (Figure 1.5).

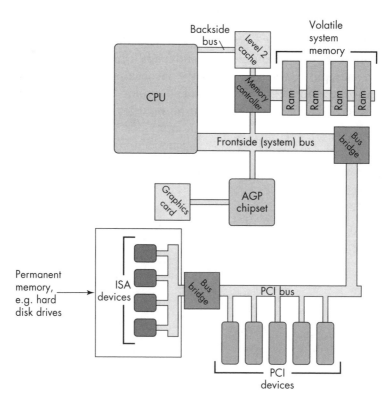

Figure 1.4 Diagram of computer schematics.

Figure 1.5 Desktop computer, monitor, mouse and keyboard.
[Courtesy of Chris Elmes]

Monitors (VDUs)

Monitors, also known as VDUs (video display units), come in many different sizes. The size is determined by measuring the distance diagonally from top left to bottom right of the screen. The quality of the picture is determined by the number of pixels (dots) on the screen and the software used to display the picture, but generally the more pixels per square inch the better the picture (also known as the resolution).

For personal use, a minimum size of 14″ is required; 17″ and 19″ are better if the computer is used frequently throughout the day. The bigger the screen, the more expensive the monitor.

Monitors are based on two major technologies, cathode ray tube (CRT) (Figure 1.6) and liquid crystal display (LCD) (Figure 1.7). Monitors based on CRT are much bulkier than those based on LCD, so if space is limited consider an LCD screen. However, LCD screens are roughly three times the price of CRT screens. The monitor represents about 15% of the cost of a PC if purchased with a CRT and 30% if based on an LCD. The monitor can be purchased separately, and so can easily be upgraded.

Figure 1.6 CRT monitor.
[Courtsey of Chris Elmes]

Figure 1.7 LCD monitor.
[Courtesy of Chris Elmes]

TFT screens are a type of LCD, so you may see the abbreviation used interchangeably.

Some monitors will have speakers built into them, so that separate speakers are not necessary.

Note on the costs of equipment: Prices quoted are based on the prices in 2004 and are given as a guide only. For comparison, the average rate for a locum pharmacist in 2004 was approximately £20 per hour. The cost of electronic equipment tends to fall significantly over time, and so the prices quoted will quickly be out of date. However, they are given so that the relative costs of different types of equipment can be compared.

Typical prices of monitors, including VAT:
17″ CRT between £90 and £120
19″ CRT between £170 and £200
15″ TFT between £220 and £330
17″ TFT between £310 and £360.

The monitor is connected to the base unit by a special monitor cable (see Graphics adapter, below). It also has its own power supply, as it consumes a large amount of power.

Case/base unit

The case or base unit houses the main components of the computer. There is space in the base unit for a power supply, a motherboard and all the drives (hard disk, floppy disk and CD-ROM or DVD). The motherboard is used to connect all the components together. The base unit can be a desktop unit which is designed so that the monitor sits on top. However, these days tower units, which are designed to sit under the desk, are more common. Most base units will have a master power switch at the back in addition to a power button on the front. There is also a reset button, which is used to reboot the computer in the event that a program malfunctions and freezes the computer. Most cases will also have a number of LEDs to indicate that the computer is switched on and when the hard disk is being accessed.

Motherboard

Inside the base unit are the power supply and motherboard. The power supply distributes power to all the components on the motherboard at the correct voltage levels. When the computer is switched on the circuits produce a large amount of heat. Cooling fans are built into the case and on to the CPU to prevent the computer from overheating.

The motherboard is the main printed circuit board within the base unit and contains all the principal electronic components that make up the computer. Some of the components are fixed on the board and cannot be removed, e.g. communication ports. Others, such as the microprocessor, memory and disk drives, plug into the motherboard. In addition there are slots for small expansion boards, such as graphics cards, which connect to the monitor and produce the picture. Figure 1.8 looks complicated and it is not necessary to understand the function of each component. It is shown so that the reader can put into perspective the components that make up the modern PC. The different components that are built into and plug into the motherboard to make up a PC will now be described.

Graphics adapter

The graphics adapter is a card that plugs into a specific slot in the motherboard and has a port into which the monitor cable is plugged. The cost can vary from under £30 to many hundreds of pounds. The reason for this large variance is the functionality built into the card. The more expensive cards are needed for graphics-intensive applications, e.g. video editing, where large amounts of data are required to be processed to manipulate pictures. For normal business applications, such as word processing and spreadsheets, a basic card is more than adequate.

Figure 1.8 PC internals of a PC computer showing the motherboard (components removed).
[Courtesy of Chris Elmes]

The monitor is connected to the graphics adapter with a special graphics cable, as shown in Figure 1.9.

Communication ports

The communication ports are used to connect peripherals (e.g. printers) to the computer. They are known as communication ports because data flows between the computer and the peripheral connected via the port. These peripherals can be anything that needs to send or receive data to or from the CPU, such as keyboards, mice and printers.

The different types of communication port will be described separately. Until recently, these were all sockets into which cables were plugged and connected to the other device. Recently, non-physical methods of connecting peripherals together have been introduced, such as infrared and wireless. This is particularly relevant when there is more than one computer in a location that need to share resources, such as the telephone line and printers (e.g. for home networking). Refer to the section on networking for more details on why this is useful. In the past the communication ports were provided as separate boards that plugged into the expansion slots, but it is becoming more common for these to be provided on the motherboard.

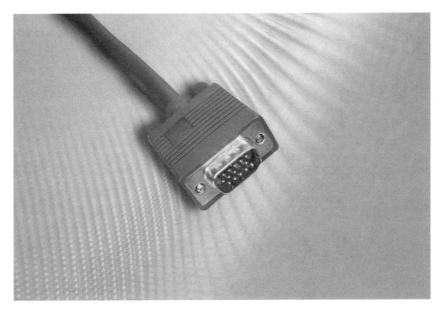

Figure 1.9 Graphics cable.
[Courtesy of Chris Elmes]

Keyboard and mouse connections

Most motherboards have dedicated ports for keyboards and mice (Figure 1.10). On modern computers these are known as PS2 connections and are colour coded (green for a mouse and mauve for the keyboard). On older computers they are larger and are known as DIN connectors. It is now possible to get keyboards and mice that connect by other methods, such as USB (see below), infrared and wireless.

Serial and parallel ports

A *serial port* (also known as an RS232 port) is either a nine- or a 25-pin D connector (Figure 1.11). On modern computers they are normally nine pins, each of which can be connected to a separate wire. Even though there are nine pins, only three wires are necessary to communicate with other peripherals and data is sent as a stream of bits, which are then combined into bytes by the software on each computer or peripheral. These ports tend to be relatively slow and are being superseded by USB ports (see below), which are much faster and automatically configured on later versions of the Windows operating system. The serial port can be identified by a symbol of zeroes and ones (10101) next to the port.

Figure 1.10 Keyboard and mouse communications port.
[Courtesy of Chris Elmes]

Parallel (printer) port

Serial port

Monitor (graphics) port

Figure 1.11   Serial, parallel and monitor ports.
[Courtesy of Chris Elmes]

Parallel ports are 25-pin D connectors and use eight wires to send data, rather than just one in a serial port. This means that the parallel port can transfer data much more quickly than a serial port. Cables tend to be thicker than serial cables, as more wires are required. They are normally used to connect printers to the computer, but like serial ports are being superseded by USB. The parallel port is identified by a small printer symbol above or below it, as it is invariably used to connect a printer to the computer.

Universal serial bus (USB)

USB is a standard which allows peripherals to communicate with the computer and was developed because of the limitations of serial and parallel ports. It is built into the motherboard of modern computers, but can be provided on an expansion card for older computers. There are currently three different USB standards that support different transfer rates. USB 1.0 supports transfer rates of 1.5 megabits per second, whereas USB 1.1 supports speeds of 12 megabits per second. Recently USB 2.0 has been introduced which supports speeds of 480 megabits per second (Mbps) and is used for high-performance devices such as high-quality video-conferencing cameras, high-resolution scanners and high-density storage devices. Until USB was introduced, these types of device had to use Firewire (see below) to obtain the transfer rates required. USB 2.0 supports old USB 1.0/1.1 software and peripherals; however, the

USB port on the computer must support USB 2.0 if transfer rates of 480 megabits are to be achieved (Figure 1.12).

The USB cable can (but not always) supply power to low-power devices such as cameras, thereby removing the need for a separate power supply. Many new peripherals, such as printers, keyboards and mice, are manufactured to connect to the computer via a USB port. Peripherals can be daisy-chained, i.e. connected together with cables that resemble a chain. This enables several devices to connect to one USB port on the computer (if they have an input and an output USB port), allowing multiple peripherals to be connected to a single USB port.

Some small devices, such as cameras and phones, have a smaller port known as a USB Mini B and are supplied with a cable which has a Mini B connector on one end and a normal-sized USB connector on the other (Figure 1.13).

One of the main advantages of USB is that (in the latest versions of Windows, e.g. Windows XP) when they are plugged in the operating system automatically detects that the device is connected and so it can be used immediately. This is referred to as 'plug and play'. Pen Drives (see later) use a USB connector to connect to the computer.

For more information on USB go to www.usb.org and click on the FAQ (frequently asked questions) link.

Figure 1.12 USB and network ports.
[Courtesy of Chris Elmes]

Figure 1.13   USB standard and mini connector.
[Courtesy of Chris Elmes]

Firewire (IEEE 1394)

Firewire ports are serial ports which are similar in function to USB but their transfer rate is much faster than USB 1.0/1.1, so they are used for devices that need a very high throughput, such as camcorders. However, with the advent of USB 2.0 they are competing in the same market. They do not require a separate power lead, as power is provided by the computer provided a six-wire connector is used. As with USB, two sizes of plug are in use, four-wire (smaller plug) and six-wire (Figure 1.14). Any device which has a four-wire connector will have to provide its own power using a separate lead.

Wireless

Wireless communications encompass a number of different technologies, such as infrared, Bluetooth and radio. They are mainly used on laptops (see below), as they are normally used for transferring data between computers and portable devices such as mobile phones and PDAs. These devices can be built into the motherboard but are usually provided on expansion cards. However, in many instances they are separate devices that plug into the computer via a USB or network port.

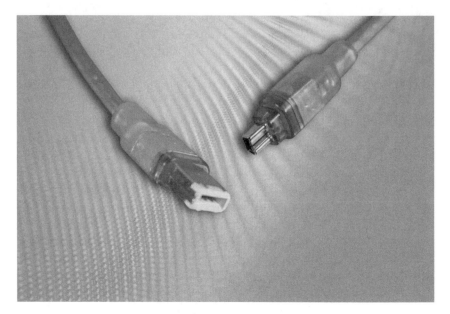

Figure 1.14 Firewire – 4 wire and 6 wire connectors. [Courtesy of Chris Elmes]

Network port

On older computers network ports were always provided on separate expansion cards. On modern computers, because of the importance of networking (see section on Networking, below), they are usually built into the motherboard and are almost always female RJ45 sockets which allow computers to be networked using cables with male RJ45 connectors (Figure 1.15). Computers in the business environment are nearly always networked to each other by connecting to a network hub, so that standard cables can be used, and as many computers as there are ports can be connected together.

Audio and microphone ports

Audio and microphone ports (Figure 1.16) are specialised communication devices that are built into the PC's soundcard. This allows the computer to play sound from WAV, MP3 or MIDI files or music from a CD-ROM. Audio ports can be built into the motherboard or provided on a separate card that slots into the motherboard. The PC's speakers plug into the audio port and the microphone port allows a microphone

Figure 1.15 Network RJ45 connectors male – female.
[Courtesy of Chris Elmes]

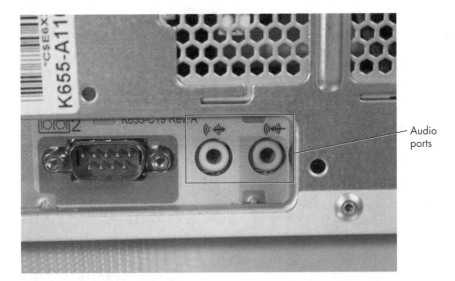

Figure 1.16 PCs audio ports.
[Courtesy of Chris Elmes]

to be connected, enabling sounds to be recorded. On some sound cards there is also an input port, which allows other sound devices (such as cassette players) to be connected to the computer.

Central processing unit (CPU)

The CPU (Figure 1.17) is the heart of the computer and interprets the instructions (programs) brought from the memory via a pathway known as the processor bus. It is plugged into the motherboard and cooled by a fan to prevent it overheating. The CPU works in a strict tempo, like a clock. One instruction is processed every clock cycle. One clock cycle is equivalent to 1 Hertz (Hz). The CPU processes millions of cycles per second (1 000 000 Hz = 1 Megahertz (MHz)). The higher the megahertz value the faster the CPU can manipulate the instructions and hence the faster the applications will run. Systems will be advertised as 900 MHz or 2.5 gigahertz (GHz), which is 2500 MHz. However, a key consideration is the amount of memory in the computer. If there is too little memory, the CPU will spend the majority of its time swapping data between the virtual memory (see Glossary) on the hard disk and the volatile memory on the motherboard.

Figure 1.17 Central processing unit (CPU) and heat sink.
[Courtesy of Chris Elmes]

Applications that move large amounts of data, e.g. games and picture manipulation programs, such as Adobe Photoshop, require large amounts of memory and processor time. If the main use of the computer is for these types of applications then buy a PC with a higher CPU speed and a large amount of memory. However, the faster the CPU, the more expensive the overall cost. Thus the choice should be made with reference to the applications that are going to be used on the PC and the budget available. CPUs for PCs are made by a limited number of companies, examples being the Pentium processor manufactured by Intel and the Athlon processor made by AMD.

Memory

Before a computer can manipulate data that data must first be loaded from a storage device such as a disk drive into the memory plugged into the motherboard. The CPU has to move data backwards and forwards from the disk to the memory. Generally speaking, the amount of memory has a significant effect on the performance of the computer, as outlined in the CPU section. When the power is switched off all the data in memory on the motherboard is lost, but can be saved on the disk drives as files. A file is a data structure or container that holds a specific number of bytes and is given a unique name. When a computer is switched on, programs (applications) and data are loaded from the numerous files on the disk drives into the memory on the motherboard.

The minimum amount of memory that should be purchased is 256 Mb. There are many different types of memory, which work at different speeds that must be matched to the motherboard. It is essential if purchasing additional memory for a PC that the correct specification is obtained.

Disk drives

Disk drives are memory storage devices that hold permanent copies of data and programs on rotating disks. There are different types of drive, the main differences between them being the capacity and the speed at which the data can be written. It is part of the job of the operating system (e.g. Windows) to store data associated with different applications in discrete files on the disk drives. These files can be created, copied and deleted by the application via the operating system.

Floppy disk drives take floppy disks (removable memory storage devices), which are flexible plastic disks coated with a magnetic oxide and protected by a rigid plastic outer cover (originally these were flex-ible, hence the name floppy) (Figure 1.18). Because the disk is remov-able it is used to store copies of data, e.g. documents and programs, stored as files that can be transferred to another computer. Many more flexible methods now exist for transferring files, such as Pen Drives, CD-ROMs and email.

Only 1.44 Mb can be stored on each disk. Many programs and documents (especially ones containing graphics) are much larger than this, so other devices with more capacity are now used. Whereas in older PCs a floppy disk drive was fitted as standard, many modern PCs are supplied without a floppy disk drive. Pen Drives, which have a much greater capacity and convenience, are used instead. These simply plug into a USB port.

The floppy disks rotate much more slowly than hard disk drives (300 revolutions per minute) and consequently the data transfer rate is much slower.

Hard disk drives are invariably fixed and cannot be seen from the outside of the PC, although it is possible to make them removable. They are known as hard disks because they consist of multiple metal disks (platters) of rotating (10 000 revolutions per minute) magnetic material

Figure 1.18 Floppy disk drive and floppy disk.
[Courtesy of Chris Elmes]

sealed inside the hard disk housing. This allows them to store much more information, and the capacity of modern PC drives ranges from 20 to 200 gigabytes (Gb; a gigabyte is 1024 megabytes, Mb).

Not many years ago 1 Gb was considered large, but as applications and the data they store increase in size the space is soon consumed. However, as with memory, so long as you do not intend to store large numbers of big files such as pictures and video, then 40 Gb is more than adequate. In addition to its capacity, the other key characteristic of the hard disk is the speed at which data can be read from or written to it – up to 20 Mb per second.

One other consideration is that the more data you store, the more you have to back up in the event of disk drive failure (see Chapter 10 on backup). It will take approximately 710 floppy disks or two CD-ROMs to back up 1 Gb of hard disk. Hard disk drives work to very high tolerances: the read/write head floats above the platter and must not come into contact with the surface. If it does it will result in a head crash, leading to loss of all data and rendering the drive useless. Because of this, hard disk drives are manufactured as sealed units, which prevents dust particles entering (Figure 1.19).

Figure 1.19 Hard disk drive with the sealed cover removed.
[Courtesy of Chris Elmes]

Hard disks have to be formatted so that the operating system and programs can be stored on them. When the computer is switched on a small program on the motherboard automatically loads the operating system from the hard disk.

Compact disk (CD) drives

Compact disks or CDs have evolved from being read-only media to read or write, hence the numerous different types of CD. Compact disks consist of a plastic disk which stores data in small pits which can be read by a laser. Each disk can store up to 650 Mb of data (equivalent to 400 floppy disks), which is one of the reasons why CDs have replaced floppies as a storage method. When an application is purchased, e.g. Microsoft Office, it will always be supplied on a CD because of the vast number and size of the files needed to install the application on the PC (Figure 1.20).

Because CDs evolved from audio compact disks the speed is quoted as a multiple of the reading speed of an audio disk (e.g. 24×).

There are a number of different types of drive. Compact disk read-only memory – *CD-ROM* – can only read CDs. *CD-R* (compact disk

Figure 1.20 CD-ROM drive and CD-ROM.
[Courtesy of Chris Elmes]

recordable write once) allow data to be written to a CD-R disk. Data can only be added to free space on the disk, i.e. when the disk is full no more data can be written to it, in contrast to CD-RW (compact disk read–write), on which existing data can be overwritten. The drives use different technology to write the data, therefore the correct type of disk for the CD drive in the PC should be purchased. CD-RW disks are more expensive than CD-R disks. However, most modern CD-ROM drives can read CDs recorded from both CD-R and CD-RW drives.

Drives can now be purchased that combine the functionality of all types into one drive. The description of the drive will be 52 × 24 × 52 CD-R/RW, which is the speed at which the drive operates (speed 52× write, 24× rewrite, 52× read).

DVD drives

Digital versatile disks are visually the same size as compact disks but have a much greater storage capacity, at least 4.7 Gb. They were originally used to store movies (and were called digital video disks), but like CDs have been adapted for use with computers. There are three writeable versions of DVD, DVD-RW, DVD +RW and DVD DVD-RAM, which can be written to many times. Combination drives are available which can write and read both CDs and DVDs. Because of their enormous capacity DVDs are useful for backing up large volumes of data. As with CDs it is important to obtain the correct type of disk for the DVD writer installed in the computer.

Modems/adapters

Modems (which can be internal or external) permit computers to communicate with each other via the public telephone network (Figure 1.21). The term is short for 'modulator/demodulator' and its function is to take a digital signal from the computer and convert it into an analogue one that can be transmitted down a conventional telephone line. The modem at the other end of the line then converts the analogue signal back into a digital one. The term modem is sometimes incorrectly used to describe modern devices that use digital signals to communicate over the telephone network (e.g. ADSL modems), but these should more correctly be described as adapters.

Analogue modem   The analogue modem is connected to the telephone socket by a lead, which normally has an RJ11 connector that plugs into the modem, and a phone jack which plugs into the standard telephone

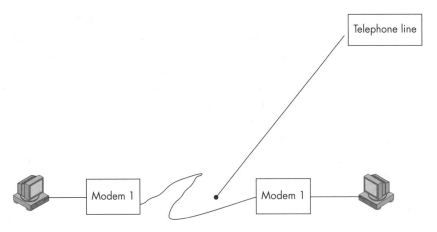

Figure 1.21 Computers communicating via modems.

socket. The majority of computers that connect to the internet do so via a modem (refer to the section on Networking for more information on how this is achieved). The speed of the modem will determine how quickly the computer can communicate with the internet. The maximum speed at which a standard analogue modem can communicate over the normal telephone system is 56 kilobits per second. Internet pages which have a lot of graphics, or large files, can be quite slow to download.

Analogue modems are used daily in community pharmacies to transmit drug orders to the wholesalers.

ISDN adapter Faster speeds can be achieved by using an ISDN modem, but a special ISDN telephone line has to be installed by the telephone company. This line has two channels, each with a speed of 64 kilobits per second, enabling a speed of 128 kilobits per second. However, when both channels are used each is charged separately, which can be expensive. BT's Highway is an ISDN-enabled product. This is being superceded by ADSL.

ADSL (broadband) ADSL adapters allow much quicker speeds than either analogue or ISDN modems. An ADSL telephone line is required, but has the advantage that it can be permanently connected to the internet (so called 'always on') and can be simultaneously used for voice calls. ADSL is not available on all telephone exchanges, so availability will depend on the geographical location of the line.

The download speed is normally twice the upload speed, but this is perfectly acceptable as more data is usually received than is sent. The download speed is normally 512 kilobits per second and upload 128 kilobits per second, however faster speeds are being introduced.

Cable modems (broadband)   A cable modem allows households with cable television and telephones to connect to other computers (i.e. the internet) via the same cable as is used to provide television pictures. These links are very high-speed connections but are normally in one direction only – downstream, i.e. from television station to home TV. Data is sent upstream by using the telephone facilities in the cable TV package, which is available when cable TV is purchased. Downstream speeds of 20 Mbps can be achieved. However, because the line is used for television data as well, the downstream speed is normally limited to 500 kilobits per second and so is roughly equivalent to an ADSL connection.

Operating systems

The components described above are the main constituents of a modern computer. However, before they can be of any use they must have software that allows them all to communicate with each other. This is known as the operating system, and it monitors and controls the input to and output from the computer. For example, when a key is pressed on the keyboard, it is the operating system that determines how that key is handled in relation to the other events taking place in the PC. It is the operating system that reads and writes data from the disk drives and communication ports. Thus when choosing a computer the operating system is a key consideration. The operating system is sometimes referred to as system software to distinguish it from the application software, which is created to perform a specific function, e.g. word processor. Application software must be written for the operating system on which it is going to be installed and used.

There are two main types of user interface by which people interact with the computer.

1.   **Command line/character based**   A character or command line-based interface is one in which the only way the user can interact (navigate) with the computer is by typing characters on the keyboard. The video display uses predefined characters which are mainly those displayed on the keyboard (Figure 1.22).
2.   **Graphical user interface (GUI)**   A graphical user interface is one in which the user interacts with the computer primarily by using a pointing device such as a mouse (Figure 1.23). The video display uses graphics and icons and is generally much easier for an inexperienced user to learn and navigate.

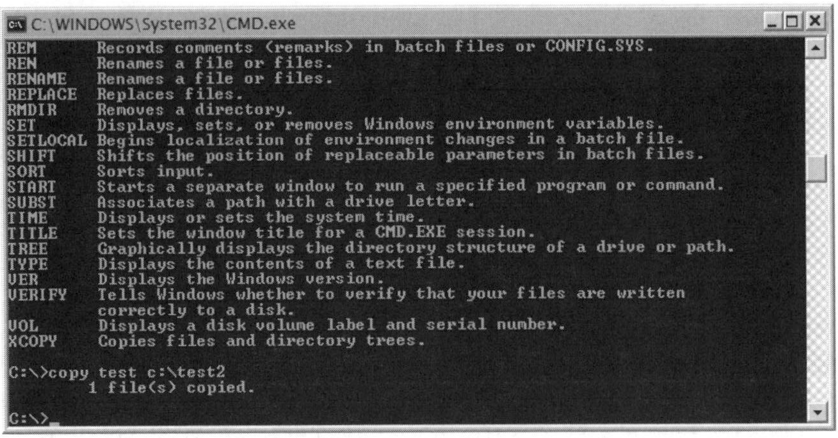

```
C:\WINDOWS\System32\CMD.exe                                    _ □ x
REM        Records comments (remarks) in batch files or CONFIG.SYS.
REN        Renames a file or files.
RENAME     Renames a file or files.
REPLACE    Replaces files.
RMDIR      Removes a directory.
SET        Displays, sets, or removes Windows environment variables.
SETLOCAL   Begins localization of environment changes in a batch file.
SHIFT      Shifts the position of replaceable parameters in batch files.
SORT       Sorts input.
START      Starts a separate window to run a specified program or command.
SUBST      Associates a path with a drive letter.
TIME       Displays or sets the system time.
TITLE      Sets the window title for a CMD.EXE session.
TREE       Graphically displays the directory structure of a drive or path.
TYPE       Displays the contents of a text file.
VER        Displays the Windows version.
VERIFY     Tells Windows whether to verify that your files are written
           correctly to a disk.
VOL        Displays a disk volume label and serial number.
XCOPY      Copies files and directory trees.

C:\>copy test c:\test2
        1 file(s) copied.

C:\>_
```

Figure 1.22 Example of a character-based interface.

Until the late 1980s the only interface available was the command line type.

Common operating systems

Microsoft Windows By far the most popular operating system for PCs is Microsoft Windows. Many versions of this have been released since the original in the early 1990s. These include Windows 95, Windows 98, Windows Millennium, Windows NT, and the latest version Windows XP. Each version has additional functionality built in. Although strictly speaking the operating system is only concerned with controlling input and output, as outlined above, it will be delivered with various general-purpose applications, such as Notepad (a very basic word processor) and other simple applications. Version naming, in Windows, is further complicated by the fact that different options are available for the same version. For example, Windows XP is available as both the professional version (which is more expensive) and the home version. The professional version is aimed at organisations that have a number of PCs to administer and maintain.

The other applications that are 'bundled' with the Windows operating system are found mainly under the Accessories menu. Some of the more significant applications are:

- Outlook Express (an email application which is a cut-down version of Outlook)
- Internet Explorer (an application used to browse the internet)

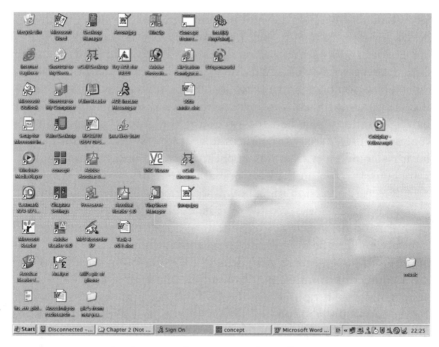

Figure 1.23   Graphical user interface – Microsoft Windows.

- Word Pad (a basic word processor which is more sophisticated than Notepad but not as sophisticated as Word, Microsoft's premier word processing application and part of the Microsoft Office suite of programs
- Windows Explorer (an application which allows the user to manage files on the computer, e.g. move, copy, delete).

MacOS   The MacOS was the first commercially available GUI operating system produced by Apple Computers. Although it was the first – and in the opinion of many the best – it has not been as popular as Windows but does have dominance in certain sectors, such as the publishing and printing industry, because of its superior desktop publishing applications. As with all operating systems there are many different versions. All versions up to MacOS 9 were proprietary, i.e. they would only run on Apple hardware. MacOS X is based on Unix and will therefore run on hardware capable of running Unix. A comparison of XP and MacOS can be found at www.xvsxp.com.

There is a small enthusiastic group of people who believe the MacOS to be far superior to Windows even though Windows has the major share of the market.

Unix/Linux   Unix is a general-purpose operating system which was developed in the 1960s by Bell Laboratories. It was widely adopted by universities and its use spread rapidly around the world. The significant difference between Unix, Windows and MacOS is that Unix is not owned by a company and as such is 'free' to anybody wishing to use it. It was written specifically for programmers, and so was adopted mainly by organisations that had the necessary computing infrastructure to support its use, thereby becoming the operating system of choice in the business community. Various applications have been written by software houses to run on the Unix operating system.

Recently a version of Unix was developed specifically for the PC, called Linux, which is created and maintained by thousands of programmers on the internet. This has all the power of Unix but has a GUI interface and can be downloaded free from the internet under the terms of the GNU public licence (see Glossary for explanation of GNU). There are a number of commercial organisations that bundle up the operating system and applications under the GNU licence and charge a small fee for the cost of distribution on CD. Among the most popular distributors are Red Hat and SuSE Linux.

Many applications written for Linux are available at modest cost and have similar functionality to those written for Windows and MacOS. Therefore the cost of ownership can be much less than for Windows and MacOS. Although this is not much of an issue for a single user, when applied to businesses having perhaps hundreds of individual PCs the savings can be significant. It may be that in the future Linux will begin to challenge the market dominance of Windows.

The choice of operating system is therefore fairly limited, but some popular applications are available for more than one system. Take, for example, the Microsoft Office suite of applications. This consists of a word processor, spreadsheet, contact management and email, presentation, database and other programs. It is available for both Windows and MacOS, but not Linux.

Buying a PC

The various components of the modern PC can now be put into perspective. There are many companies that supply PCs and who will advertise in the media, primarily in newspapers, but also in the computer press and on television. They will describe their systems in a similar manner to those described in Table 1.3. Understanding the function of each of the components will allow an informed comparison to be made about different systems.

Table 1.3 Comparison of two PC systems

	System 1	*System 2*
Name	Dell™ Dimension™ 2400	Dell™ Dimension™ 4600
Processor	Intel® Celeron Processor 2.40 GHz	Intel® Pentium 4 Processor 2.66 GHz (512 kb cache)
Operating system and additional application packages	Microsoft® Windows XP Home Edition and Microsoft® Works 7.0	Microsoft® Windows XP Home Edition and Microsoft® Works 7.0
Memory	128 Mb (333 MHz) DDR RAM	256 MB dual-channel DDR (333 MHz) RAM
Hard drive	40 Gb IDE hard drive	80 Gb IDE hard drive
Monitor	15″ Colour monitor (13.8 vis, 0.28 dot pitch)	17″ flat panel monitor (17.0″ vis)
Network	Integrated 10/100 NIC	Integrated Intel Pro 10/100 NIC
Graphics card	Intel® Integrated Extreme Graphics	Intel® Integrated Extreme Graphics
Audio	Integrated audio	Integrated audio
CD-ROM	20/48× CD-ROM drive	20/48× CD-ROM drive

The cost of system 2 is nearly twice that of system 1. The foregoing text should have explained the difference between the two system specifications and why there is a difference in price.

The examples in Table 1.3 are given so that comparisons can be made between specification and price, and it is possible to buy systems that are more than twice the price of system 2. Some suppliers tailor the system to the specific requirements of the customer.

The specification of the PC will be determined by its use. Therefore, it is essential to make a list of the uses to which the PC is going to be put, in the same way that a buyer would when purchasing a car. However, when purchasing a car the basic function is to get from A to B. The choice of car is determined by secondary functions, such as the number of seats, comfort, performance, etc., but a PC is so versatile that it can be used for hundreds of basic functions.

The checklist in Table 1.4 can be used to determine what/where/ how the PC is going to be used.

Other equipment

The previous sections described the different components that make up a PC. There are many other pieces of equipment that may be purchased in addition. These will depend on the uses to which the computer is

Table 1.4 PC checklist

Prime use	*Notes*
Home	
Business	
Home/business	
Applications/functions required	
Word processor	
Spreadsheet	
Database	
Presentation software	
eMail	
Browse the internet	
Printing	
Creating music CDs	
Storing digital photgraphs	
Accounts	
Desktop publishing	
eBooks	
Single PC	
Use with other PCs	
Number of users	
When	
Where	
How	
Convenience	
Reliability	
Dependence backup	
Personal/business/corporate use	
Use	
Dedicated/multipurpose	
Networked or standalone	
Static/portable	
Work/home/both	

going to be put. Some will be essential, e.g. a printer, so that anything displayed on screen can be printed – email, letters, etc. Others will be optional. These other pieces of equipment are known as peripherals, as they do not form part of the main PC and can be bought from suppliers other than the manufacturer of the PC itself. All of them require a driver, a special piece of software that allows the operating system to communicate with the device, and will always be delivered with a CD-ROM containing the driver software. The peripheral is connected to the computer by one of the methods described above – serial or parallel port, USB or Firewire, or even wireless. If the peripheral is connected to a PC running a later version of the operating system, such as Windows XP, the computer will automatically detect that a new peripheral has been connected and prompt for the CD-ROM containing the driver software to be put into the CD drive. This is known as 'plug and play' equipment. If an earlier version of the operating system is used the driver software will have to be loaded manually by running the 'Setup' program on the CD.

Printers

Nearly all applications software provides a print function, so it is essential to have access to a printer. By far the majority of printers are designed to take stationery which is A4 or smaller. There are also specialist printers for specific functions such as label printing. The choice should be made taking into account the purchase cost, running costs, quality, and suitability for the application being used. Depending on the application, the computer may be supplied with more than one type of printer. For example, a computer used to produce labels in a community pharmacy may have one printer for printing labels and one for endorsing scripts.

Generally the printer is connected to the computer by a parallel or a serial cable, depending on the interface supplied on the printer. Recently printers have been introduced which connect to the PC via a USB interface.

It is possible to place a printer on a network, so that any PC on the network can use that printer, thereby reducing the need for one printer for each PC (see section on Networking).

Dot matrix printers   These printers have a print head that fires pins (normally 24) at the paper to make the shape of the characters. A ribbon impregnated with ink is placed between the print head and the paper. When the pins hit the ribbon the ink is transferred on to the paper, thus creating an image. The paper can be fed via tractors (sprockets) or in single sheets.

Dot matrix printers are the cheapest type to buy and run. Generally they will only print in black and the print quality is not very good, owing to the method by which the ink is transferred to the paper. Also, the image tends gradually to fade as the ribbon is a continuous loop and is constantly reused.

Because dot matrix printers can be used with continuous stationery they have been used to print dispensary labels. However, they are not really designed for this, and many problems can occur when they are used in this manner. Dot matrix printers are gradually being superseded by thermal transfer printers, which are specifically designed for the purpose of label printing.

Dot matrix printers are also used when more than one copy of a printout is required. Special multipart stationery is used in these situations.

Dot matrix printers tend to be noisy, and when being used to print large volumes require acoustic hoods to contain the noise.

Inkjet printers Inkjet printers are the most commonly used type for printing good-quality documents and will print in black and colour. They do not take continuous stationery and so cannot be used to print dispensary labels in an efficient manner. Inkjet printers have separate cartridges for black and the coloured inks. The colour cartridge is composed of three primary colours, which are combined to give any other colour. The image is formed by spraying the liquid ink at the paper. The ink then needs to dry, otherwise it will smudge, making inkjet printers slower than laser printers (see below).

Although the cost of inkjet printers is relatively low the cost of the ink cartridge can make them expensive to run. Many manufacturers set the price of the printers very low but the price of the replacement cartridges very high. When selecting a printer, be sure to take into account the ongoing running costs.

Laser printers Laser printers are high-speed printers which until recently printed only in black and white. They work in much the same way as photocopiers, the image being formed by electrostatic transfer of powder from the toner cartridge to the paper. The powder is then heated to set it. This is the reason why laser printers have to 'warm up' before they can start to print. Like inkjet printers, they cannot be used with continuous stationery. They are the most expensive printers to buy and run, but produce high-quality prints and can produce the pages much faster than inkjet and dot matrix printers. The toner cartridges are relatively expensive.

Recently the price of colour laser printers has started to fall, so that if colour is a requirement they can be considered instead of an inkjet. However, the running costs can be considerably higher.

Thermal printers Thermal printers are generally made for specialised functions such as label printing, and produce high-quality print. As they are specifically designed for printing labels they do not suffer from the problems associated with dot matrix printers, such as labels peeling off the backing and getting stuck on the roller. There are two types of thermal printer. *Thermal printers* work by heating up specially treated paper to form the image. One problem with this type of printer is that the image can fade as the label ages, especially when it is put in the fridge. Therefore these printers should not be used to produce dispensary labels.

Thermal transfer printers, on the other hand, work in much the same way as a dot matrix printer. These printers have special thermal ribbons. The print head transfers the pigment from the ribbon on to the paper or label using heat. Special paper is not required and the image produced is of high quality and does not fade with time. However, although they are more expensive to run than dot matrix label printers the quality is far superior and they are subject to fewer operational problems.

Running costs   Table 1.5 shows a comparison of the different types of printer and their running costs.

Scanners

A scanner is a device that can read text or illustrations printed on paper and translate the information into a form the computer can use (Figure 1.24). A scanner works by digitising an image and storing it in a bit map file on the computer. Once the image has been scanned the file can be manipulated with software to convert it into other file formats, such as GIF, JPEG or TIF, which are more efficient at storing the image, resulting in smaller file sizes.

Text stored as an image cannot be edited using a word processor. However, optical character recognition software can analyse the scanned image and convert any text to ASCII characters, which can be then manipulated in a word processor. Scanners are packaged with software and functionality described above.

Scanners have a footprint which is slightly bigger than an A4 sheet of paper, as this is the most common size of document scanned. They have a glass screen on which the document is placed and are very similar to a photocopier. Most scanners can be purchased for less than £100. The most important aspect when considering the alternatives are the resolution and the speed at which the document can be scanned. The higher the resolution quoted in dots per inch (DPI), the better the quality of the scanned image.

Table 1.5 Comparison of printer types

Type	Typical purchase cost	Pence per page	Max typical speed pages per minute (ppm)	Quality	Paper type	Consumables	Other	Notes
Dot matrix	–	–	–	Poor quality	Continuous or sheet fed	Printer ribbon	Can be configured to print less than a page at a time on continuous stationary. Paper can move backwards as well as forwards	These days have been superseded by Inkjet. Only used where quality is not an issue, e.g. delivery notes or inkjet inappropriate, e.g. dispensary labels
Inkjet	£80–£150	1.1–3p per page	10.9 ppm	Quality determined by the type of paper used and the quality setting on the printer	Quality of the output is dependent on the paper used and the quality setting on the printer. Better the quality the slower the speed of printing	Black cartridge. Colour cartridge	Has to print full sheet, so not appropriate for labels. Prints colour as well as mono black	
Mono laser	£240–£300	–	–	–	–	Toner cartridges	–	
Colour laser	£500–£600	–	20 ppm in mono. 12 ppm in colour	–	–	Toner cartridges black + colour	–	

Figure 1.24 Scanner.
[Courtesy of Chris Elmes]

Combined scanners and printers are available which can also be used as photocopiers. Some also combine fax facilities.

Pen Drives

Pen Drives are permanent memory storage devices (but without any moving parts) which, as the name suggests, are about the size of a small pen and connect to the computer via a USB connector (Figure 1.25). They are used like a floppy disk but have the advantage that they are smaller, have much greater capacity, are much faster (higher transfer rate) and can be accessed without having to load any software (on later versions of Windows, e.g. XP). The Pen Drive is plugged into any available USB port on the computer and is allocated a drive letter just like a hard disk or a floppy disk. Files can be saved and deleted as on any hard or floppy disk. Pen Drives are available in different storage capacities (e.g. 64 Mb, 128 Mb, 256 Mb) and the maximum size is increasing all the time. A 64 Mb Pen Drive is equivalent to approximately 40 floppy disks.

Notebook (laptop)

The term notebook or laptop computer has been used to describe computers that are self-contained and which generally have a footprint (i.e. area)

Figure 1.25 Pen drive.
[Courtesy of Chris Elmes]

less than that of an A4 sheet of paper (Figure 1.26). All the components described for a personal computer – base unit, keyboard and screen – are built into one unit. The main advantage of these computers is that they are portable and can be used in any location, as they can be run from internal batteries. To make them portable the components need to be much smaller and lighter, which means that generally the cost of a laptop is more than that of an equivalent desktop/tower PC of the same specification.

Notebooks are generally 'clam shelled' in design, that is, they are hinged down one side. When opened up the keyboard is built into the main body of the notebook and the monitor is built into the top part. In addition to the keyboard there will be a touchpad and two buttons, which give the functionality of a mouse (although it is possible to use a normal mouse with most notebooks).

Notebooks used to be very expensive compared to static desktop PCs, but in recent times prices have started to fall considerably. The changing role of pharmacists means that notebooks are becoming an essential tool, especially when their jobs are performed in more than one location.

Portability brings its own issues, which need to be considered particularly in relation to backup, connectivity with other computers and the internet. As it is portable, it is much easier to lose or have the PC

Figure 1.26 Notebook computer
[Courtesy of Chris Elmes]

stolen. It is essential that any documents/files the user needs are backed up to a secondary device or permanent storage device. The later versions of Windows, e.g. 2000 and XP, have functionality built into the operating system that synchronises the data held on the notebook computer with that on another computer, such as a network drive or static computer (see Networking).

It is becoming common for users to become dependent on email and access to the internet. In a static PC this is catered for by physically locating it next to a network point or a phone line. With a notebook computer this is more of a problem. For this reason, notebooks need to have different ways of connecting to other computers or devices.

It is becoming more common for notebook computers to have a wireless adapter built in which allows connection to a wireless network without the need for cables. More and more public places, such as railway stations and hotels, are providing wireless access points so that users can access the internet and ultimately emails, etc. If wireless networks are not available then the internet can be accessed via a modem, which connects to a standard telephone line. Sometimes modems are built into the notebook, or can be added separately in the form of a PCMCIA card (Figure 1.27a). This has a standard connector and is about the same size as a credit card.

Figure 1.27a PCMCIA card.
[Courtesy of Chris Elmes]

PCMCIA slot

Figure 1.27b PCMCIA slot.
[Courtesy of Chris Elmes]

Notebooks have PCMCIA slots (Figure 1.27b) that allow devices such as modems to be plugged into them. The devices are always of a standard size, have the footprint of a credit card, and can be plugged and unplugged from the PCMCIA slot when required.

It is now possible to buy a PCMCIA card (Figure 1.28) which allows access to the mobile phone network using a general packet radio service (GPRS). This also allows access to the internet from anywhere where the card can receive a signal from a transmitter. A service provider contract is required to access the GPRS network. Costs are generally based on the amount of data moving across the link.

Docking stations

The size and weight of portable computers vary enormously, depending on the facilities built in, from less than 2 lb in weight and 0.5 inches thick to 7–8 lb and 1.5 inches thick. This selection is determined by what compromises the user is prepared to make. There is a big difference between carrying a 7–8 lb notebook around and one weighing less than 2 lb. For example, if the CD drive is only used occasionally then a notebook could be selected in which the CD drive is external and can be

Figure 1.28 GPRS PCMCIA modem card (in situ).
[Courtesy of Chris Elmes]

plugged in only when required, thus reducing the weight of the note-book.

Docking stations (Figure 1.29) are available, which are useful if the user has a main place of work. The notebook clips into the docking station, which has connections for all the interfaces of a normal desktop PC, such as keyboard, mouse, network and printer. This allows the notebook PC to be used like a desktop PC without having to unplug cables each time it is taken to another location. In addition, the docking station may contain a CD-ROM and floppy disk drives, which allows the size and weight of the notebook to be reduced.

PDA (portable digital assistant)

PDAs or palmtop computers are designed, as the term suggests, to be used in the palm of the hand (Figure 1.30). Typically these computers are no more than 3 inches wide, 5 inches long and 0.5 inches thick, weigh only a few ounces, and will fit easily into a shirt pocket. Instead of using a keyboard (although versions exist that have very small key-boards) to input text, a stylus is used in conjunction with handwriting recognition software. One of the fundamental design aspects of a PDA

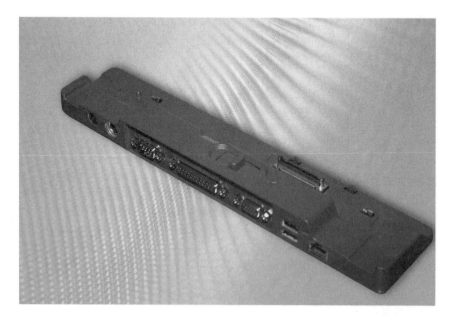

Figure 1.29 Docking station.
[Courtesy of Chris Elmes]

Figure 1.30   Example of a tungsten palm-based device.
[Courtesy of Chris Elmes]

is that it is meant to be used in conjunction with a personal computer, and so they are supplied with cables and software that enable them to be connected to the PC. Typically they are provided with four major applications, but many more are available, e.g. calendar (appointments), contacts list, to-do lists and notes. The four applications are also available on the desktop or notepad PC, so that the data associated with each application can be viewed on either the PC or the PDA. The fundamental principle of this type of device is that the PDA is kept in synchronisation with the PC. If any data is changed on the PC then it is marked as having been changed, and similarly on the PDA. The PDA is placed in a cradle, which is connected to the PC via one of the communication ports. A button is pressed on the cradle that activates synchronisation software (a process known as hotSynching) which adds any changes made on the PDA to the PC and vice versa. It does not matter whether the change has been made on the PC or the PDA, all data is synchronised so that it is as up to date as the last time synchronisation took place. This effectively copes with the backup of the information as well. If the PDA is stolen or lost, a replacement can be obtained, placed in the cradle, and all the data from the PC will be synchronised with the new PDA.

The main benefit of these devices is that the information the user requires is immediately available in a device that fits into a pocket. There is no need to wait for the operating system to load, as with a desktop or notebook PC: the applications are available instantly when the device is switched on. PDAs do not have hard disk drives and consequently have much less permanent memory than a PC. The applications software used on PDAs is much smaller than the equivalent PC software and consequently uses much less memory. There are two main types of device, based on two different operating systems, Palm or Microsoft Windows CE (a cut-down version of the Windows operating system; Figure 1.31).

PDAs are manufactured by different companies and will use either the Palm or Windows CE. Table 1.6 lists some of the hardware manufacturers and the operating systems used on the various devices.

Many of the PDAs have slots that take memory cards, such as the SD cards used by Palm devices. Some PDAs can be used as phones and are equipped with communications hardware and software, enabling access to the internet via GPRS, a radio system used to send data to mobile phones and devices such as PDAs.

This also allows email to be received while on the move or away from the office. Any emails sent to the normal PC email address can

Figure 1.31   HP Ipaq – Example of Windows-based device.
[Courtesy of Chris Elmes]

Table 1.6 PDA manufacturers

Palm	*Microsoft*
Tungsten	Compaq iPaq
Handspring	Hewlett Packard Jordana
Zire	Toshiba
Sony Clie	

automatically be sent to the PDA and the user alerted. There are two types of technology available, known as 'push' and 'pull'. In 'pull' technology the user must request that any emails in the mailbox are sent to the PDA, whereas in 'push' technology the email is automatically sent when it arrives in the mailbox, allowing the user to be alerted immediately.

There are thousands of applications written specifically for the Palm device, many of them medical applications and databases. Recently the *British National Formulary* was released as an electronic version on an SD card (Figure 1.32).

The capacity of these devices has increased enormously over the last few years, thereby enabling many reference texts to be stored on the same device. Adobe Reader is available for both platforms and allows

Figure 1.32 eBNF on a PDA.
[Courtesy of Chris Elmes]

any PDF document to be read on a PDA. The screens have benefited from colour and the resolution has improved significantly, making text much easier to read. It is anticipated that these devices will replace the paper-based reference books in the near future.

PDAs are powered by batteries, usually rechargeable, but some use standard alkaline batteries. The life of the battery between charges is one of the most important considerations when purchasing a PDA. The life of the batteries is determined by many factors, such as which operating system is used, the amount of memory and the type of display used. Therefore, the more features used, such as playing music, the more frequently the device will have to be recharged.

Pocket PCs tend to use more power than the palm-operating system because of their increased memory requirements.

Many mobile phones are beginning to offer the facilities available on PDAs, and it is quite likely that in the future the technologies used in PDAs and mobile phones will converge:

www.palmone.com/us/products/compare/palmos-vs-pocketpc.html

2

Operating systems and security

What is an operating system?

All computers have some type of operating system which allows the computer to boot when power is applied. (Boot is the term used to describe the actions by the computer when it is switched on. These are usually in the form of a set of instructions that are stored in permanent memory and are carried out when the power is applied.) The operating system is the software that controls all input and output from the computer. When the computer is switched on it activates a small program called the basic input/output system (BIOS), which is permanently stored on the motherboard. This program checks that all the components that make up the computer are working correctly, and then automatically loads the operating system, which is stored on a permanent memory device such as a hard disk. It is responsible for making sure that all the different components of the computer, e.g. memory, disk drives, keyboards and other peripherals such as printers, can communicate with each other in an orderly manner (Figure 2.1).

The operating system also loads the applications software, which fulfils specific functions, e.g. word processor and spreadsheet. Applications must be written for the specific operating system. An application written for the Windows operating system will not work on the Unix operating system, and vice versa. However, there are examples where an application may be written for more than one operating system. For example, Microsoft Word is available for both Windows and MacOS and is supplied as completely separate products even though the functionality is nearly identical.

The majority of modern electronic equipment, such as televisions and washing machines, have a central processor unit (CPU) which controls the operation of the device. These types of device have a limited range of options which can be used to control them, but do not have an operating system as such. The difference between these devices and a computer is that a computer has a great many options and uses to which it can be put. A PC, for example, is a general-purpose tool built around a microprocessor. It has lots of different parts – memory, hard disk,

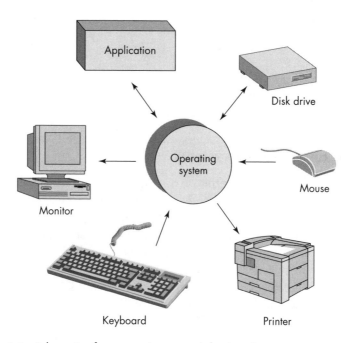

Figure 2.1 Schematic of an operating system's basic tasks.

modem, etc. – that work together. 'General purpose' means that you can do many different things with a PC. It can be used to type documents, send email, browse the internet, etc.

The operating system provides the building blocks and infrastructure on which a software application can be built, much as in the way that the foundations and basic utilities such as water, electricity, gas and drainage are provided for houses. In exactly the same way that it takes enormous resources to create the basic utility infrastructure, it takes enormous resources to create an operating system. The complexity of many operating systems means that it may take years from inception to introduction, and many more years before it is stable and bug free.

All PCs have operating systems, the most common of which are the Windows family, the Macintosh family and the Unix family. Note that these are called families as there are different versions of a particular operating system. A software application will be written for a particular version of the operating system. When new versions of operating systems are produced the developers will always try to ensure that programs written for an older version will still work with the newer version, but this cannot be guaranteed.

At the simplest level, an operating system does two things:

- It manages the hardware and software resources of the computer system. These include such things as the processor, memory, disk space, etc.
- It provides a stable, consistent way for applications to deal with the hardware without having to know all the details of the hardware.

The first task, managing the hardware and software resources, is very important. In a multitasking operating system such as Windows, more than one software application can be running at the same time. Each of these applications competes for the attention of the CPU and demands memory, storage and input/output (I/O) bandwidth for its own purposes. In this capacity, the operating system ensures that each application gets the necessary resources.

The second task, providing a consistent application interface, is especially important when there are many manufacturers of IBM-compatible PCs, or if the hardware making up the computer is ever likely to be changed. A consistent application program interface (API) allows a software developer to write an application on a computer supplied by one manufacturer and have a high level of confidence that it will run on one supplied by another, even if the amount of memory or storage is different on the two machines. Even if a particular computer is unique, an operating system can ensure that applications continue to run when hardware upgrades and updates occur, because the operating system and not the application is charged with managing the hardware and the distribution of its resources. Windows '98 is an example of the flexibility an operating system provides. Windows '98 runs on hardware from thousands of manufacturers. It can accommodate thousands of different printers, disk drives and special peripherals in any possible combination.

User interface

The operating system determines how the user will interact with the computer and is referred to as the 'user interface'. There are two main types of user interface: character based and graphical.

Character based A character-based interface treats the screen display as an array of boxes, each holding one ASCII character. There are ASCII characters for each letter of the alphabet, plus all the punctuation characters. Interaction with this type of system is via a series of commands in the form of special words that the operating system recognises (Figure 2.2).

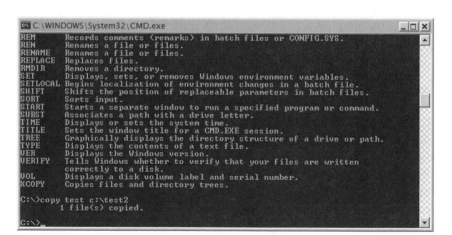

Figure 2.2 Character-based command line interface.

Character-based systems can be programmed to give a list of options known as menus (Figure 2.3). The user selects the number or letter corresponding to the option on the menu and may be taken into further menus or into an application. The interaction with the application is purely through the keyboard.

Character-based systems can also use an extended range of characters, which include shapes for drawing pictures. This allows these systems to display menus, windows and other shapes consisting mainly of straight lines. The menu options are usually selected by pressing a combination of keys, such as 'ALT' and 'F' to access a menu and then using the arrow keys to move through the options. In some of these

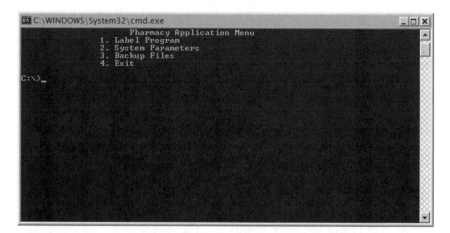

Figure 2.3 Character-based menu driven interface.

types of interface the options can be selected by using a mouse as a simple pointer (Figure 2.4).

Graphical Graphical interfaces (known as GUIs – graphical user interfaces) treat the display as an array of pixels (dots) (Figure 2.5). Characters and images are formed by illuminating patterns of pixels to create the image. There are a number of fundamental concepts when interacting with a GUI:

- Pictorial representation of objects as small icons, e.g. a printer, and the use of menus.
- Use of a pointer on the screen which is moved around to select menus and icons. The shape of the pointer changes depending on its location on the screen.
- Use of a pointing device such as a mouse, which is used to control the pointer and to select a menu or icon by clicking a button on the mouse.

The pictorial nature of the GUI makes it easier for the inexperienced user to interact with the computer without the need to learn complex commands.

Types of operating system

There are three types of operating system which can be categorised based on the type of computer they control and the sort of application they support:

- **Single-user, single task** As the name implies, this operating system is designed to manage the computer so that one user can effectively do one thing at a time,

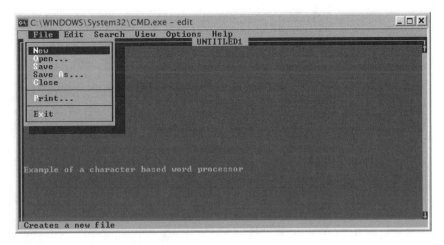

Figure 2.4 Character-based menu/window system.

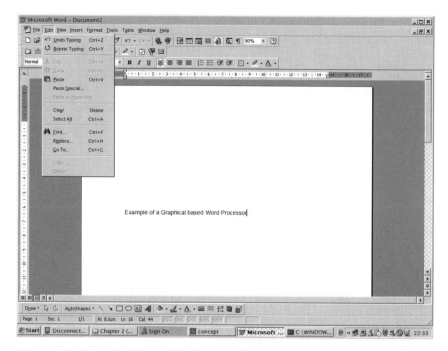

Figure 2.5   Example of a graphical user interface.

that is, it can only run one program at a time. When the user starts an application, the program that is already running is closed and the new one opened. The Palm OS for Palm PDAs is a good example of a modern single-user, single-task operating system.

- **Single-user, multitasking** This is the type of operating system most people use on their PCs. Windows '98 and the MacOS are both examples of an operating system that will let a single user have several programs in operation at the same time. For example, it is entirely possible for a Windows user to be writing a note in a word processor while downloading a file from the internet and simultaneously printing the text of an email message.

- **Multiuser** A multiuser operating system allows many different users to take advantage of the computer's resources simultaneously. The operating system must make sure that the requirements of the various users are balanced, and that each of the programs they are using has sufficient and separate resources so that a problem with one user does not affect the entire community. Unix is an example of a multiuser operating system.

It is important to differentiate between multiuser operating systems and single-user operating systems that support networking. Operating systems such as Windows NT and Netware can support many networked users, but they are not true multiuser systems. For this type of operating system the system administrator is the only 'user'. All the logins by the remote users are handled by one process run by the system administrator.

Facilities provided by the operating system

As mentioned earlier, the operating system provides the basic building blocks that the software developer can use to produce software without any in-depth knowledge of the hardware and devices that will be connected to the computer. For example, there are many hundreds of different printers available: if the operating system did not take care of the interface between the computer and the printer a software developer would need to create different programs for each different type of printer. However, it is only necessary for the program to communicate with the operating system in a standard manner, i.e. via the application program interface, for the computer to be able to print to any printer. The manufacturer of the printer has to provide a small program called a device driver, which is loaded on to the computer when the printer is installed. This acts as a translator between the operating system and the printer. This means that when a user selects the print command in an application it will work with any printer. All devices that are used with the computer must have a driver to act as a translator between them and the facilities provided by the operating system.

On its own the operating system does not do anything particularly useful, but it does provide facilities that can be used by applications such as file handling and printing. Some operating systems, such as Windows, are sometimes bundled with basic applications. For example, Windows is delivered with Internet Explorer, which allows a user to connect to the internet and browse the World Wide Web. Internet Explorer is an application that uses the facilities of the operating system, e.g. its networking capabilities, to communicate with the web. Microsoft, the suppliers of Windows, choose to deliver it with the operating system because most users will require the use of a web browser.

Filing system One of the most important aspects of the operating system is to manage the storage of data. This is known as the filing system. In most operating systems data is stored in files, although on some, such as the Palm OS, the data is stored as records. A file is a structure used to store data on storage devices such as hard disks and CDs. It is the operating system's function to manage all aspects of file handling, such as creation, modification, copying and deletion. Each file is given a unique identifying name. On a typical computer there will be thousands of files. If they were all stored in one location it would be very difficult to manage them. The operating system stores the files in structures called directories (or folders), which are analogous to the use of filing cabinets to store related information in folders. Directories are given names to identify them in the same way as files. A directory created within another directory is known as a subdirectory. This gives rise to a filing system that has an inverted tree structure, each directory being a branch. To access a particular file the operating system will need to know the device (e.g. hard disk), directory and subdirectory in which a file is stored. This route to the file is known as the path (Figure 2.6).

A filename cannot be used more than once in the same directory or folder. When a software application needs to store data, it passes the data and the name of the file to the operating system, which checks the file name is valid. The operating system is responsible for actually storing the data. In graphical user systems there is usually a facility for viewing and manipulating files which allows the user to browse the directory structure. In Windows this is called Windows Explorer (Figure 2.7).

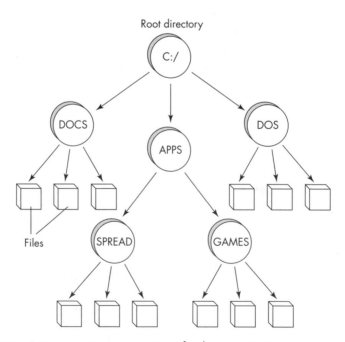

Figure 2.6 Diagrammatic representation of a directory structure.

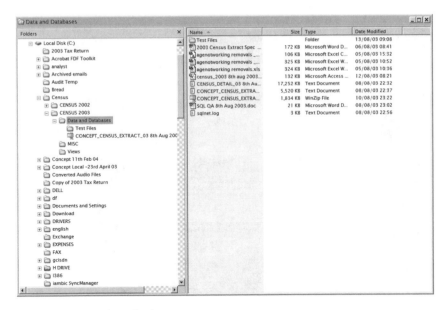

Figure 2.7   Windows Explorer.

The operating system and the installed software applications will create many directories and files that contain programs and data. Most applications allow the user to save data created by the software. For example Word, a word processor developed by Microsoft, stores each document in a separate file. The user is given the opportunity to decide the name of the file and the directory in which it is stored. It does this by opening a 'window' that allows the user to browse the directory structure. It also lets the user create directories and subdirectories. Although this appears to be part of the Word application, it is the operating system that is doing most of the work to display the directory structure, etc. The Word application is responsible for the interface between the user and the operating system functionality (Figure 2.8).

It is essential for the user to create a directory structure that allows them to locate files easily. If these are kept in a logical series of directories then they are much easier to manage and locate. This is analogous to making sure that all physical documents are stored in the same filing cabinet and organised in a way that allows them to be found easily. This is particularly important in relation to backing up files. If the files are stored in one directory with a series of subdirectories it is very easy to back them up with one copy command. Any subdirectories and files below the parent directory are automatically copied. Many applications, when storing files, choose a default directory in which to store them.

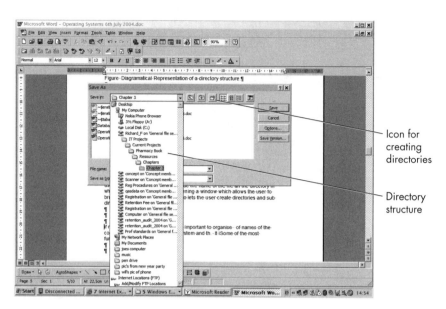

Icon for
creating
directories

Directory
structure

Figure 2.8 Saving a document file in Microsoft Word.

This is usually different for each application, and results in fragment-
ation of a user's files in many different directories. When saving a file the
user is given the opportunity to change the directory. It is advisable, for
the reasons given above, to store the file in a directory of the user's
choice.

Networking subsystem Although the user sees very little visual indication of networking, it is one of the most important aspects of any
modern computer. The networking facilities allow computers to communicate both with each other and with other devices such as printers.
It is the network subsystem that handles all the requests by applications
to access other computers, and vice versa. Without this subsystem the
computer would not be able to access the internet, share files with other
systems or access network printers. Sometimes there is a delay between
requesting information from another computer and receiving it, giving
the appearance that the application that issued the request has hung or
crashed. This is due to the speed at which the request is serviced, and is
dependent on the amount of data being requested and the speed of the
network link. Large files, for example, can take many minutes to be
requested over a standard telephone line. Most computers use a protocol known as TCP/IP to communicate with other systems. When two
computers exchange information in this way, one is said to be the client

and one the server. The client is the computer requesting the data, and the server the computer providing the data (Figure 2.9).

The client must identify itself to the server by supplying a user-name and password, to ensure that access is only given to authorised users who are already known to the server system. The server system will have previously set up the username and password in some sort of registration process.

Printing subsystem   Another essential facility provided by the operating system is the ability to print. The majority of applications have a print option, which allows data manipulated by the application to be printed. The formatting of the data is the responsibility of the application, whereas the responsibility for the actual printing is the operating system's. Modern operating systems such as Windows XP have facilities to allow the use of a printer connected either directly to the computer or via a network (Figure 2.10). If the printer is on a network the operating system will also use the network subsystem. This enables many computers to share a single printer placed in a convenient location and reduces the number of printers required by an organisation.

When the print command is selected the user is given the opportunity to select the printer to which the document should be directed (Figure 2.11). The operating system shows all printers that have been set up to be accessed by the computer, so the user can choose the printer depending on its facilities and the type of document to be printed.

For example, if the document has no colour it can be directed to a normal laser printer, which prints much faster than an inkjet, which

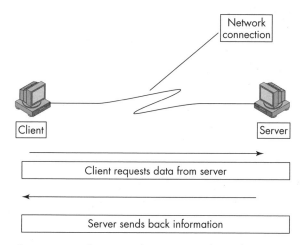

Figure 2.9   Computers working in a client–server relationship.

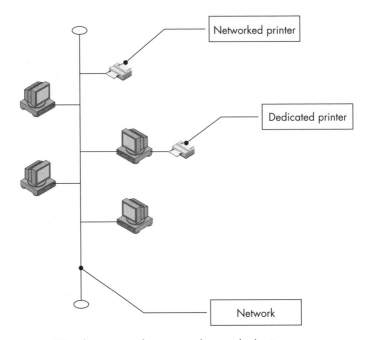

Figure 2.10 Directly connected printer and networked printer.

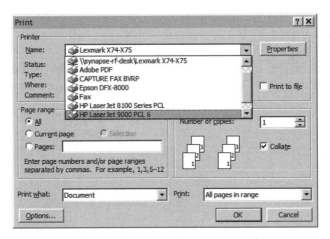

Figure 2.11 Printer dialogue selection window.

would be required for colour. Most modern operating systems, such as Windows XP, have 'wizards' to guide the user through the process of adding a printer.

If more than one printer can be used by a computer, one of them is selected as the default printer. This is the one that will be used if the user does not select an alternative. The default printer can also be selected by the user, and in Windows is indicated by a 'tick' icon next to the printer name.

Once the application has sent the file to the printer the user can carry on using the application even though the document has not physically been printed. The operating system is responsible for managing and queuing all documents sent to the printers, in a process known as spooling. Modern operating systems have a two-way communication between them and the printer which allows the system to determine the state of the printer and display appropriate messages, e.g. if the printer is offline, or has run out of paper. It prevents documents from being 'lost' if the printer is offline. There is usually a function in modern operating systems to determine the status of all documents that have been spooled and not yet printed. In Windows this can be accessed by clicking 'Printers and Faxes' from the control panel menu (Figure 2.12).

General functions and utilities   The operating system is responsible for providing many functions, such as the ability to copy and paste between applications. Once again, the application is responsible for providing the options to copy text or an object. The copied item is then placed in

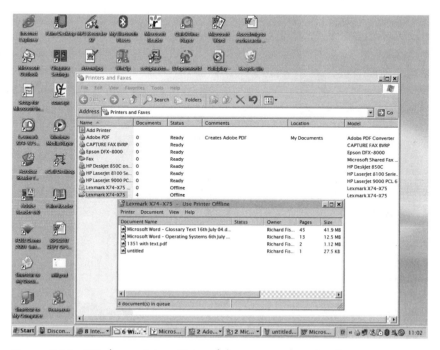

Figure 2.12   Windows printers. Status of documents to be printed.

a temporary area of memory known as a clipboard. The user can then switch to another application and paste the copied item into the new application. In Windows the content of the complete screen display at any point in time can be copied to clipboard by pressing the 'Print Screen' button. This can be pasted into a document and is very useful for producing pictures of a particular window. Pressing the ALT and the Print Screen buttons together copies only the active window.

Keyboard shortcuts and accelerator keys   Although GUI systems are designed to be used with a mouse, there are many times when it is more efficient to use the keyboard to complete a menu option, especially when it is used repeatedly. For example, when creating a document it is normal to keep saving it periodically so that any changes are not lost. This is usually achieved by using the mouse to access the File menu and clicking Save, which means taking the hands off the keyboard. The same action can be completed by using the accelerator keys (or keyboard shortcuts) (Figure 2.13). These are usually displayed to the right of the menu option. In Windows, a file can be saved by pressing the 'CTRL'

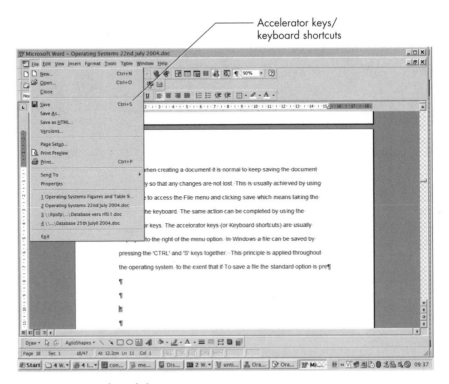

Figure 2.13 Keyboard shortcuts.

and 'S' keys together. This principle is applied throughout the operating system.

Operating systems used on PCs

The main operating systems a user is likely to encounter on the devices described in Chapter 1 will now be described.

MS-DOS

MS-DOS was the original operating system used on the first IBM-compatible PCs and was developed by Microsoft. It was a huge success and has provided the basis for Microsoft's continuing dominance of the global software market. It was a single-user, single-tasking character-based operating system, and was eventually replaced by Microsoft Windows, which had a graphical user interface and originally ran on top of MS-DOS. As subsequent versions of Windows have been released, the MS-DOS component has been replaced. However, applications designed to run on MS-DOS can still be used on a Windows system by running in a window called a DOS Shell (Figure 2.14), but are still character based.

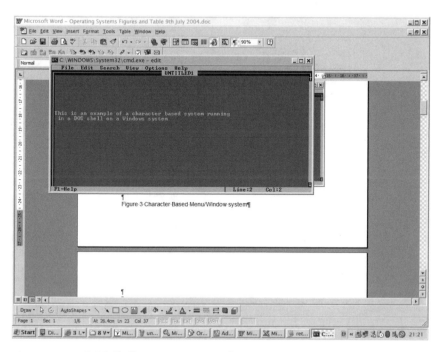

Figure 2.14   DOS Shell running on a Windows system.

Microsoft Windows

Microsoft Windows is the most widely used operating system for personal computers and accounts for Microsoft's dominance of the PC market. It is estimated that nearly 90% of all PCs are running a version of Windows. Application developers thus tend to develop applications for the Windows platform, as this gives them a much bigger market in which to sell. Therefore, in many instances the choice of operating system will be governed by the applications to be used.

Windows provides a graphical user interface and a multitasking environment that allows many programs to be run at the same time in separate 'windows', hence its name (Figure 2.15). Windows has certain user interface conventions to which application suppliers conform, so that the 'look and feel' and the navigation around the application are generally the same. For example, menu options are always displayed on the top left of the window underneath the title bar. It is often said that Windows is 'intuitive' because of the same 'look and feel' of the applications, and the implication is that it will be easy to learn. In the

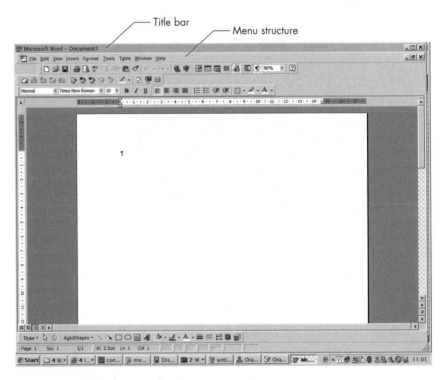

Figure 2.15 Windows application – menu options.

author's opinion this is a complete misnomer, as each application is designed to perform completely different functions (even though there may be common functions such as copy and paste). This results in users not being adequately trained, with the result that the application is not used properly or efficiently. There is no substitute for training if the application is to be used to its full potential.

Many versions of Windows have been developed since the original in 1985, each of which has introduced new enhancements. Many of these were technical and not visible to the end user. Windows '95 was a major release and is still used on many PCs today. It was the first version to introduce the concept of 'plug and play', which automatically detects new equipment inserted or attached to the PC and loads the appropriate drivers, which greatly simplified the process of configuring the PC. Windows '95 also changed the 'look and feel' of the previous versions, which is fundamentally still the same on all subsequent versions. 'Look and feel' is a term used to describe how the windows and menus, etc. are presented to the end user, and the way that they interact with the system. Windows '95 was the first version to introduce the concept of the 'desktop', where icons can be placed on the screen and used to start programs. Although there have been minor cosmetic changes in sub-sequent versions the 'look and feel' have remained fundamentally the same. The next version, Windows '98, was fundamentally the same as '95 but introduced support for USB devices and, more significantly, the integration of the Internet Explorer web browser, which allows users to access resources on the World Wide Web. Minor revisions to '98 were produced, called Windows '98 Second Edition (SE) and Windows '98 Millennium Edition (ME). Windows '95 and '98 were essentially aimed at the home market. Microsoft also produced a version of Windows aimed at the professional market. This version, called Windows NT, was introduced in 1993 and used completely different technology from that used to create '95 and '98. It was much more stable when multi-tasking, which resulted in its use as a server for business networks. It also used a different method of filing data on hard disks called NTFS, which allowed much larger hard disks to be supported. Its other major feature was its increased security, whereby users had to log on to the operating system by entering a username and password. Various ver-sions have been released since 1993 and retained the same name except for the version number, until Windows NT version 5 was renamed Windows 2000. The latest version of the Windows operating system is Windows XP, which is built on the technology used to develop Windows NT. Windows XP is designed to satisfy the requirements of both the home and the professional market, and is sold as Windows XP Home Edition and Windows XP Professional. There are many other versions of Windows which are used to satisfy specific market sectors, for example Windows 2003 Server, which is used on computers that act as servers to other PCs. Windows CE is a version designed to run on handheld computers, but is built on completely different technology from that used on PCs. Some of the major versions of Microsoft Windows are listed in Table 2.1.

MacOS

The Macintosh operating system was introduced in 1984 for a range of computers known as 'Macintosh', manufactured by Apple. It was the

Table 2.1 Versions of Microsoft Windows

Product	Type	Notes
Windows XP Home Edition Windows	Home	Latest version of Windows for home use
Windows XP Professional	Professional	Latest version of Windows for professional use
Windows XP Tablet PC Edition	Professional	Includes support for entering data using a stylus on a touch-sensitive screen
Windows XP Media Center Edition 2004	Home	
Windows Server 2003 Standard Edition	IT departments	Used by IT departments to provide computer resources to networked PCs
Windows Server 2003 Enterprise Edition	IT departments	Used by IT departments to provide computer resources to networked PCs
Windows Me (Millennium Edition)	Home	
Windows 98 SE (Second Edition)	Home	
Windows 98	Home	
Windows 95 OSR2.5	Home	Latest version of 95 which included support for Internet Explorer 4
Windows NT 4.0 Enterprise Server	Professional	Used by IT departments to provide computer resources to networked PCs
Windows NT 4.0 Workstation	Professional	Used on networked computers in business environment instead of 95 or 98

first commonly available operating system to use a GUI and used 'icons' – pictorial representations of common real-world objects – such as a 'Waste Bin' into which unwanted documents could be placed. Many of the visual elements were subsequently incorporated into versions of Windows.

Although MacOS was the first GUI, the PC market was and still is dominated by Microsoft Windows, and MacOS holds less than 10% of the market. Consequently there are far fewer software applications available for MacOS than for Windows, but it is used extensively by the publishing industry, where it has created a niche market. However, an application is available called 'Virtual PC' which can be loaded on to a Macintosh system and emulates the Windows operating system. This allows Windows applications to be run on a Macintosh computer.

The latest version, MacOS X, has been developed from a Unix-based operating system and consequently is compatible with Unix systems.

Unix/Linux

Unix is a multiuser multitasking operating system developed at Bell Laboratories in the early 1970s. It was designed to be a small, flexible system used exclusively by programmers, and portable, which meant that it could be run on virtually any type of computer with any type of hardware. This and its low price made it a popular choice for universities and led to its adoption throughout the world. However, because it was intended to be used by programmers it was not initially used on PCs. The history of Unix means that it is an open-source operating system, i.e. the source code is available to anyone wishing to add functionality to the operating system, and this in part has led to its success. In contrast to Windows and MacOS it is 'free' and its standardisation is governed by the 'Open Source Group'. Its robust design and networking capabilities have led to its being used on many internet servers. Recently a version of Unix for PCs has been developed which has a graphical user interface and is known as Linux. Again this is free, but is usually distributed by a number of organisations (e.g. Red Hat, SUSE, Mandrake) which charge a small fee for it. As it is 'free' its use in large organisations can result in significant cost savings. As with the Macintosh, the majority of commercial applications have been written for the Windows operating system, even though there are 'free' versions of popular Windows applications. For example, Star Office has much of the functionality of Microsoft Office and is available at a significantly reduced cost. It remains to be seen whether Linux can make inroads to become one of the operating systems of choice and reduce the dominance and near monopoly of Microsoft.

Personal digital assistant operating systems

The hardware used to create personal digital assistants (handheld computers), despite fundamentally performing the same tasks as a PC, is very different because of the need to make the components very small. In addition, they are powered by batteries rather than being connected to the mains supply, and have very small screens and in many cases do not have keyboards. All these factors mean that the operating systems used in these devices are very different from those used in conventional PCs. The devices are intended for use by people who are on the move, are very small, will fit into a shirt or coat pocket, and are designed to be used in conjunction with a desktop or notebook computer. The two main operating systems used are Palm OS and Pocket PC (formerly called Windows CE); they are designed to work with specific hardware and as such are always delivered with the PDA. The design of the operating system enables the data on the PDA to be backed up to and synchronised with the desktop computer (or notebook), as being portable means they are more vulnerable to theft, loss and breakage. The synchronisation is required so that any changes made on the PDA are reflected on the desktop computer. Most PDAs are delivered with four standard applications: calendar, contacts list, memo pad and to-do list. These applications can be synchronised with the desktop versions so that any changes on either the PC or the PDA are reflected on both devices. On Palm devices this process is known as 'hotsynching'. The PDA is placed in a cradle attached to the desktop computer and the 'hot-synch' initiated. This synchronisation process is a fundamental part of the operating system. PDAs generally use a stylus for input on a touch-sensitive screen, which means that handwriting recognition software is a fundamental part of the operating system. The Palm OS system dominates the PDA market in the same way that Windows dominates the PC market, although the Pocket PC OS is starting to make inroads. Many developers produce applications for both systems.

Security and audit

Security is an all-encompassing term used to describe all aspects of regulating access to, and ensuring the preservation of, data on computers.

Regulating access to data is achieved by using a number of different techniques.

Authentication

Authentication ensures that only authorised persons can access data on a computer. This is usually achieved by creating a 'Login' or 'Logon' screen into which the user must type a username (or user ID) and a password. The username and password are associated with a 'user account', which identifies the user and is set up on the target system by a person identified as the system administrator. Only a valid combination of username and password will allow the user to gain access. In large organisations where there are hundreds of PCs, for example a hospital, there may be a team of system administrators whose function is to maintain access to the network resources and any other systems used by the organisation. The username is analogous to a bank account number in that it identifies the person. The password is associated with the account and is personal to the user, and is analogous to a PIN number. Passwords should be stored on the target system in an encrypted form, so that not even the system administrator knows the password associated with a particular username. This ensures that the only person who can log on with that username is the person who 'owns' the password. Audit trails identify the user from the username, and if the password were to be disclosed to another person they could impersonate the real user. This is why passwords should never ever be disclosed. It is also why, if the administrator initially supplies the password, the user is instructed to change it at the first opportunity. Anybody who banks over the internet will know how rigorous the banks are in ensuring that only the account holder can access the account, by having additional information known only to themselves. The process of verifying the identity of a user or computer is known as authentication.

It has become a feature of many client applications that require users to athenticate themselves, to store the username and password so that the user does not have to enter them each time they access the system. For example, when a user connects to the internet on a PC running Windows using a telephone line they will invariably connect via an internet service provider, who will allocate them a username and password. The system can be set up so that when the user requires access to a web browser or email, which requires them to be connected to the internet, it is performed automatically. The system automatically dials the number and enters the username and password already stored on the computer. This is not a situation which should be encouraged, as it means that an unauthorised user can access an account if the computer is left unattended. Although the username may be stored the password should always be entered manually and the software configured to always prompt for the password.

The username is linked with account details, which will normally be associated with certain privileges and permissions on the target system and is dependent on how the security subsystem has been designed and programmed. Many systems will limit certain menu options to a particular category of user. For example, the creation of new user accounts may be limited to the system administrator. There are many different ways of designing security systems which are dependent on the functionality required, but they are all based on the principle of authentication.

One of the problems associated with modern-day computing is that a person may use many systems, each requiring authentication, thus requiring them to have many different usernames and passwords.

Encryption

Authentication ensures that only authorised users can access the data stored on a computer or in a system. However, owing to the enormous growth of networks and the internet, large volumes of data are transferred from one system to another. Much of this is of a sensitive and confidential nature, for example medical records, credit card details and bank account details, and could be intercepted and monitored by computer programs. Encryption is a process of encoding data so that it can only be read by a person (or computer) with the key to decode it. Computer encryption is based on the science of cryptography, which has been used for centuries to make and break secret codes. Most forms of encryption used today rely on computers, as it is too easy for human-based codes to be deciphered by computers. There are different types of encryption system, the most commonly used being based on public key encryption, and this is one of the principal means of ensuring the security of many types of confidential transaction. In the majority of cases the user is unaware that encryption is being used. However, the user should ensure that where confidential information is being moved, underlying systems are in place to ensure that the data is encrypted. This applies not only to financial transactions carried out over the web, but to any information that is moved from one system to another, e.g. emails. This is particularly important when medical details are sent by email. However, security is like a chain: it is only as strong as its weakest link. Make sure that some of the obvious methods of protecting the data are not overlooked, such as leaving a computer unattended and logged on. NHSnet is a network service developed for the NHS which ensures that only authorised users can gain access to it and that the data being exchanged is encrypted and secure.

Malicious threats

Another aspect of security relates to malicious attempts to corrupt data or bring down a computer system. There are many methods by which an unauthorised user may try to gain access to a computer and the data stored on it. Generally the methods used exploit 'holes' in the operating system. Many different techniques are used, depending on the individual's ultimate objectives, including the use of viruses, worms, Trojan horses, etc. There are also different techniques to prevent these attacks, which include firewalls and antivirus software.

Viruses A virus is a program that can copy itself from one computer to another in the same way as a biological virus replicates itself in different hosts, hence the name. In the same way that a biological virus cannot exist in its own right and must use the DNA of a cell to replicate itself, so too does a computer virus, by attaching itself to another computer program. Viruses are almost always written with malicious intent, but some are written to counteract the effects of another virus. A virus is written for a specific operating system and the programmer uses their detailed knowledge of that system to write the virus programs, which exploit some weakness or functionality. The effects of a virus depend entirely on the aims of the programmer who created them, and can range from no noticeable impact to the user, to the total destruction of the machine by erasing the files on the hard disk drive. Many viruses remain dormant but replicate themselves on more and more computers when some event triggers their activation, such as a particular date in the future being reached. Erasure of the hard disk, although a relatively low risk, is a possibility and one of many reasons why files and data should be backed up on a routine and regular basis.

Viruses were originally transmitted from computer to computer by attaching themselves to files on floppy disks. However, nowadays almost all viruses are promulgated through the use of the internet, embedded into emails, piggybacked on email attachments, or by downloading files from a web site. Many email viruses automatically email themselves to all addresses in a user's address book. A whole industry has developed to produce antivirus software, which is installed on the computer (see Virus software).

Worms   A worm is very similar to a virus and again is usually created with malicious intent. A worm copies itself from computer to computer by using the fact that almost all computers access networks. Using a network, a worm can expand from a single copy incredibly quickly. In July 2001 the 'Code Red' worm replicated itself over 250 000 times in approximately 9 hours.

A worm usually exploits some sort of security hole in a piece of software or the operating system. For example, the 'Slammer' worm (which caused mayhem in January 2003) exploited a hole in Microsoft's SQL server by creating such a volume of useless network traffic that much on the internet ground to a halt, as it could not cope with the volume.

Trojan horses   A Trojan horse is a malicious computer program which is similar to a virus. It purports to be a normal program, but when executed causes damage to the computer, for example by erasing the hard disk. A Trojan horse has no method of replicating itself. Most email viruses are usually Trojan horses, as they rely on the user opening them to execute the program.

Adware   Adware are programs that have the same effect as web browser pop-ups which are displayed when surfing the internet. Pop-ups are usually intentionally displayed by the developer of the web page being viewed, whereas adware are programs located on the user's PC and contact specific sites to advertise something totally unrelated to the site being viewed. Adware is usually installed on a computer by the user clicking a website link and the program being downloaded and installed in the background without the user being aware. Both pop-ups and adware can become very annoying, and it is difficult to distinguish between them. Pop-ups can be blocked by configuring the web browser to prevent their display (or only allow pop-ups from certain sites). Adware, on the other hand, must be removed from the computer using a program to detect their presence in much the same way as a virus scanner.

Spyware   Spyware is software which is very similar to adware and is installed on the PC in the same way, without the knowledge of the user.

Rather than using pop-up windows, this type of software works entirely in the background without the user being aware. It is designed to gather information about the user's activities when using the PC which is then relayed to advertisers or other interested parties. As with adware, spyware can be detected by special programs that identify and remove them.

Methods of protecting computers

As can be seen from the preceding text there are many ways that the data and information on a computer can be compromised. Protecting data should be viewed in the same way as protecting one's home: it is possible to make it totally impregnable, but this has to be balanced against the associated costs and ease of accessibility. If a burglar still manages to breach the security, the householder will hopefully also have insurance to cover any losses. So it is with protecting computer data, in that for the computer to be useful it will need access to the internet, thereby putting itself at risk. Although there are many ways to reduce this risk it is still possible that these could be breached, and so the equivalent of house-hold insurance is that any vital data is regularly and routinely backed up. Security is like a chain, in that it is only as strong as its weakest link: it is no good putting the latest and most sophisticated locks on a door if it is easy to get through the windows. Protecting computer data from unauthorised users is exactly the same: whereas there is much antivirus software which protects the computer from attack via the internet, do not ignore the simple precautions of leaving it unattended and logged on. Data protection needs to be thought about and planned. It is very easy to become dependent on the tools and information provided by IT without considering the risks in the event of loss.

The security of data can be broadly considered in relation to two groups of users.

- People who have physical access to the computer, such as work colleagues and family.
- People who do not have physical access to the computer but who try to gain access via programs attached to legitimate files or software.

Physical access Authentication is the most common type of security used by this group, controlling access to the computer, a server or an application (Figure 2.16).

Many Windows-based programs offer to save the password so that it does not need to be entered every time access is required. This option

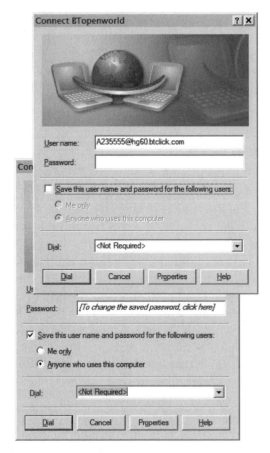

Figure 2.16 Access control screen to internet service provider.

should never be ticked, and nor should a password ever be written as a note attached to the computer (a common occurrence), otherwise anyone can access the system. Authentication software is built into most software applications, especially in multiuser applications such as hospital pharmacy systems. Community systems of the past do not tend to have this type of authentication, but this will need to be introduced as the systems are developed, such as for electronic transmission of prescriptions.

Earlier versions of Windows, such as '95, had no concept of different users accessing the same machine. However, it has become common for more than one person to use the same machine and want to connect to the internet. This means that each user may wish to prevent access to their files by other users. This is clearly relevant where a home machine is used for work-related activities and is also used by the children for personal use. This is catered for in later versions of Windows, such as XP, which allows each user to be given an account with a username and password. The files for each user can be protected by setting permissions on each file or group of files. The allocation of the accounts is controlled by the machine's 'administrator'. This reflects the way computers are set up in most large organisations that incorporate networks.

Non-physical access

Antivirus software   One of the most common ways of protecting against viruses is to install antivirus software. However, because there are so many different methods of infecting computers there are almost as many different products to combat them. Some of the more common suppliers of antivirus software are companies such as McAfee and Symantec, who produce software which is installed on PCs just like any other application. When they are first installed they will usually check the whole of the PC for viruses, and this may take some time. Subsequently they are set up as a background task that monitors all activity on the computer and compares it to the activity of known viruses. This means that as new viruses are discovered, the antivirus software must be updated so that the PC is protected. Nowadays this is carried out automatically by the software contacting the company's web server and downloading the latest updates. If a virus can replicate itself before the virus protection updates are sent out it is still possible to be infected. Therefore, although virus protection software is not foolproof, it is better than nothing at all.

Other simple commonsense methods can also reduce the risk from attack by viruses, for example:

- Avoid programs from unknown sources (such as the internet), and instead stick to commercial software purchased on CDs: you eliminate almost all of the risk from traditional viruses.
- If using Windows software, make sure that Macro Virus Protection is enabled in all Microsoft applications; and you should *never* run macros in a document unless you know what they do.
- Never double-click on an attachment that contains an executable that arrives as an email attachment. Attachments that come in as Word files (.doc), spreadsheets (.xls), images (.gif and .jpg) etc., are data files and can do no damage (unless they have macros embedded, but if Microsoft's Macro Virus Protection is enabled the user will be warned about this when opening the attachment). A file with an extension such as EXE, COM or VBS is an executable, and an executable can do any sort of damage it wants. Once you run it, you have given it permission to do anything on your machine. The only defence is to never run executables that arrive via email.
- Delete emails from unknown sources.

Installation of a firewall A firewall is software that is configured to monitor all network traffic between a local area network (LAN) and the outside world to prevent security breaches. Home users who have broadband connections such as ADSL and cable modems are effectively LANs even though there may only be one computer, because they are permanently connected to the internet and are vulnerable to attack by malicious persons. Any messages that do not meet the specified security criteria are blocked by the firewall. Firewalls can be implemented as software only, sitting on a computer and monitoring traffic. For example, Windows XP has firewall capability installed as part of the operating system which can be switched on or off by the user. It is much more common these days for firewalls to be included with some other piece of network equipment, such as routers, ADSL modems and wireless access points.

3

Database fundamentals

What is a database?

The term database is defined in most dictionaries as 'a structured set of data held in a computer'. Many people use the term to describe any collection of data stored on a computer, for example a list of names and addresses. Although this is indeed a structured set of data, it is not strictly speaking a database. The term is further blurred by the fact that some applications, e.g. spreadsheets, appear to have facilities that mimic the functionality of databases. In this section we will be trying to differentiate and explain the difference between a true database and a collection of stored records. Therefore, for the purposes of this book the definition of a database is 'any collection of integrated records that has a self-describing structure and has tools and functions to allow information to be retrieved'.

Types of database

There are many different types of database 'models' which have developed since the early days of computing. The three main types are:

- Relational
- Hierarchical
- Network.

Each model has its own strengths and weaknesses, but the overwhelming majority of databases nowadays are based on the relational model. This book will concentrate on the relational model, as it is by far the most common one readers are likely to encounter.

The relational database model was first formulated in 1970 by E F Codd, who was a researcher at IBM. He defined the rules that must be applied to the data stored in a relational database.

The principles of relational databases are the same irrespective of the size or the number of records they contain. They may contain a few records, such as in a personal contacts database, or millions, such as in banking systems. However, as the number of records increases so does the complexity of managing and updating them, and can require significant resources. For example, in a personal contacts database there may be only one user accessing the data, whereas in a banking system there will be thousands, all accessing the same data. In the early days of computing each application/program was written to perform a specific function, for example pharmacy labelling. This type of application typically produced dispensing labels with the details of the drug, dosage instructions, etc. The names of the drugs and any information that needed to be recalled were stored in a file so that they could be selected by the user when a label was required. The programmer not only had to program the user interface, but also had to write programs to store the drug names on a permanent storage device such as a hard disk. The files that contained data such as drug descriptions were known as flat files, and the structure that described the organisation of the records and data was held within the program. The structure is needed so that the program knows where one record ends and another begins. In a flat file all of the information is stored as text, with the end of a record marked by a special character called a delimiter. The delimiter usually used to mark the end of a record is a 'newline' character. This character is not normally visible when viewed on a screen, but is present in the file and is used to instruct the computer to move the screen display to the next line down when it is encountered. Table 3.1 shows an example of three records all on separate lines.

In addition, each field within the record is marked with a different delimiter. A field is used to describe an area that stores information. In the example in Table 3.1 there are four fields for each record. Field 1 stores the drug name, field 2 the strength, field 3 the drug form and field 4 the pack size. The best delimiters are those that are not usually used in text, e.g. the bar character '|', but for historical reasons a comma was frequently used, which is also often used to separate text, such as different lines of an address. As text contains commas, the whole field (or variable) is normally enclosed in quotes. These types of file are often referred to as comma-separated variable (CSV) files even when the fields are separated by different delimiters.

These are known as flat files because they do not store structural information on the organisation of the records, and are not true databases if compared with our definition of a database.

Table 3.1 Three drug name records in CSV format

"Amoxicillin","250 mg","Capsules","500"
"Paracetamol","500 mg","Tablets","1000"
"Chlorpheniramine","4 mg/10 ml","Syrup","150 ml"

As computing developed, rather than building the structure into the program, the specific part of the program that was responsible for storing and retrieving data was separated from the user interface programs and sold as a separate application. Such programs were known as database management systems (DBMS) and were sold separately by different suppliers. These systems would include facilities (application program interfaces – API) to allow programs to interface with the DBMS. When the application program required data it would request it via the API (see Figure 3.1).

This interface is analogous to a bank system. The only way to deposit and withdraw money is through the bank's interfaces, i.e. the cashier or equivalent.

The data structure as well as the data itself is held in the DBMS. Common DBMSs include Oracle, Sybase and SQL Server, which have developed over the years to be very complex and sophisticated systems. The complexity is usually related to the amount of information stored, and raises the issue of scalability. A DBMS such as Access, which is provided by Microsoft as part of the Microsoft Office suite of software, is fine for holding relatively small amounts of data, for example up to about 250 Mb. (This is a significant amount of data, but compared to the volumes stored in a banking system it is relatively small.) Access is not designed to cope with concurrent users and the volumes of data that may be required to be held for applications such as banking. Millions of banking transactions occur daily in the UK alone, so that the amount of

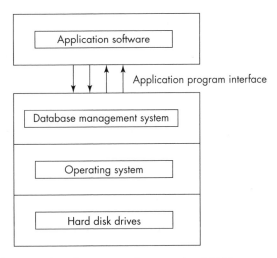

Figure 3.1 Schematic of application interfacing with a DBMS.

data needed to be stored and to keep track of these transactions is enormous. This is why Microsoft also provide a DBMS called SQL Server, which can cope with much larger volumes and competes against scalable DBMSs such as Oracle and Sybase. SQL Server is scalable, i.e. it is designed to cope with small or large volumes and the performance does not deteriorate as the volumes increase. Whereas Access is designed to work on a single computer (although it can be networked), the more scalable products are designed to work with many hundreds of computers accessing the same database. The facilities available to manage the database increase as the volume of data increases. A complex database needs to be managed and can consume significant manpower resources. The person coordinating this management is known as the database administrator (DBA). It is their responsibility to ensure the functionality, integrity and security of the database. In small systems such as a pharmacy system there will generally be no need for a full-time person to have this role, as the system supplier should ensure that these responsibilities are performed automatically or by instructing the customer to follow a set of documented procedures. However, the organisation does need to appoint an administrator who looks after the system and understands the relationship between the data stored and the business processes it supports.

One of the most important aspects of DBMS is the ability to retrieve data so that it can be presented in a way that is meaningful to the end user. This is achieved by using a query language to interrogate the data. One of the more common languages is known as SQL (pronounced 'sequel'), which stands for structured query language. SQL is a standardised language and was originally developed by IBM. It is covered by both ANSI and ISO standards, which means the same commands can generally be used on any SQL-compliant system. Although the name implies that it is query language, only a limited number of the commands relate to the querying of data held in the database: there are many others that allow the creation, updating and maintenance of that data.

Structure of data

Any software application or program running on a computer that stores and manipulates information has to store the data so that it can be recalled and viewed at some time in the future.

The data is stored in an organised form so that it can be retrieved when required. This is known as a database. The data is stored as series of records in a series of tables. Each record consists of one or more related fields that hold the data. The records can be visualised as a table with a row (horizontal) representing a record and columns (vertical) representing the different values held in each field. A column is given a name to identify the data held within it (Figure 3.2). In the example given there are three fields: Drug name, Strength, and Drug form. It should be clear that the fields are related, in that a drug has a name and also has a strength and a form which, when combined together, give a description of that particular drug.

Many readers who have used spreadsheet applications will recognise this structure. In a spreadsheet it is common to store all data being viewed in one table. A spreadsheet is not a database (measured against our earlier definition) because it does not store information about the structure of the data. Owing to the sheer amount of data that needs to be stored in many systems, it is inefficient to store it all in one single table. Thus data is stored in separate tables, which have relationships to each other. This is said to be a relational database. Each table is given a unique name, and their management is achieved by software known as the database management system (DBMS).

Take, for instance, a pharmacy system used to produce dispensing labels and medication history. There will be many different tables that store the information used to produce a dispensing label and the medication a patient has received. An example of a table used to hold data about drugs is given in Table 3.2. This is an example only and the actual table would contain many more columns.

Compare the table shown with the format in a flat file (Table 3.3).

A flat file makes it difficult to search for specific information or to create reports that include only certain fields from each record, whereas the database table allows specific information to be found easily. It also allows DBMS to sort the data based on any field and generate reports that contain only certain fields from each record.

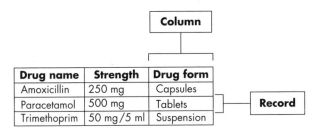

Figure 3.2 Structure of a table.

Table 3.2 Sample Drugs table

Drug name	Brand	Strength	Form	Pack size	Current stock	Reorder quantity
Amoxicillin	Amoxil	250 mg	Capsules	21	147	84
Paracetamol		500 mg	Tablets	1000	700	200
Atenolol	Tenormin	100 mg	Tablets	28	280	112
Chlorpheniramine	Piriton	4 mg/10 ml	Syrup	150 ml	280	150
Amoxicillin	Amoxil	500 mg	Capsules	21	90	63

Table 3.3 Drugs table – data shown as a flat file

"Drug name","Brand","Strength","Form","Pack size","Current stock","Reorder quantity"

"Amoxicillin","Amoxil","250 mg","Capsules","21","147","84"
"Paracetamol"," ","500 mg","Tablets","1000","700","200"
"Atenolol","Tenormin","100 mg","Tablets","28","280","112"
"Chlorpheniramine","Piriton","4 mg/10 ml","Syrup","150 ml","280","150"

In the example Drugs table, the system can easily sort the records by either the generic name or the brand name because of the arrangement of data in columns.

In Table 3.2 there are only a few drugs, but in a typical system there will be many thousands. There will only be a limited number of drug forms – probably fewer than 100 – associated with the drug names. In the example Drugs table, every time a drug with a capsule form is entered, the word 'capsule' would have to be retyped. One of the key principles of a relational database is that the data is held only once if possible. In Table 3.2, each time another drug is added to a database, using a Drugs Maintenance function provided in the pharmacy application, the form must be specified each time. Each time it is entered it is repeating the same information and there is the possibility of its being typed incorrectly or misspelled. The database and system designer ensures that the details of drug forms are held in a separate table and maintained independently (i.e. a Drug Form Maintenance function would be provided). When the Drugs table is updated the maintenance function would be written so that the user could select only a valid drug form from the table (Table 3.4).

The Drugs table structure would then look like that shown in Table 3.5, with the Drug Form Description column replaced by one called Drug Form Code.

The Drug Form Code column in both the Drugs table and the Drug Form table is known as key field, as it is used to relate one table to another. The column name in both tables must be identical. Although

Table 3.4 Drug Forms table

Drug Form code	Drug Form description	Type
TB	Tablets	units
CA	Capsules	units
SY	Syrup	ml
ET	Enteric coated tablets	units
IJ	Injection	units

Table 3.5 New structure of Drugs table

Drug name	Brand	Strength	Drug Form code	Pack size	Current stock	Reorder quantity
Amoxicillin	Amoxil	250 mg	CA	21	147	84
Paracetamol		500 mg	TB	1000	700	200
Atenolol	Tenormin	100 mg	TB	28	280	112
Chlorpheniramine	Piriton	4 mg/10 ml	SY	150 ml	280	150

this is how the data is stored, the developer of the pharmacy application will ensure that whenever a drug name is displayed, it will be displayed wherever possible with the Drug Form Code in the Drugs table replaced by the Drug Form Description from the Drug Forms table (Figure 3.3). So, in the case of the drug amoxicillin in Table 3.5, the full drug description would be: 'Amoxicillin 250 mg capsules', the Drug Form of

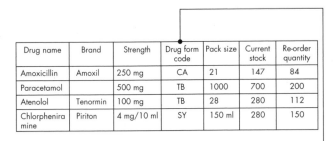

Figure 3.3 Relationship between the Drug and Drug Forms tables.

CA in the Drugs table being used as a reference in the Drug Forms table to give the Drug Form description of 'Capsules'.

Thus a relationship exists between the Drugs table and the Drug Form table based on the key field Drug Form Code, hence the reason why this type of database is called relational. The DBMS provides commands and functions to manipulate the data in the different tables. These commands and functions are collectively known as the query language. One of the most widely used query languages is SQL. Although the name implies that it is only used to look at and display the data, it is also used to create and update tables.

The principles described for Drug and Drug Forms tables are used throughout the database. A typical relational database has anywhere from 10 to more than 1000 tables, each containing a column or columns that other tables can key on to so as to obtain information from that table.

Views

When data from more than one table is combined to create a new virtual table using a common key field, the tables are said to be 'joined'. This concept is one of the fundamental aspects of the relational database. The tables can be visualised as a single table even though the data is stored in separate physical tables. The columns used as keys are not normally displayed. The Drug Form code for a particular drug from the Drugs table is used to find the record with the same Drug Form code in the Drug Forms table. For example, the Drug Form code 'CA' will be used to find the record with the same Drug Form code in the Drugs Form table. The Drug Form description can then be used in the joined table instead of the code. This is repeated for every drug form code in the Drugs table. Any other columns from the Drug Forms table can be displayed in the joined table if required. The joined table is shown in Table 3.6.

The joined tables are said to give a view of the data. Query languages allow all or only selected columns to be displayed. In the example in Table 3.6 the Drug Form code is redundant and could be excluded from the view. The DBMS allows views to be created that display the columns required from any tables where a relationship exists. In Microsoft Access, a view is known as a query.

Use of primary and foreign keys

In an application such as a pharmacy labelling system, when a drug is dispensed the stock level of that drug needs to be updated. If the drug

Table 3.6 Joined Drug and Drug Forms table

Drug name	Brand	Strength	Drug Form description	Type	Drug Form Code	Pack size	Current stock	Reorder quantity
Amoxicillin	Amoxil	250 mg	Tablets	units	CA	21	147	84
Paracetamol		500 mg	Capsules	units	TB	1000	700	200
Atenolol	Tenormin	100 mg	Tablets	units	TB	28	280	112
Chlorpheniramine	Piriton	4 mg/ 10 ml	Syrup	ml	SY	150 ml	280	150

dispensed is amoxicillin, for example, then the system will need to locate the correct record to update. In a Drugs table there will be many occurrences (or records) of the drug amoxicillin because of the different strengths, drug forms and pack sizes. If the current stock level of the amoxicillin 250 mg capsules needs to be updated to reflect that the drug has been dispensed, how will the DBMS know which amoxicillin record to update? There must be something in the record to uniquely identify the record (row) so that the correct drug can be selected and the current stock level updated. In the example Drugs table the drug name, strength, drug form and pack size would need to be used to select the correct drug. Pack size is required as there are many products that will have the same drug name, strength and drug form but which are supplied in different pack sizes. The combination of the columns that make a row unique is known as the primary key. If more than one column is required to uniquely identify the record it is known as a compound key. To have to specify all the columns becomes unwieldy, and therefore it is usual to make sure that each row has a column that uniquely identifies that row. This can be a column which is guaranteed to be unique, such as a PIP code, or it can be generated by the DBMS. In pharmacy applications it is usual for the developer to generate a unique number for each different drug, because even though the PIP code is unique it may not be readily available for new products. The column containing this unique reference is known as the primary key. Therefore, adding a primary key to the Drugs table would give the table as shown in Figure 3.4.

This primary key then makes it easy for the DBMS to uniquely identify a drug in the Drugs table, which can then be used and stored in other tables to uniquely identify a drug. An example of another table that references the data in the Drugs table would be one containing drug orders – Drug Orders. Rather than store the description every time a drug is ordered, a column will be included which contains the primary key of the Drugs table (Figure 3.5). Similarly, the Supplier ID would reference the Supplier table. Therefore, the Drug ID column from the

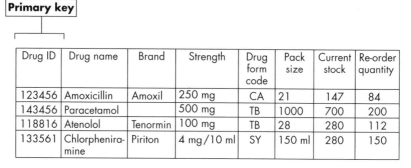

Drug ID	Drug name	Brand	Strength	Drug form code	Pack size	Current stock	Re-order quantity
123456	Amoxicillin	Amoxil	250 mg	CA	21	147	84
143456	Paracetamol		500 mg	TB	1000	700	200
118816	Atenolol	Tenormin	100 mg	TB	28	280	112
133561	Chlorphenira-mine	Piriton	4 mg/10 ml	SY	150 ml	280	150

Figure 3.4 Drug table with primary key column added.

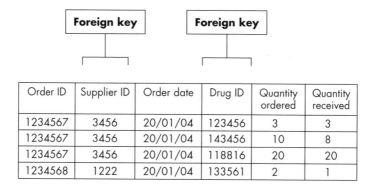

Order ID	Supplier ID	Order date	Drug ID	Quantity ordered	Quantity received
1234567	3456	20/01/04	123456	3	3
1234567	3456	20/01/04	143456	10	8
1234567	3456	20/01/04	118816	20	20
1234568	1222	20/01/04	133561	2	1

Figure 3.5 Drug Orders table showing foreign key columns.

Drugs table is said also to be a foreign key into the Drug Orders table. Similarly, the Supplier ID in the Supplier table is also a foreign key.

These tables are examples only, and in reality would actually contain many more columns.

Referential integrity

In the example above the Drug Orders table is dependent on both the Drugs table and the Supplier table. If a record in either table is deleted and the Drug Orders table contains a reference to either of those records, the drug name and supplier name cannot be displayed as the relationship no longer exists. The DBMS can be used to ensure that this situation cannot arise and hence to ensure the referential integrity of the system, i.e. a record cannot be deleted if it still has a relationship with a record in another table.

Performance and indexes

The concepts of the relational database are relatively simple, and the examples given show only a small subset of the data stored in a database. In order for the DBMS to join two tables it must scan the values in the foreign key columns and make a join based on matching values. This would be a very slow process, and in the early days many people said that relational databases were too slow to be of any practical use. The DBMS enables indexes to be created on certain key fields, and in many instances does this automatically. This means that when the DBMS needs to find a record it can use an index to go to it, rather than have to search through the whole table.

Data types

When a table is created, the columns that make up that table have to be given names. In addition, each column is allocated a data type, which determines the type of data that can be stored in it. For example, a column defined as data type 'Integer' can only store whole numbers, e.g. 37, whereas a column defined as data type 'Character' can store text. This is necessary, as a computer needs to know what legitimate computations it can perform on different columns. For example, it is legitimate to add two numbers stored in a column defined as integer data types, but not to add two values which are stored in a 'character' data type. Storing the text characters '3' and '7' in character data type is allowed. However, in this form they could not be added to another number. The character data type would first have to be converted into an integer before the computation could proceed. There are many different data types:

- Numerics, e.g. interger, real
- Strings, e.g. character
- Booleans, e.g. true, false or null
- Datetimes, e.g. date, time.

Columns defined as character data types also have to be defined with the maximum number of characters that can be held, so that memory space is used efficiently.

Database schema

When any application stores data that is subsequently going to be used to produce reports and information, it is essential to understand the relationships between the tables holding the data. The description of the

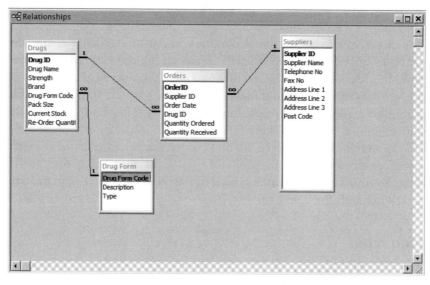

Figure 3.6 Graphical database schema.

relationships is known as the database schema and is often supplied as a diagram showing the tables and columns and their interrelationships. Other supporting documentation is also required to show the data types, etc. associated with each column. An example of a diagrammatic database schema is shown in Figure 3.6.

In this example the relationships are shown by lines joining the column names. The characters '1' and '∞' show what type of relationship exists. For example, the relationship between 'Drug ID' in the Drugs table and Drug ID in the Orders table is a one-to-many type: the 'Drug ID 12345' will appear in the Drugs table only once, as this is unique to a particular drug, but may appear in the Order table many times, i.e. each time the drug is ordered.

In reality the database schema will be far more complex than the example given, and it is essential that if the data in the application is to be used to provide and produce reports the schemas are provided with the application, so that the relationships can be understood. It is impossible to design and produce a meaningful report of the data required if the schema is not available.

Database design and data collection

Databases are used as repositories for the data collected by an application, such as a pharmacy system. The design of the database, i.e. the tables and relationships required to support an application, will be dictated by the business processes with which it is used. The business processes used in pharmacy are different for each sector, which means that the systems designed for one sector will not necessarily be applicable to those used in another. Take, for example, hospital and community pharmacy. Whereas both sectors have a requirement to produce dispensing labels, the processes involved in producing the final dispensed prescription that is given to the patient are very different. This is one of the reasons why a pharmacy system designed and sold for community use is very rarely used in hospitals, and vice versa. When designing a computer system the designer must first look at all the components of the business process, paying particular attention to the data requirements and their relationship with real-life events. This process is known as systems analysis and is a subject in its own right, requiring that an analyst consult and observe the people who will use and interact with the computer system. This can be a time-consuming and expensive exercise, and on large projects whole teams of analysts are employed. However, this is essential if vital aspects of the processes are not to be overlooked, which would be expensive to correct once a system is built. Once all the requirements have been fully identified, the functionality of the system can be specified and the database designed to support that functionality. One of the major uses of computer systems is to produce reports based on the data collected as part of the business process. If these reports are to accurately reflect what has happened and make informed decisions, the system must be designed and used properly. For example, if a mistake is made in creating a dispensing label it is important it is rectified in the correct way. Many users just create another label, rather than rectify the original. This can have many implications, such as incorrect usage figures, stock levels and patient records, to name but a few, and clearly would give inaccurate and misleading information. Thus it is important to ensure that functionality is available within the application that enables mistakes to be rectified easily, and that users are properly trained in the correct procedures for maintaining the data. It is not uncommon for computer systems to be blamed for producing incorrect information by users who do not fully understand the relationship between the business processes and the data stored in the system. This has led to the term garbage in garbage out (GIGO), which is used to remind users that computers are tools that manipulate the data they are given. If data input is incorrect it will give erroneous results.

Thus when producing information in the form of reports from computer databases it is essential to understand not only the relationships of tables in the underlying database, but also the mechanisms by which the tables are populated with data. The results of the reports should always be reconciled and validated by reference to other independent data. It is common when suppliers are trying to sell their systems for them to give demonstrations that purport to show how easy it is to create reports using query tools. In reality, although the tools allow the data to be accessed, the production of meaningful and accurate reports requires a significant amount of time and effort in understanding the underlying business processes and their relationship with the data. Do not underestimate the resources required to produce useful and meaningful reports.

Reporting tools

Any application that runs on the Windows operating system and uses a relational database will invariably provide facilities to allow third-party reporting tools to access that database. This is usually achieved by using an application program interface (API) created by Microsoft and is known as open database connectivity (ODBC). Any application which is ODBC compliant will, subject to the correct driver being available, be able to access the data in a relational database. This allows computer systems that use different database management systems to access databases supplied by different manufacturers, thereby allowing the creation of reports that use data stored in separate computer systems.

Many tools and software applications support the use of ODBC, the most common of which is Microsoft's Access. ODBC is used to link a table in an Access database to a table in an external database. Data in spreadsheets and text files can also be accessed in this way. Queries and reports can then be created using graphical tools and wizards provided as part of Access, using data stored in external databases and files. There are many sophisticated tools supplied by companies such as Business Objects and Cognos that allow reports to be written using these graphical tools. The skills and knowledge required to use these are quite significant and the resources required should not be underestimated. As outlined earlier, a detailed knowledge of the business processes and the underlying database structure of the computer system is essential if meaningful reports and information are to be produced.

4

Networks and communications

What is a network?

In computing the term network refers to one or more computers connected together so they can communicate with each other. When connected they can exchange data and use each other's resources (e.g. printers, disk drives, etc.). Also, many software applications depend on a network to enable them to function, for example email and web browsers. Without a network infrastructure these applications could not receive and send data from one computer to another, which is fundamental to their usefulness. The most common and largest example of networking is the internet.

Millions of computers form the internet, which allows them to exchange and access each other's data. The information is normally presented as web pages, which can be accessed by a browser such as Internet Explorer or Netscape Navigator, but there are many other ways of accessing the data, such as downloading files.

All the computer's other equipment that makes up the internet is usually represented diagrammatically as a cloud, as the route taken by

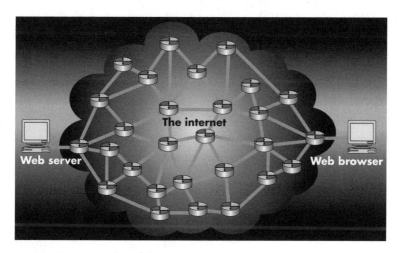

Figure 4.1 Representation of the internet.

the data from one computer to another is transparent. Although a great deal of technology is required to get data from a web server to a browser, the route is irrelevant to the computers involved (Figure 4.1).

How networks evolved

The simplest form of network is formed by two computers connected together via a cable between one of the communications ports, such as the serial port, on each. In addition to the cable, software must be installed on each computer so that they can exchange information (Figure 4.2). This is essentially how networks began.

However, the limitation of this method is that only two computers can be involved, as additional communication ports are required for each additional computer. To enable more computers to exchange information the method of connection and the software required had to become more sophisticated. Different manufacturers produced their own proprietary hardware and software for communicating with other computers. The arrangement by which computers are connected together is known as the topology (Figure 4.3).

When all devices are connected to a central cable using a T connector, the arrangement is known a 'bus' topology. When all computers are connected to another in the shape of a ring the arrangement is known as a 'ring' topology, whereas when computers are connected to a central hub it is known as a 'star' topology.

The topology employed is determined by the hardware (physical topology) and software (logical topology) requirements of the network protocol being used, i.e. the rules by which the network should be physically connected and the rules by which the data should logically be sent to other computers on the network.

The computers must be connected by some physical medium, i.e. the cable, and have equipment (i.e. the network card) to send out electrical signals via the cable. These signals are picked up by the computers attached to the cable and represent the bits of data being transmitted. One of the most popular architectures is Ethernet, which can be used in both bus and star topologies. The most common physical topology is the bus, which uses a T connector (it has three branches) to

Figure 4.2 Computers connected by a cable using communications port.

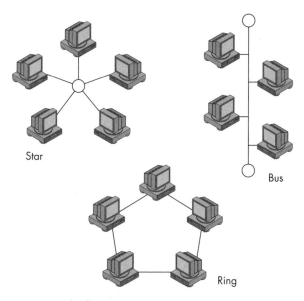

Star

Bus

Ring

Figure 4.3 Examples of different network topologies.

connect the computer to a central cable. Adding another T connector allows another computer to access the cable, and so on. This type of connector allows any number of computers to be connected together using a common cable. In some networks this is simply a T connector; in others it is actually a box into which connectors can be plugged, but it performs the same function as a T connector. Bus technology is relatively inexpensive and easy to install for smaller networks and is almost invariably the type that is likely to be encountered (Figure 4.4).

Each topology had its advantages and disadvantages, and it soon became clear that there would be major benefits if all computers could exchange data irrespective of the manufacturer. In order for this to happen standards had to be agreed which covered the exchange of data. From 1978 onwards a model of the different elements required to enable computer systems to communicate with each other was developed by a subcommittee of the International Standards Organisation (ISO) and is known as the Open Systems Interconnection (OSI) Reference Model. This is broken down into seven different layers, each layer performing a specific task. For example, the first layer defines the standard relating to how the hardware is physically connected, i.e. the cables, sockets, plugs and the electrical characteristics.

The standards have enabled networking to progress to the level of sophistication that enables the World Wide Web to operate. Enabling a

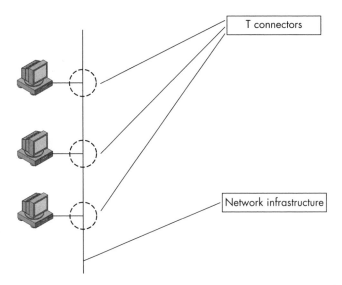

Figure 4.4 Computers connected to network using T connectors (bus topology).

network on a computer these days is simply a matter of purchasing a network card and configuring the networking software. The networking software that uses the card is usually part of the operating system, and is known as the network subsystem. Later versions of Windows, such as XP, have much more support for networking than earlier versions such as '95.

Although there are many advantages to sharing data between computers there must be a way to ensure that only authorised users can access a computer or its data. This is achieved by allocating a username and password to an individual/computer which is authorised to access all or certain parts of that computer.

Why are networks important?

The main reason why networks are important is that the resources available on one computer are available to others. Resources are any facility provided by the computer. They can be in the form of information and files, but can also include other devices such as printers, telephone lines, etc. This means that instead of having to have a printer for each computer in a small office, a network allows all computers to use one printer. These are called local area networks (LANs), as the computers are all in the same building or in close proximity to each other. LANs can be connected to the internet via telephone lines, thus enabling all users to access the internet (Figure 4.5). In large networks where there are many users, the telephone lines are of a special type which are able to handle high data transfer rates. BT and other telephone operators supply special digital lines which do not need to be dialled and can support differing throughputs depending on the requirements of the business. These types of line are generally 'always on', i.e. are permanently available and used exclusively by the business or organisation, and are known as leased lines. In order to prevent unauthorised users from the internet accessing the LAN a device known as a firewall checks all the data passing along the telephone line and only allows authorised traffic to pass through.

Every time a person accesses the internet they are relying on the ability of computers to network. Every time an email is sent or received

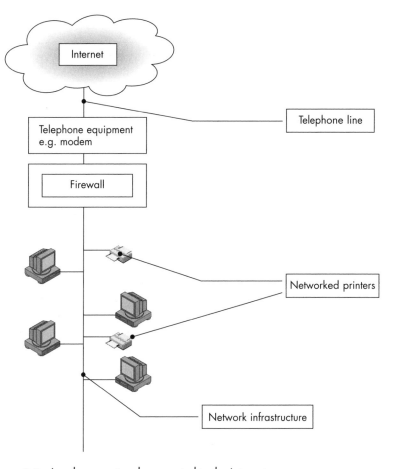

Figure 4.5 Local area network connected to the internet.

the computer must be networked to other computers to access the email server (i.e. equivalent to a post office box where letters can be collected).

Computers used in hospital pharmacy systems will almost invariably be networked so that they can access a central database. For example, the patient medication records will be held on one central computer and the other computers will access the same information via the network. In the home environment, until recently, the only use of network technology was to access the internet through the telephone line, as most homes only had one computer. As people start to work from home, more families are beginning to have more than one computer and all want to access the same resources, such as the internet and printers. Home networking enables all the computers in the home to access the internet at the same time, and to share other resources such as files and printers. This is often referred to as small office/home office (SOHO) networking and uses exactly the same principles as large networks in businesses and hospitals.

In the changing world of pharmacy, many pharmacists are starting to become mobile and have notebook computers which are used in many locations as well as at home. These notebooks need to access a network so that they can send and receive email. At some time they will also want to be able to print documents wherever they are working. Access to a network will allow these users to use a printer or any other network resource, such as the internet. Until recently these notebooks had to be physically connected by a cable, but now it is possible to use wireless access. Wireless access allows the computer to connect to a network via a piece of equipment known as a wireless access point, which is used instead of a physical cable. Notebooks can be equipped with wireless network adapters that allow the computer to access a network if it is within 100 metres of a wireless access point, thus removing the restriction of a physical connection.

Many public places, such as railway stations and hotels, are starting to provide wireless access points so that users can access the internet. Wireless access points can also be purchased for the home environment and are relatively cheap (less than £100), thus enabling pharmacists with notebook computers to access the home network (without cabling), which in turn can access the internet. This gives all the advantages of networks without the need to run cabling throughout the house.

In the home environment, to access the internet a computer will normally have to connect to an internet service provider (ISP), for which a charge will be made. Each computer that accesses the ISP is given a username and password unique to that computer, thereby ensuring that only authorised users can access the service. Once connected to the ISP the computer can access any other computer on the internet, which is essentially a public place or a public network. These computers are almost always accessed through a web browser.

It is possible with networking to provide a link to a private network, e.g. a hospital or Primary Care Trust network, which uses the internet as a transport mechanism. This is known as a virtual private network (VPN). All the data travelling on this channel is encrypted and cannot be seen by any computer on the public internet. This means that once a computer has access to the internet the computer has the potential to connect to any other private network, whether business or a small home network.

The internet can be accessed by telephones and PDAs using the GPRS telephone network. This means that any facilities available via a desktop or notebook computer are available from a handheld device. The limitation is the fact that most content from the internet is formatted for a large screen and not for a small device, but the advantage is that the device is always available and switches on instantly. It is already possible to read, write, receive and send emails from a PDA device while the user is out of the office. This means that anybody away from their normal desktop or notebook can receive and send emails while on the move, avoiding the need to trawl through all their emails when they get back to their office (see PDA for more details). As technology progresses it is easy to envisage that the PDA linked to a network will become an essential part of the pharmacist's toolset.

Networks allow computers to act as servers to other computers, print server, file server, database server, mail server, fax server, etc.

How do networks work?

The best analogy that can be used to describe and understand how a network works is the way a letter or parcel is sent from the sender to the recipient. The sender addresses the letter or parcel with a unique address, i.e. there is no other person in the world with that same address. If the address on the parcel is not unique then it may be delivered to the wrong recipient. Each computer or device on a network has to have a unique address. Computer networks work by bundling the data into small packets or parcels, each addressed with the unique identifier of the recipient computer. In the postal system a letter is sent to a Post Office sorting centre, which determines the most efficient route to send the letter based on the address on the envelope. In a computer network the role of the post office is fulfilled by specialised computers called routers. These routers look at the address of the recipient and send the packet to the next router, and so on until the packet is received by the recipient. If a particular route is blocked for any reason the packet will be resent until acknowledgement is received that the packet has been delivered. The design of networks was influenced by those used by the military, which needed to be resilient in case of nuclear attack, which could destroy major sections of a network. If a packet cannot be delivered by a particular route another route is tried until it is delivered. Thus if the route chosen by a router is blocked because that part of the network is not working, it will try to resend the packet by a different route.

Physical equipment

Each piece of equipment that connects to a network needs to be given a unique address, which is allocated when the equipment is manufactured. This is known as the media access control (MAC) address. In a PC, there is a network card which is allocated a MAC address by the manufacturer and is used to connect the computer to the network. This card, as well as consisting of electronic components, also has a port into which a cable can be connected so that the computer can be physically connected to the network.

Many modern computers have the network card built into the motherboard, rather than a separate card. Notebook computers also have the network card built in, or they are provided on PCMCIA cards.

In the early days of computing the cable used to connect computers together was known as a coaxial cable (very similar to that used to connect a television to an aerial), as this was the only type that could shield the electrical signals from interference by external electrical fields. This type of cable was quite thick, difficult to work with, and has largely been replaced by Category 5 twisted pair cable with RJ45 connectors on each end. RJ45 connectors consist of both female and male ends (Figure 4.6).

Category 5 (often abbreviated to CAT 5) cables are easy to run and can be used for telephones as well as data. Many organisations run a backbone of Category 5 cables from the main computer room to each floor of the building, terminated at each end by a female RJ45 connector. For convenience they are grouped together in racks. Twisted pair cables are then run from each cabinet to various points in each office

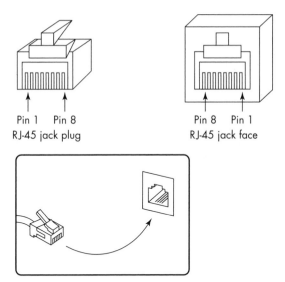

Figure 4.6 Male and female RJ45 connectors.

and terminated at a wall or floor socket with female RJ45 connectors (Figure 4.7). This arrangement is known as structured cabling and has the advantage of being very flexible. If a computer needs to be connected to the network it is just a matter of finding a free RJ45 socket and connecting it to the computer with a CAT5 cable with male RJ45 ends (Figure 4.8).

Network hub

If all the network points in a room are used, extra connection points can be created by installing a network hub, which effectively creates additional wall sockets (Figure 4.9). Network hubs are available with different numbers of additional sockets and are analogous to mains electrical four-way adapters. The network hub is connected to the wall socket and the computers or printers to the additional female RJ45 sockets.

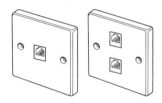

Figure 4.7 RJ45 wall/floor sockets (female).

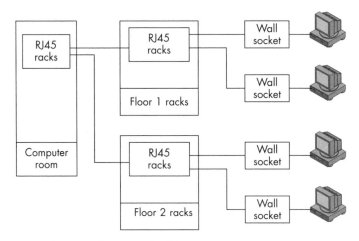

Figure 4.8 Schematic of structured cabling.

Figure 4.9 Network hub.
[Courtesy of Chris Elmes]

When all the equipment described above is connected together it is known as a local area network, as it is located in the same building or in close proximity. To be able to connect to computers on other networks such as the internet there has to be a way of connecting one LAN to another. This is usually achieved by using the public telephone infrastructure. However, this requires special equipment at each end of the telephone line. The telephone system was originally designed to carry voice signals and uses analogue signals. In order for it to be used to transfer the digital data used by computers, the signals have to be converted to analogue and then back into digital. The device that performs this function is known as a modem (see Chapter 1), and there needs to be a modem at each end of the link. In addition to the physical connection a device known as a router (or gateway) is connected to the modem. The router is usually a combination of hardware and software which looks at the address associated with the data packets and routes them to the appropriate computer.

In a simple home environment, the computer is connected to a modem, which is then used to connect to an internet service provider (ISP), that has modems and routers on their network to enable the rest of the internet to be accessed. In a business environment there will be many users requiring access to the internet. The maximum speed at which a modem can transmit data is 56 kilobits per second, which is far too slow if many users are accessing the network at the same time. In these instances special telephone lines and equipment (which are used instead of modems) are purchased from telephone suppliers which can work at speeds of more than 1024 kilobits per second. The link is usually located in the organisation's computer room and managed by dedicated computer staff. The equivalent type of telephone line for a small business or home user which allows greater throughput of data (maximum of 128 kilobits per second) is an ISDN (integrated services digital network) line. This must be installed by BT and uses special devices at each end which replace the modems. It is packaged as 'BT Highway' and, like conventional lines, is a dial-up connection. These lines are charged on the basis of the amount of time connected, unless using an ISP that offers a fixed charge per month. (Note: With ISDN, to get the maximum throughput of 128 kilobits per second two lines are used, incurring two charges.) ISDN is being superseded by ADSL (asymmetric digital subscriber line), which allows voice and data to use the existing telephone system at the same time. The availability of ADSL is governed by whether the BT telephone exchange has been converted for ADSL use, and is not yet available in all parts of the country. ADSL lines use special ADSL modems and microfilter/line splitters which connect both the normal phone and the ADSL modem to one telephone socket. ADSL is referred to as 'always on', i.e. no dial-up is required, and the charges incurred are fixed on a monthly basis irrespective of the length of time the line is used. ADSL lines are also known as broadband because the data transfer rate is much greater than that of conventional and ISDN lines. ADSL lines are equivalent to the type of telephone line used in businesses which are 'always on', and allow the home user to set up mini home networks that allow all computers to access the internet and receive voice calls at the same time, using one telephone line. The fact that these lines are 'always on' means that additional considerations need to be taken into account to prevent unauthorised access, for example the inclusion of a firewall. Households that have access to cable TV can get the same facilities as ADSL telephone lines by using cable modems instead of ADSL modems to connect to the cable bringing in the TV picture.

Network software

The physical connection between the computers is only one aspect of the operation of a network. Computers communicate by using software to send data from one computer to another. This software has to be able to send and receive data in a form that can be understood by each computer involved. This is achieved by using a protocol, which is a set of rules that govern how the two communicating devices can exchange data with each other. This is analogous to two people communicating to each other using a walkie-talkie, who must agree when each can speak. They cannot speak at the same time, and so will use the word 'Over' to signify that they have finished. They must also decide which language they are going to use. There are hundreds of different protocols in use that enable computers and computing equipment to communicate with each other. However, the most common suite of protocols used in the internet and small networks is the transmission control protocol/internet protocol, nearly always referred to as TCP/IP. Each piece of network equipment worldwide has a unique address, and as part of the IP is assigned an address. This address consists of four numbers separated by a stop, e.g. 192.168.100.1. When a computer connects to the internet via an ISP an IP address is allocated to the computer by the ISP. This address is used in all communications with other computers. When a computer on a LAN wishes to communicate with one on the internet it does so using a router (or gateway). A router is a piece of equipment that connects one or more networks together. Its job is to forward data packets from one network to another so that they arrive at the correct destination. A router is analogous to a post office sorting centre, used to deliver letters to the correct address. The sorting office looks at the address on the letter and determines the most appropriate route for the letter to take. The router does the same thing with the data packets by looking at the IP address and determining the most appropriate route based on routing table stored in its memory. Routers are extremely sophisticated devices, even though for home or small business use they can be purchased for less than £100. They are often combined with other devices such as ADSL modems to provide multiple functionality.

On PCs, the network software required to connect to other networks is provided as part of the operating system. All modern PC operating systems, such as Windows, MacOS and Linux, have a network subsystem which uses TCP/IP.

There are millions of LANs that use the same IP addresses to communicate with each other on a local basis. The range of addresses usually used and reserved for private networks starts with 192.168.x.y (where x and y are different numbers for each computer on the local network). If these addresses were used on the internet they would not be unique, as there are many LANs with the same address. This situation is resolved by using network address translation (NAT) software. This allows a local area network to use one set of IP addresses for internal traffic, i.e. on the LAN, and another set for external traffic to another network. This fufils two main functions: it adds security by acting like a firewall, hiding internal LAN addresses from the external world, and it allows business or home networks to employ IP addresses that will not conflict with those used by other organisations.

Different types of network that may be encountered

The ways in which networks can be configured is infinite, as can be seen from the above. In many organisations the management of computer networks is a full-time job and, depending on the size of the network, can have whole departments dedicated to it. However, the functionality and principles involved can be applied to small networks used for business and home. This section details some of the ways in which network technology can be used and configured to allow resources such as the internet and printers to be shared in a convenient way.

Small office/home office (SOHO) networks can be set up in a variety of ways, and the following factors will affect the way in which the network is configured and its functionality.

- **Internet access availability** The network configuration can be limited by the options available for connecting to the internet. Almost all home and small business users will connect via an ISP. Whereas standard modems and dial-up access are available to nearly everyone and require little additional investment, higher bandwidth (i.e. speed of data transmission) requires that the household or business has access to a broadband link using ADSL or cable TV. ADSL is not yet available on all telephone exchanges, and cable is not available to all households. Broadband allows much faster connection speeds than conventional dial-up analogue modems, and has different speeds for download and upload. Download speeds are typically 512 and 256 kilobits per second, although other speeds are available. In contrast, the maximum speed of a dial-up modem is 56 kilobits per second. The telephone connection is usually the slowest part of any network and will determine how quickly data is transferred.

- **Equipment and cost** In the past the equipment and software required to provide the functionality of networks cost many hundreds or thousands of pounds. These costs have fallen dramatically over the last few years, so that it is cost-effective for most people to consider setting up a small network.

- **ADSL/CABLE telephone lines** One of the most significant advances is the provision and cost of high-speed telephone links that allow multiple users to access the internet at the same time and at a price within the reach of most people. Typical costs for 'always on' access are around £30 per month.

- **ADSL modem** ADSL modems are available from the supplier as part of the ADSL service. However, ADSL modems are also available combined with a network hub and router software, which allows a number of devices to form a small LAN with access to the internet. These are available for less than £100.

- **Hub** A hub is simply a device that allows multiple devices to be connected to the same physical piece of wire, acting as a junction box for network cabling. However, most modern hubs have inbuilt intelligence (hence requiring a power supply) which allows simple management of the data packets. Hubs are made with variable numbers of female RJ45 ports into which cables with male RJ45 terminators are plugged. The most common numbers of ports for home and small business are four and eight.

- **Routers** Routers look like hubs but have more inbuilt intelligence, which allows them to take data packets from one network and send them on to another.

- **Wireless access point** A wireless access point is a device that connects to a LAN and allows devices such as notebook computers with wireless network cards to access the LAN without the need for a cable. These have a range of about 100 metres, and so have the advantage of being able to be used anywhere in a domestic household and connect to the internet via the ADSl link. A wireless access point and wireless network card for the notebook are available for less than £100.

- **Combined ADSL/hub/router/ADSL modems** Devices that combine the functionality of a network hub, ADSL modem, router and wireless access point into one unit are available for just over £100. It is important when selecting equipment to understand the functionality included in the device.

- **Configuration simplicity** Most small office/home office networks do not have people with the expertise of a managed IT department. The configuration that is eventually chosen must therefore be simple enough for the average user to install and maintain.
- **The environment of the network** Environmental factors can affect the choice of equipment used. For example, some buildings might have restrictions on installing cabling, or it may be difficult to run cabling. Some locations, such as hospitals, might restrict the use of wireless network devices because of electrical shielding or interference.
- **Security for the internet connection** Connecting a network to the internet via an 'always on' connection has implications regarding security and protecting the computers on the network from attack. The network can be protected by using a combination of network address translation and firewall technologies.
- **Preferences and knowledge of the installer** The network configuration is invariably influenced by the knowledge, experience and personal preferences of the person installing the components.
- **Internet service providers** An ISP is a company that provides access points to the internet via dial-up telephone lines, ADSL telephone lines or optical cables (also used for cable TV). They will also offer other facilities, such as email and web hosting services. The cost of providing these services will vary depending on the type of access being used and the services provided. There are many different pricing plans, ranging from those based on the time connected via the telephone line to those that offer unlimited access for a fixed monthly fee. There are hundreds of ISPs, some of the most common being America On Line (AOL), BT, Yahoo, and Wanadoo. To look at the full range of ISPs available visit http://www.uk-isp-directory.co.uk/. It is essential to understand which services are required from the ISP. As a minimum most ISPs will provide email services and an initial amount of disk space that can be used to create a small web site. The ISP will create an account and allocate a username and password to each subscriber. Before a user can use the account they must log in using this username and password. When connecting via a dial-up modem, the software used to connect to the ISP must be configured to dial a telephone number and supply the username and password. ISP providers usually provide a setup disk, which takes care of this configuration and guides the user through the process. It is usual to configure the software so that the ISP is dialled automatically (if not already connected) when an application requires access to the internet, the software supplying the username and prompting for the password. The system is often configured to remember the password so that the system can automatically log on to the service provider without any intervention. This is not an option to be recommended, as anybody with access to the PC will be able to access the ISP account without knowing the username and password.

The account created on the ISP is normally accessed using a web browser (Figure 4.10). This means that it is usually possible to access the

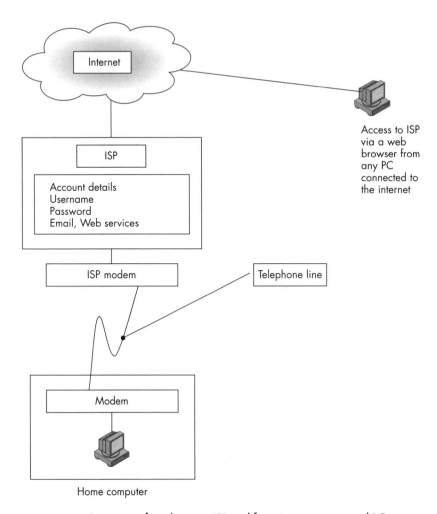

Account details
Username
Password
Email, Web services

Access to ISP
via a web
browser from
any PC
connected to
the internet

Figure 4.10 Connection from home to ISP and from internet-connected PC.

user's email from any PC that has access to the internet by logging in to the ISP's home web page and entering the username and password.

When an ADSL or cable connection service is purchased the connection is 'always on', that is, there is no need for the computer to dial the ISP. However, as with dial-up connections the subscriber will still have an account and username and password to enable access to email, and will still be able to access the account from any PC connected to the internet.

There are many different pricing plans charged by the ISPs and it is important to compare like with like and to check what is being offered.

Many ISPs offer unlimited access for dial-up lines for a fixed monthly charge, as opposed to a cost per minute. ADSL tends to be a fixed monthly charge, but new pricing models are being introduced which also take into account the amount of data transferred. Always check the terms and conditions of the service.

There are many different ways of making a physical connection with another computer. The configurations described below show how small businesses and home users can configure equipment to create small networks that offer significant benefits.

Small office/home office network configurations

Single computer connected to an ISP via a dial-up analogue modem

This is the most common configuration of a home network used to access the internet and is the way that the majority of people initially set up their computers (Figure 4.11). It consists of a single computer connected to an ISP using networking software which is supplied as part of the operating system. In the majority of cases this will be Windows. The ISP provides modems that allow a home computer to dial a telephone number. To connect to these ISPs the user has to enter a username and password, which identifies the computer to the ISP and prevents

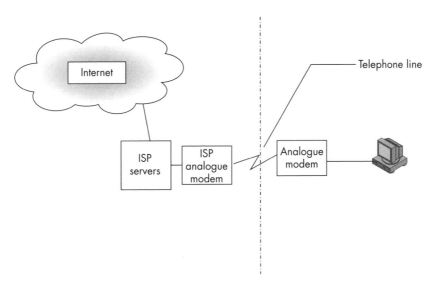

Figure 4.11 Usual network access – single computer connected to an ISP via a dial-up analogue modem.

unauthorised access. The software that connects to the ISP is part of the network subsystem of the operating system being used. PCs running earlier versions of Windows, such as '95 and '98, have an option called Network Neighbourhood, whereas later versions such as XP have an option called Network Places. The modem will be internal to the computer, or may be external and connected via one of the communications ports, such as the USB or serial ports.

The disadvantages of this arrangement are that the link is relatively slow and the telephone cannot be used for voice calls while the computer is connected to the internet. In households where there is more than one computer, only one can be connected to the telephone line at any one time.

Single computer connected to an ISP via an ADSL modem

This configuration (Figure 4.12) is exactly the same as the previous one except that the modem is replaced by an ADSL modem. ADSL modems are available which can be fitted internally, but these days it is more common to use an external modem connected to the computer via a USB cable.

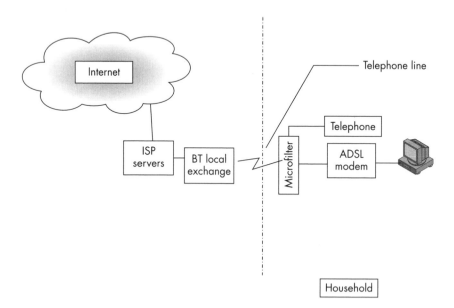

Figure 4.12 Network access – single computer connected to an ISP via an ADSL modem.

This method has the advantage that the speed is ten times faster than a standard analogue modem for a 512 kilobit broadband connection (other broadband speeds are available which are priced accordingly). It also has the advantage that the connection is 'always on' and there is no delay in dialling the ISP. The telephone line can also be used for voice calls at the same time.

The disadvantage is that because the connection is 'always on' the computer is more vulnerable to attack by hackers. A firewall therefore needs to be installed to prevent unauthorised access. Many firewalls are available either cheaply or free, and Windows XP includes a simple firewall capability within the operating system.

Multiple computers with an ADSL connection via one of the computers

This arrangement (Figure 4.13) means that each of the computers will need a network adapter so they can be connected together, thereby creating a network of at least two computers, one of which is connected to the ADSL modem. All the computers are connected together using a small hub and CAT 5 cables with male RJ45 ends. One end of the cable connects to the network card and the other to the hub.

In this arrangement each computer needs to be assigned an IP address. This can be achieved by accessing the configuration screen on

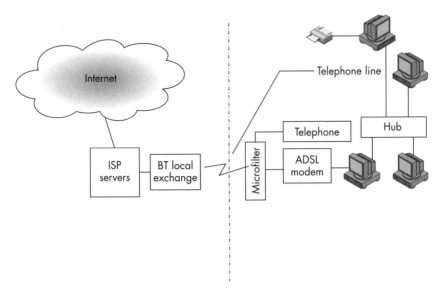

Figure 4.13 Network access – multiple computers organised into a network.

each computer via the operating system. In later versions of Windows this can be achieved automatically by using one of the computers as a dynamic host configuration protocol (DHCP) server. The DHCP software automatically assigns a unique IP address to each computer from a range reserved for private networks (e.g. 192.168.1.0). All computers can have access to the resources of the others, provided each one has granted sharing permission.

In this arrangement all the computers can access the internet at the same time through the ADSL link. In addition, they can print to any printer connected to any computer. This means that different types of printer can be attached to different computers but be used by all the others.

The disadvantage of this arrangement is that because the resources – e.g. printers and ADSL connection – are connected to individual computers these computers must be switched on if the others are to be able to use them. The computer connected to the ADSL line should be configured to use a firewall in order to protect the others on the network.

Multiple computers with an ADSL connection provided in a combined router, hub and firewall

This type of configuration (Figure 4.14) gives all the benefits of the previous one but has the added advantage that not all the computers need to be switched on. The ADSL modem in the previous configuration is replaced by a standalone ADSL modem, which also acts as a hub, router and firewall. It is possible to have separate devices for each function, but an ADSL modem with the combined functionality costs less than £100.

In this example configuration one of the printers is connected directly to the network. In this arrangement the printer must have an internal network card or be connected to an external card so that an IP address can be allocated and the printer accessed through it.

Multiple computers with an ADSL connection and wireless access point

The only difference between the previous configuration and this one (Figure 4.15) is the addition of a wireless access point, which is connected to the combined hub/ADSL modem/router by a standard CAT 5 cable with male RJ45 ends. It is possible by buy a wireless access point combined with the hub/ADSL modem/router for little over £100. Any

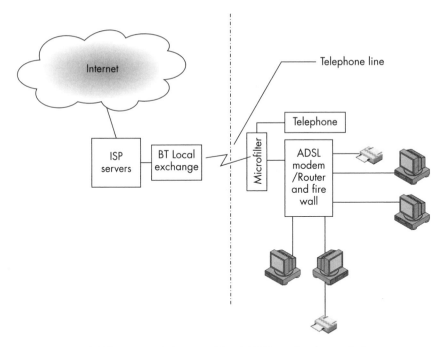

Figure 4.14   LAN connected via a combined ADSL modem/router/hub.

device equipped with a wireless access card can then gain access to the network and all its resources. Wireless access points are often referred to as Wi-Fi. The most common standard used is referred to as 802.11, which has different variants signified by a letter suffix. The two main variants are 802.11b, which provides transmission rates of 11 megabits per second (Mbps), and 802.11g, which supports higher transfer rates of 20 Mbps and is compatible with 802.11b equipment.

The distances these types of device can cover is approximately 100 metres. Many modern laptops have Wi-Fi built in, but PCMCIA cards can be purchased which can convert a laptop into a Wi-Fi device. This means that a laptop equipped with Wi-Fi can be used anywhere in the household and still have access to all the network resources such as printers and the internet, and is not constrained by physical wires. It is also possible to get Wi-Fi adapters for desktop PCs, thereby creating a network which is totally wireless. Wireless access points are also available in public places such as railway stations, airports and hotels. A laptop equipped with a Wi-Fi adapter can access these public wireless access points for a small charge, enabling users to access the internet and also collect their email.

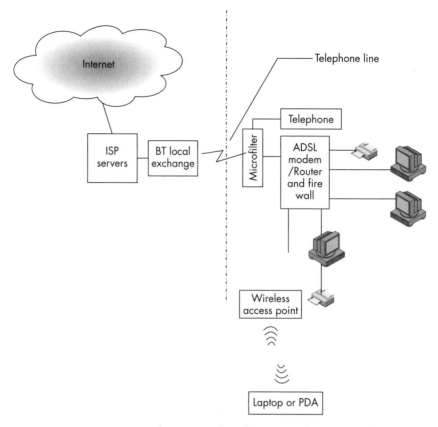

Figure 4.15 LAN connected via a combined ADSL modem/router/hub + wireless access point.

Virtual private network

A virtual private network (VPN) is a private network that uses a public network such as the internet to connect remote sites together using a 'virtual' channel. The virtual channel is totally protected from the external network and allows remote users to connect to a corporate or business network from any point where they can access the internet. This means that the remote user has all the facilities of a user who is on the corporate LAN. In the past this would have required special dial-up modems installed in the computer. With the advent of ADSL modems and Wi-Fi it means that remote workers can have exactly the same facilities as a local user provided they have access to the internet. A server is required at the corporate site to deal with VPN requests. On the later versions of Windows such as XP it is a simple matter to connect to a VPN server.

5

Application software

Introduction

Application software are programs written to fulfil a particular function, e.g. a word processor, which is used to produce documents such as reports and letters. There are hundreds of thousands of different applications produced by software developers, who can range from multinational organisations to a hobbyist creating an application to meet their particular requirement. Applications should be seen as tools to enable some end objective to be achieved. When selecting any tool it is important to understand how it will be used and why it will be of benefit. Applications can be broadly split into three categories:

- **General-purpose applications** such as word processors and spreadsheets, which can be used by many different types of user and business. The market for these types of applications is measured in millions.
- **Specific applications**, such as hospital pharmacy systems, which are used by a specific type of user and are usually designed to integrate with some business process. The market for these types of applications is fairly limited. In the UK the market for hospital pharmacy systems is measured in hundreds, whereas for community pharmacy systems it is around 15 000.
- **Bespoke applications.** These are designed and built to the user's own requirements. They are the most expensive of all, as ultimately a single organisation is paying for all the development costs, which can be considerable. They include analysis, design, specification, programming, quality assurance, documentation (system and training) and training. Usually this is done by specialist software development companies. Sometimes organisations may have an employee who develops a system to meet a particular need. The problem with this approach is that they are usually the only person who knows how the system works, and invariably do not provide sufficient documentation to enable it to be maintained should they leave. If the organisation relies heavily on the application, this can have a major impact on its ability to operate efficiently if the developer leaves.

The size of the market ultimately determines the revenue potential for the developers and hence the cost of the applications. General-purpose applications tend to be relatively inexpensive given the functionality included, whereas specific applications tend to increase in price as the market size decreases. The resources available to get the best use from an application, such as books and training courses, mirror the size of the market. There are many books and training courses available for general-purpose applications at a relatively low cost. Training for specific applications is usually provided by the developer and the costs tend to be much higher. The support and maintenance of the product is also governed by the size of the market. All software will have errors (bugs) that will need to be fixed. If there are many thousands of users these bugs are more likely to be identified and fixed by the developer, who usually provides a web site where software to fix the problem can be downloaded. Normally there is no charge for this. Support and maintenance for specific or bespoke applications, however, is usually chargeable on an annual basis. Suppliers typically charge support and maintenance at 10–15% of the actual cost of the application.

The purchase of software applications needs to take into account all aspects of implementing and using them, not just the cost of the software. The additional costs will be significantly higher for a specific or bespoke application, which will invariably require additional resources such as project management if the implementation is to be successful and meet the overall objectives.

It is important to understand why a particular application becomes the 'standard'. This is also related to market share and marketing. The application software may not be the best or most efficient, but because of the marketing and its uptake it becomes the market leader. For example, Microsoft estimates that worldwide it has 300 million users of its Office suite of software, which has five major products:

- Word – a word processor
- Excel – a spreadsheet application
- Access – a database management application
- Powerpoint – a presentation application for producing slideshows
- Outlook – personal organiser software and email application.

These types of application can be used by many different types of business and thus can be considered general-purpose applications which have a huge market. The price of the application is usually based on the number of copies likely to be sold. Therefore, even though considerable costs and resources may be involved in developing an application, these costs can be recouped and the revenue measured in tens of millions of pounds per year. As more and more users adopt an application it encourages others to do the same, especially when the application produces files in a particular format. For example, Microsoft Word produces documents in a particular format which has a file extension of '.doc'. If somebody wants to read a Word document produced by another person they will need to purchase a copy of Word to read it (or convert it into some other format), which encourages the adoption of that particular product. If the majority of people use the same applications it is easy to exchange documents, particularly as email attachments.

Application software is designed and programmed to work with a particular operating system, even though some popular applications may be available for more than one system. For example, Microsoft Office is available for both Windows and Macintosh operating systems. The operating system provides the building blocks and infrastructure on which the application can be built, in much the same way as the foundations and basic utilities such as water, electricity, gas and drainage are provided for all houses. In exactly the same way that it takes enormous resources to create the basic utility infrastructure, it takes enormous resources to create an operating system. The complexity of many operating systems means that it may take years from inception to introduction, and many more years before it is stable and free from bugs. The uptake of a particular operating system also drives the market for applications. Software developers will develop applications for the operating system with the biggest market share, as this gives them a bigger market. The more applications that are available for an operating system, the more people select that system, which is why a particular system ends up dominating the market.

The most widely used operating system used on PCs is Microsoft Windows. Many different versions of Windows have been developed over the years. Table 5.1 gives a list of the major versions with the year of release. Many of them such as NT, 2000 and XP Professional, were aimed at business users rather than home users and contained functionality that allowed IT departments to manage large numbers of computers on a network. They were designed to work with *server* versions of Windows. Most applications produced for the later versions of Windows are backward compatible and can be used on the older Windows operating systems.

Although Windows holds the largest market share there are other operating systems, the most common of which are MacOS and Linux. Mac (short for Macintosh) systems have carved out a niche market among graphic designers and publishers. This is because when desktop publishing applications were in their infancy, the best applications were

Table 5.1 http://www.computerhope.com/history/windows.htm

Windows version	Year of release
Windows 3.1	1992
Windows '95	1995
Windows '98	1998
Windows '98 Second Edition	1999
Windows Me	2000
Windows NT® Workstation 3.51	1995
Windows NT Workstation 4.0	1996
Windows 2000 Professional	2000
Windows XP Home Edition	2001
Windows XP Professional	2001

produced for the Mac operating system and resulted in Macintoshes being purchased specifically for this purpose. MacOS is generally only seen on machines in the range supplied by Apple, i.e. when a Macintosh PC is purchased it always comes preloaded with the MacOS system. Whilst this is generally true of PCs – i.e. the computer is normally bought with a copy of Windows already loaded – machines can be bought from many suppliers without any operating system. The user can then choose which they wish to purchase. For the PC user, one of the more popular alternatives to Windows is Linux, which is based on the Unix operating system. Unix uses a command line user interface, which is difficult for the novice to learn. However, Linux has a graphical user interface (GUI), which is far easier for the novice to use and much more like Windows. Even though Linux is free the number of users is minute compared to the number of Windows users, mainly because of the availability of applications. However, more applications are being developed for Linux, which are generally free, and it will be interesting to see if it becomes more widely adopted in the future.

In addition to operating systems for PCs there are also operating systems written specifically for personal digital assistants (PDAs). As the computer architecture of a PDA is completely different from that of a PC the operating system must be specifically designed for it. PDAs are for the most part designed to work in conjunction with a PC, and the operating system is written with this and the portability of the PDA in mind. All the data on the PDA needs to be backed up and synchronised to a PC, as the PDA could easily be lost, stolen or broken.

The market for PDAs closely mirrors that of the PC in that the Palm became the dominant operating system. This was because developers of the Palm device encouraged software developers to create applications by giving free support. There are literally thousands of applications designed for the Palm, many of which have a medical use, e.g. drug knowledge bases. The two major operating systems for PDAs are Palm and Pocket PC. When a PDA is purchased it will already have the operating system installed.

There are many more applications available for the Palm operating system than for the Pocket PC, and generally devices based on the Palm operating system are cheaper than those based on the Pocket PC. The choice of PDA will depend on how you intend to use it and the software applications available. The eBNF (electronic *British National Formulary*), for example, is only available for Palm-based PDAs and is supplied on a secure digital (SD) card. Many of the software applications for PDAs are available over the internet and are downloaded on to a PC and then on to the PDA by synchronising with the PC.

Developing software applications

All software applications are written in machine code, which consists of binary instructions that the computer's processor can execute to produce the required functionality. Programming languages, which are more readable by humans than machine code, are used to develop the applications. Programming languages are described as high or low level, depending on how close they are to the machine instructions of the computer on which they run, machine code being the lowest level. Programs written in a programming language must first be translated into machine code for the specific processor on which they are to run. The original high-level program instructions are known as the source code. The translation is performed by another computer program called a compiler or an interpreter. Compiled programs result in a file known as an executable. For example, in Windows file names ending in the extension .exe are executable machine code files. Double-clicking the file 'excel.exe' will start the Microsoft Excel spreadsheet application. There are hundreds of different programming languages which are used to develop software applications.

Obtaining application software

General-purpose applications

There are many different ways of purchasing and obtaining software. The traditional way of purchasing general-purpose commercial software is buying a boxed set from a shop or mail-order company. The software is almost always supplied on a CD-ROM, together with any document-ation about the application. The CD is inserted into the PC and a setup program run which installs the software and configures the application for use. Some Install routines require a software key to be entered, which is supplied with the software.

Application software can also be obtained directly from the inter-net by accessing any web site that allows software to be downloaded. There are many sites dedicated to providing software for PCs and PDAs. In many cases the software can be tried before purchasing, either with a limit on the time it can be used or having limited functionality. The soft-ware available from these web sites falls into three main categories.

Commercial

Some companies who provide boxed software also provide download sites from which either a trial or a full version can be downloaded. Trial versions usually have limited functionality or can be used for a limited period only. Once the trial has ended the software must be purchased at the commercial rate.

Shareware

Shareware is software that is distributed free on a trial basis, with the understanding that the user may need or want to pay for it later. Some software developers offer a shareware version of their program with a built-in expiry date (after 30 days the user can no longer get access to the program). Other shareware is offered with certain capabilities disabled, as an enticement to buy the complete version.

Many companies and individuals worldwide develop software applications and distribute them from their web site, or from one that specialises in distributing software for all types of operating system. Others specialise in software for specific types of computer, such as PDAs.

Freeware

This is software that is offered at no cost to the user. Freeware may be subject to copyright, which may prevent modification or resale. Freeware is not to be confused with free software, which means that software should be free from copyright and licensing, and the source code should be available to the end user for them to modify and improve. Many companies allow older versions of their software to be used free of charge in the hope that a user will purchase the latest version with more advanced features.

Demonstration/trial software

Many companies create a demonstration version of the software which can be downloaded from the internet and tried free of charge. The difference between this type of software and shareware is slight.

Purchasing and downloading software

When downloading software be aware of the size of the file being downloaded and the speed of the internet link. Some software is many tens or hundreds of megabytes, which will take hours to download over a normal telephone line with an analogue modem.

When selecting software always check that it is compatible with the system on which it is going to be installed. All application software is written for a specific operating system, and also requires that the hardware conform to a minimum specification. 'Minimum system requirements' should be displayed as part of the technical information describing the software. A typical example is shown below.

System requirements (Table 5.2)   The specification of a Windows PC on which software is to be loaded can be determined by looking at the system details in the Control Panel. Click Start, Control Panel, System, and look at the details shown in the General tab (Figure 5.1).

To determine the amount of free disk space available, click My Computer. Highlight Local Disk C: and click the right mouse button. A menu will be displayed. Click Properties, and a window will show how much disk space has been used and how much is free (Figure 5.2). The details obtained can be compared with the system requirements quoted for the application software to be purchased.

Some popular applications will be available for more than one operating system. For example, Microsoft Office, which includes a word processor and a spreadsheet application, is also available for both Windows and MacOS. Microsoft, the software developers, are prepared to create a version specifically for the Mac operating system because the volume of sales justifies the extra development and QA costs. However, it is not available for Linux because Linux is free. If Microsoft offered a

Table 5.2 System requirements

Component	Requirement
Computer and processor	Personal computer with an Intel Pentium 233 MHz or faster processor (Pentium III recommended)
Memory	128 Mb of RAM or greater
Hard disk	180 Mb of available hard-disk space; optional installation files cache (recommended) requires an additional 200 Mb of available hard-disk space
Drive	CD-ROM or DVD drive
Display	Super VGA (800 × 600) or higher-resolution monitor
Operating system	Microsoft Windows 2000 with Service Pack 3 (SP3), Windows XP, or later
Other	Microsoft Exchange Server is required for certain advanced functionality in Microsoft Office Outlook; Microsoft Windows Server 2003 running Microsoft Windows SharePoint Services is required for certain advanced collaboration functionality; certain inking features require running Microsoft Office on the Microsoft Windows XP Tablet PC Edition; speech recognition functionality requires a Pentium II 400 MHz or faster processor and a close-talk microphone and audio output device; Information Rights Management features require access to a Windows 2003 Server running Windows Rights Management Services
Internet connection	Internet functionality requires dial-up or broadband internet access (provided separately)

Linux version it would probably reduce the sales of the Windows operating system. There are packages that have similar functionality to Microsoft Office, such as StarOffice. StarOffice is available for both Linux and Windows, and the functionality is very similar to that provided by Microsoft Office at a fraction of the cost. However, because most businesses and organisations standardise on the use of Microsoft Office for interoperability, training and support reasons, there is a reluctance to try other products because of perceived problems with compatibility.

Specific/bespoke applications

The types of application described so far are generally used by a single user on a single PC or PDA and are used to perform a specific task. However, many applications are designed to provide a solution to a business requirement. The way in which the user interacts with these types of application depends on the business process with which they

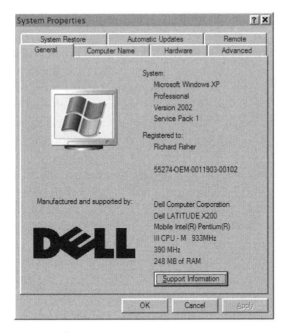

Figure 5.1   System specifications.

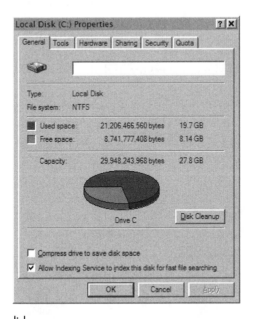

Figure 5.2   Free disk space.

are being used. Generally these applications are designed to allow more than one user to access the same information, and are referred to as multiuser systems. For example, a hospital pharmacy system will have many users who may at some time want to access the same information for different reasons. The dispensary staff, for example, will want to use the system to create labels, whereas the stores staff will want to create orders based on usage of drugs in one or more dispensaries. This means that the applications must be written to perform specific tasks aligned to the business process. As a result, the interrelationships between these types of application and the business process are much more complex than PC applications, which are used as general-purpose tools and do not affect other users. Multiuser applications are usually loaded on to a separate computer known as a server, which is connected via a network to all the PCs or terminals wishing to access the system. The application software runs on the server, which handles requests for information from the separate PCs, known as clients, in an orderly manner. Figure 5.3 shows a typical configuration.

The configuration of this type of software is much more compli-cated than a single-user application installed on a single PC and normally requires a much more complex installation procedure. Because of this, the installation and setup is usually performed by support personnel employed by the company supplying the system, and as a result is much more expensive. It is essential that implementation of these types of system is properly project managed because of the inter-action with the business processes and the potential impact on many users.

It is also essential that there is a system manager who understands how the system operates and can take appropriate action if problems occur. Support and maintenance of the software is essential when the business is dependent on the application to fulfil its business objectives.

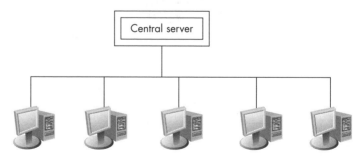

Figure 5.3 Multiuser client–server configuration.

General-purpose PC applications

Many applications are used on a daily basis to enable users to fulfil their everyday jobs.

Web browser

A web browser is an application whose purpose is to read pages published on the World Wide Web. There are many different suppliers of web browsers, but the two most popular are Microsoft's Internet Explorer and Netscape's Netscape Navigator. Internet Explorer is bundled with the Windows operating system (but is also available for the MacOS), so that any PC using Windows will already have a browser that is ready for use, and this is one of the reasons why it is one of the most popular. Netscape Navigator is available free for both the Windows and Mac operating systems.

The two main functions of a web browser are:

- To request a page from another computer whose URL has been typed in to the address field of the browser. URL is short for universal resource locator, and is the unique address of any section of a page that is available to be viewed on the World Wide Web. If a *hyperlink* is clicked by the user, it has the same effect as typing in a URL. A hyperlink is any text or object (such as a logo) that stores the URL of a page, so that it is easy for the user to navigate from page to page.

- To interpret the *HTML* page sent back by the *web server* from where the request was made and display it in the browser window. HTML is short for hypertext markup language, which is a protocol used to describe how the pages and documents published on the World Wide Web should be displayed. This is a series of instructions written in plain ASCII text which is interpreted by the web browser and creates the page as designed by the author of that page. There is usually a menu option which allows the HTML text to be viewed. Figure 5.4 shows a simple example of a page created in a text editor and the display it creates.

This is a very simple example, but the principles used are exactly the same for complex pages with many graphics. The instructions for each element are usually contained between two tags, one that switches the effect on and another that switches it off. A tag shows as two angled brackets < > which contain the instructions. An end tag has the same instruction as a start tag but is preceded by a slash (/) to switch the effect off.

Web browsers have many additional functions, such as the ability to download files, and can be enhanced with additional programs called

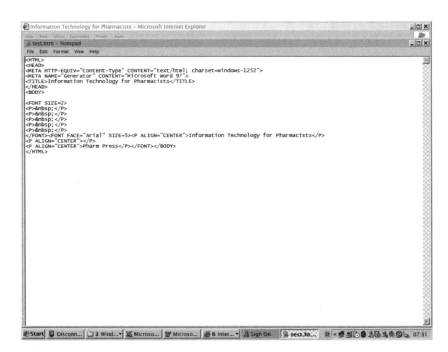

Figure 5.4 Example of a simple HTML page and the markup language.

plug-ins, which allow video and sound to be played. Many applications, such as Adobe Reader, have functionality that allows documents to be viewed in the browser window with all the functions of the normal application. Clicking on a hyperlink that references an Adobe document, i.e. a PDF file, transfers the file from the web server and displays the document in the browser window. If the PDF file is large, which is quite often the case, it may take some time over a slow link (such as one connected via a conventional modem) and it sometimes appears as though the browser has stopped working. When transferring or viewing files it is important to be aware of the size of the file being transferred.

There are many additional features included in browsers that allow web pages that have previously been visited to be easily recalled. There is an 'Add to favourites' menu option, which allows a particular page to be stored, and most browsers automatically keep a history of sites and pages recently visited which can easily be recalled without the need to remember the URL. As with any application it is essential that the user is trained to make the best use of the facilities available.

Email

Email (electronic mail) applications allow the exchange of computer-stored messages between users. The messages are sent from one computer to another utilising network technology, and therefore a prerequisite is that the computer must have access to a network. The basis of an electronic mailing system is fairly simple and works in much the same way as the postal service. In the conventional postal system each household has a unique address. The person writes a letter and puts it in an envelope with the name and address of the addressee on the front. This is then placed in a postbox, collected by the post office and taken to the sorting office. The address is scanned and the best route for the letter determined. It may go to several sorting offices before it is delivered to the final one, which can deliver the letter to the actual address.

In an email system, a mail server is the equivalent of the sorting office. The server is located on a particular computer with a unique domain name and has a mailbox for each user registered with that server. A domain name has to be unique for each computer in the world, and is one of the reasons why domain names must be registered so that nobody else can use the same name. The format of an email address is always the same, having two main parts separated by the '@' symbol. The first part of the address is the name of the mailbox. The second part is the domain name of the mail server on which the mailbox is located.

Emails are sent and received from the mailbox and will sit in the box until they are retrieved using an email application capable of accessing the mailbox. Email is a classic example of a client–server technology where two separate programs, one on the client computer and one on the server, communicate with each other. The client will run the email application which allows the email messages to be created and read, and the server will run the mail server application which handles the actual sending and receiving of the messages. In this case the mail server can operate independently of the client application. When a user wishes to send email or look at the contents of their mailbox they must connect to the mailbox using the client application.

There are many different types of email client application and it is important to understand them, as they have different methods of accessing the mailbox.

As explained above, all mail is sent or received from a mailbox on a mail server. There are two main types of email client that allow emails to be sent and received. Mail servers are usually provided by ISPs, but larger organisations will provide their own. For example, the NHS provides an email service as part of NHSnet, but because of security aspects relating to the transfer of sensitive patient information, there are strict rules governing the computers that can connect to and use the service.

PC-based email clients

Email application clients such as Outlook, Outlook Express, Eudora and Pegasus are loaded on to the user's PC and configured to connect to the mail server. One of the most confusing aspects of email clients is the multitude of ways this can be done, depending on a number of different factors such as how the PC connects to the mail server. Computers that are attached to a LAN in an organisation or small business will usually be configured to connect to the mail server automatically when they are opened, whereas home users who use an ISP as their mail server will need to connect via the telephone line. The software will automatically detect if the computer is not connected to the ISP, and dial the appropriate number if not. Home users using ADSL will effectively always be connected. The email messages are usually left on the mail server, but there are many ways in which they can be managed to make it convenient for the end user.

To access a mailbox the user will have to supply a username and password, which prevents unauthorised users from accessing the contents of the mailbox. If the software connects automatically without intervention from the user it means that the username and password are saved somewhere on the machine, a point to be borne in mind if others use the same machine. The configuration issues surrounding the setup of a standalone email client means that it is usually only practical to use these types of email client applications on the computer from which the mailbox is normally accessed.

Browser-based email clients

Web browsers are the other main means of accessing mailboxes. Many organisations, such as Microsoft (Hotmail) and Yahoo (Yahoo!MAIL), allow users to create mailboxes for personal use, free of charge. These are accessed through a web browser on any PC connected to the internet by entering a previously created username and password. The functionality of these web-based browsers is much more limited than that of PC-based clients, but they have the advantage that email can be sent and received using any PC connected to the internet.

Some providers and organisations allow a user to connect either via a PC-based client email application or by using a web browser (using additional software on the mail server). This gives the advantages of both methods and allows someone who does not have access to their PC to still access their emails with no configuration problems.

The functionality included in email applications varies depending on the product selected. Many, such as Outlook, part of the Microsoft Office suite, are integrated with personal information managers (PIMS), which allow diaries and contacts to be maintained, as well as a 'to-do' list. Outlook Express, which is a standalone email client, is bundled with the Windows operating system and allows a contact list of names, addresses, email addresses, telephone numbers, etc. to be maintained as well as the ability to send and receive emails.

The way in which the emails are initially displayed can be changed according to the user's preferences. Most applications have a series of folders into which emails can be placed or moved (Figure 5.5). The two main folders are known as the Inbox and the Outbox. The Inbox receives emails from other email users. The Outbox is used to store any that are ready to be sent.

The folders show a list of messages in the mailbox by displaying their headers. The header shows the email address of the person who sent the message, the subject, and the date and time sent. The content of each email can be viewed by double-clicking the header. The appearance

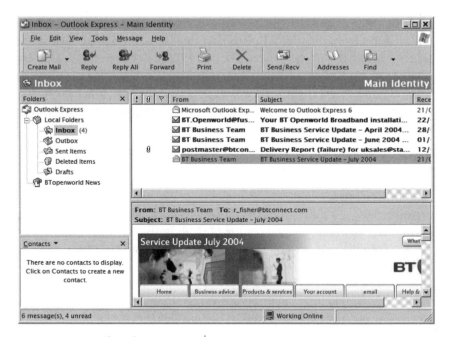

Figure 5.5 Email application.

of most PC-based email clients is highly configurable and can be changed to meet the user's requirements. New folders can be created and given a name. This allows the user to organise emails by subject or any other convenient method, so that they can be reviewed or recalled in the future.

One of the major benefits of emails is that attachments can be added to the message. Attachments are files, which can be of any type – text documents or photographs, for example. However, for the recipient to view the content of the file they must have an application on the PC that can understand its format. For example, if a person is sent a document produced in Word it will have a '.doc' file extension. To view this file, the recipient's computer must have a copy of Word. This is one of the reasons why documents are converted into Adobe PDF format, which allows any document to be read using Adobe Reader. Adobe Reader is available free of charge so that any document converted to PDF format can be read. Email has become a common method of transferring files, as attachments can be saved on the recipient's computer.

Used correctly, email is an extremely efficient method of communication, but in common with other systems it has its strengths and weaknesses. Used incorrectly it can be a drain on resources. Email addresses are stored in a contacts list and it is very easy to select and add an address to an email that is to be sent. As this is so easy, many users send copies of emails to people without first considering whether it is really necessary and the impact on the recipient. The recipient has to read the message to see whether it is relevant to them, and decide whether they need to take any action. This is compounded by unsolicited emails (known as 'spam') sent by organisations trying to advertise their products. In many respects email has become a victim of its own success. It is essential for any organisation to develop policies on email usage and that users are trained on these policies and adopt them. An email is no different from a letter, except that it is much easier to create and send. If email is used as a formal method of communication, the organisational policies, procedures and standards applied to sending them should be consistent with the sending of letters. Most organisations have 'style guides' that outline the format and content of documents used to communicate externally. Emails are electronic documents and should be part of the 'style guide'. There is usually a policy for physically storing copies of official letters of communication; there should also be a mechanism for storing and retrieving emails if required in the future.

Many people are lulled into the belief that once an email is sent it will be delivered instantaneously and immediately read by the recipient. However, the speed of delivery depends on the efficiency of the mail servers used. It is not uncommon for it to take hours where there are problems with the mail servers. Incorrectly typed addresses also mean that emails will not be delivered. Just because an email is delivered does not mean that it will be read by the recipient, although if requested by the sender some servers will send back a message to say that the message has been read.

Personal information management system (PIMS)

PIMS applications are used to replace the functions of a diary or Filofax by storing the information used in everyday life, such as contact addresses, telephone numbers, appointments, etc. A PIM is the classic example of how important it is to understand how all the elements of IT are used in practice. One of the most important aspects of a diary is that it is small, compact, and can easily be carried around so that it is always available when required. Although the functions of a diary or Filofax can be replicated in a PC application, it is of limited use if the user is frequently away from their PC and needs to update or refer to information stored. However, with the advent of PDAs and mobile phones, which are similar in size to a diary and portable, the deficiencies of the PC-based system can be addressed by the use of synchronisation software. The functionality of addresses, telephone numbers, appointments, etc. on the PC is replicated on the PDA or phone, which is periodically connected to the PC. The 'synchronisation' software then compares the contents of the PC with those of the PDA or phone, and vice versa, and any differences are updated on both. Thus the user always has the information to hand in a convenient form. This process also means that if the PDA/phone is lost or stolen a backup copy is available on the PC, and vice versa. If a PDA is lost all the user has to do is obtain a new one and synchronise the devices. Many PDAs are supplied with their own PIM software. However, because many users use PIM systems such as Outlook, PDAs are also supplied with software that will synchronise with other PIM systems, such as Outlook and Lotus Notes. Intellisynch is one of the most popular PIM synchronisation software applications. This allows users to use the most popular PIMS, such as Outlook, and have the same information on a handy PDA when away from the PC.

Using the same principle of synchronisation it is possible to obtain software such as Adobe and Microsoft Reader, which allow the download of books, PDF documents, etc. that can be read on the PDA. In addition, other reference materials such as the eBNF are available for reading on a PDA. The PDA then starts to become an information centre for the mobile user. As wireless technology for PDAs improves the options to access information from any location become limitless.

Word processors

A word processor is a software application that allows documents to be created, edited and printed. It is probably the most common application used on PCs and has virtually wiped out the use of typewriters. The major advantage of word processors is that changes can be made without having to retype the whole document.

All word processors support basic text editing functions, such as:

- Inserting text at any point in the document.
- Deleting text by either deleting single characters or selecting a whole block to be deleted.
- Cutting and pasting allows text to be selected and removed (cut) and then inserted (pasted) into another location.
- Copying text and pasting into another location.

- Search and Replace allows text to be searched for a particular word or phrase.
- Automatically moves to the next line when a line is filled. This is known as word wrap.
- The user can scroll through the length of the document when it becomes longer than the screen.

Word processors that support the basic functionality described above are usually described as text editors (Figure 5.6).

The Windows operating system is bundled with a basic text editor called Notepad.

Modern word processing applications support many more additional functions and features that enable documents to be formatted in more sophisticated ways (Figure 5.7). For example, different fonts can be used and changed to any size. Many other different objects can be added to the documents, such as tables and pictures. The documents appear on the monitor screen exactly as they will appear on the printed page, often referred to by the acronym WYSIWYG (what you see is what you get).

Text and graphics from other applications, such as pages in a web browser, can easily be copied and pasted into word processors.

One of the problems with fully functional word processors is that there is so much functionality that much of it is never used, or the application is used incorrectly. As with any other application, it is essential that the user is properly trained.

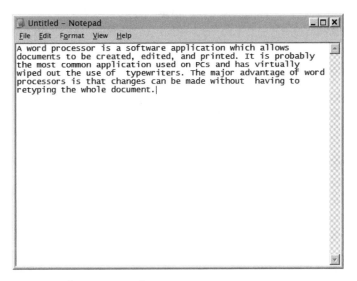

Figure 5.6   Text editor – Notepad.

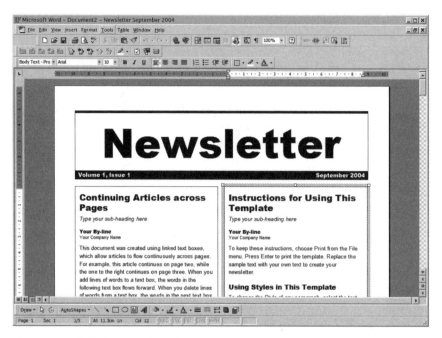

Figure 5.7 Fully functional word processor.

The most popular word processor today is Word, which can be purchased as part of the Microsoft Office suite of applications or on its own. It can be purchased for both Windows and MacOS operating systems. Other less popular word processors are WordPro and Word-perfect. Many other word processors are available free of charge.

Spreadsheet

Spreadsheets are used primarily to display and manipulate numbers, which are arranged in rows (horizontal) and columns (vertical). The first row usually contains headings. The intersection of a column and a row is known as a cell, which is given a reference that identifies its location. Columns are identified by alphabetic characters (left to right) and rows by numbers (top to bottom) (Figure 5.8).

The reference 'A1' refers to the first cell in the spreadsheet. Cells can contain data or mathematical formulae. The formulae act on the data in other cells. For example, a cell may contain a formula to add up a list of numbers to give a total. The cells can also contain text and dates, which are used to give meaning to the numbers. This means that they can be used as a tool to display records extracted from a database.

Row
references

Formula
uses cell
references
but cell
displays
the result

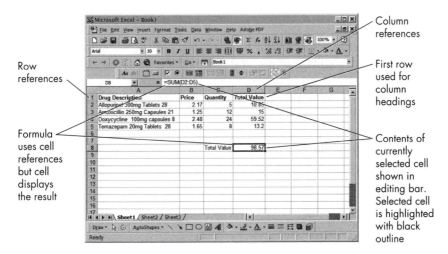

Column
references

First row
used for
column
headings

Contents of
currently
selected cell
shown in
editing bar.
Selected cell
is highlighted
with black
outline

Figure 5.8   Spreadsheet.

The most popular modern spreadsheet is Excel, which is part of the Microsoft Office suite of applications but can also be purchased separately and has many more features than the basic functionality described above. It has many inbuilt mathematical formulae and has the ability to produce graphs and charts from the data in the spreadsheet.

Adequate training is essential if the application is to be used to its fullest potential.

Utility applications

Some applications have become de facto 'standards' in certain situations.

Adobe Reader

Adobe Reader (previously known as Acrobat Reader) is a free application provided by Adobe which is used to read PDF files. The PDF format allows documents containing both text and graphics created by many different types of application to be viewed and printed in a uniform manner on different computer systems. It has become an accepted method of viewing documents. Much of the information provided on the internet is in PDF format. The application can be downloaded free of charge from the Adobe web site. Adobe Reader is also available for PDAs, which enables PDF documents to be read on a handheld device.
www.adobe.com

Winzip

Winzip is an application used to compress files. Compression reduces the size of a file and is very useful if a file is large and needs to be sent to another computer via a network. Compressing reduces the time taken to send a large file. Files that have been compressed using Winzip have a '.zip' extension. The application also allows any number of directories and files to be compressed into a single file. Large attachments sent by email are often 'zipped' before sending. To read the contents of a zipped file the recipient requires a copy of Winzip. Early versions of Winzip can be obtained free of charge.

Useful web sites
www.microsoft.com
www.apple.com/uk
www.unix.org
www.linux.org
www.pharmpress.com/bnfpda
www.tucows.com
www.handango.com

6

Information retrieval and data mining – reporting

Introduction

One of the fundamental uses of computers is to collect, store and disseminate data. Normally this data is collected as a byproduct of some business process. Take, for example, pharmacy dispensary systems, which were originally designed to produce labels as part of the dispensing process. Very little data was stored except that necessary to produce the labels, such as the drug description, dosage instructions and warnings. The additional requirements to produce a label, such as patient name and quantity, were entered each time a series of labels was produced. None of the label information was stored, and thus valuable information such as drug usage and patient labelling history was lost. It was soon realised that with very little additional input this data could be collected and used for both operational (e.g. patient medication records) and managerial benefit (e.g. reports of drug usage). Managerial information is usually required initially at summary level (i.e. subtotals and totals), whereas operational information is usually required at the detailed level.

As IT systems have developed the amount of data stored has grown exponentially. The key to obtaining meaningful information and knowledge from this data is understanding the relationships between the data stored and the business processes used to collect that data. There are many different names and terms given to the techniques for analysing data, such as business intelligence, data mining and online analytical processing (OLAP), but all are essentially software tools that allow data to be accessed and manipulated to produce information with which to make informed business decisions. However, these tools can only be used effectively if the person creating the report has a thorough understanding of the structure of the underlying database and how the data is collected. Even though the amount of data collected is vast, there may still be occasions when information is not available because the application has not been designed to collect the relevant data. The underlying structure of the data will dictate whether information can be retrieved. For example, it would be very useful when a drug is recalled to be able to search the computer system for the batch number of the drug, to see if it has been issued. Most pharmacy systems do not collect batch numbers, either when the goods are received or when they are issued. Even if the system does have the ability to collect the batch numbers, the processes involved in dispensing make it impractical to collect. Although this may seem obvious, it illustrates why it is important to understand the relationship between the business process and the data used to support it. The amount of work and resources required to understand the requirements and produce meaningful reports should not be underestimated. One of the requirements of most pharmacy systems is the ability to produce ad hoc queries, i.e. one-off reports to show specific information, usually as a result of some exceptional circumstance. Most system suppliers will demonstrate the use of report writing tools, which are usually graphically based and give the illusion that reports can be constructed in seconds. Although this is generally true, whether the information is meaningful and useful is another matter. What is not shown is the amount of time and effort required to define, design, construct and quality assure the report. The skills required to produce meaningful and useful information with these tools are considerable. It is also vital that any reports that are produced should be quality assured and reconciled against other sources of the same data, all of which can be very time-consuming.

Before a report can be produced the designer must understand how the data is being collected and stored. Without documentation on file specifications or data base schema it is virtually impossible to produce meaningful reports. The schema documents the relationships between the tables in the database from a technical point of view, but this alone is not sufficient. The designer of a report must also understand the business processes and the way that the data entered into the system is related to these processes. The reports will only be as good as the data on the system. Inadequate validation of the data when it is entered, from both a system and a procedural point of view, will result in poor reports, hence the term 'garbage in, garbage out' (GIGO).

The report designer needs to be aware of the effect on the data when users make errors. For example, when a dispensary label is produced which has an error it is very easy to create another one rather than rectify the original. Any reports created that give information on usage will then be incorrect, as they will contain an entry for both the correct label and the incorrect one. This has other knock-on effects if the label generation process is also being used to update stock control information, as the stock level will be incorrect. This is why it is essential to have robust procedures in place that users can follow when errors are made. Training in the use of these procedures and the consequences of non-adherence are vital, as it is all too common to blame the computer for inaccurate information when in fact it is due to lack of understanding of how the system operates. This is a point to bear in mind when evaluating software. The developers should provide functionality that allows common errors of this type to be easily rectified, as if the process is long and complex there is less likelihood that the users will bother. The correct use becomes more important as businesses rely more and more on IT. Take, for example, the consequences of incorrect data when pharmacists start to transfer prescriptions to the Prescription Pricing Authority (PPA) electronically (electronic transmission of prescriptions – ETP). If the data sent to the Pricing Authority is generated as a byproduct of label production (a logical assumption), then it will be essential that any mistakes are rectified, otherwise it will result in an incorrect claim.

In summary, the key to obtaining accurate meaningful information is understanding how the system collects the data and interacts with the business processes using that application, i.e. the whole system, not just the database. Although software tools are essential to get at the information they are only one small element of the information retrieval process. Considerable skills, knowledge and time are required to produce meaningful information.

Database information

Many software tools or applications are used to analyse the data stored in databases. The majority of these are very sophisticated and use graphical displays and 'drag and drop' techniques to manipulate the data. For example, a column in a table can be dragged to a different position. The tools are designed to work with many different types of database and data sources, which can usually be purchased separately from an application or database. The tools are usually used to supplement predefined reports, which are part of any computer system and are used to answer ad hoc queries, but can also be used to provide summary data from a system in a form and style that meets the user's requirements. Many suppliers will integrate these tools so that they appear to be part of the system. Some are also integrated with familiar Microsoft Office products such as Excel, Access and Word, which are then used to display and present the information. Microsoft products such as Excel and Access can also be used on their own to access the data in an underlying database. Indeed, there are so many different ways of producing the same information that the choice can be overwhelming. The one point to bear in mind with all these tools is that it requires a considerable amount of training, skills and knowledge to produce anything other than simple reports, which may be contrary to the impression given by the suppliers, who are trying to sell the product. The production of any report requires a certain amount of 'development', with all its different elements, i.e. definition of requirements, analysis, specification, production, quality assurance and testing. This can take a considerable amount of time, but it is the only way of ensuring that the information produced is reliable and accurate.

Different types of tool

As mentioned earlier, many different types of tool can be used to produce and analyse data. In the majority of modern systems the data stored by an application such as a pharmacy system is stored in a database management system (DBMS), which is completely separate from the application itself.

The majority of modern systems run on the Windows operating system. Microsoft have developed a standard and method by which the data in all major databases running on Windows can be accessed. This is known as open database connectivity (ODBC) (Figure 6.1).

The functionality is implemented by loading a program (driver) which is specific to the type of database being accessed. The majority of software reporting tools use ODBC to access the data in databases.

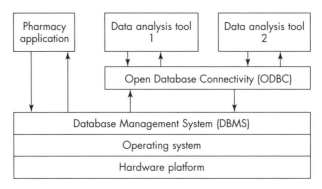

Figure 6.1 Schematic of access to data in DBMS.

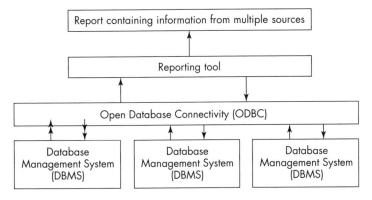

Figure 6.2 Schematic of report produced from multiple sources.

There are even ODBC drivers that allow data from spreadsheet files and text files to be accessed, which means that data from different sources can be accessed and combined. Therefore, a report can be created from multiple databases as well as other information sources such as spreadsheets (Figure 6.2).

The use of ODBC has become so widespread that it has effectively become a 'standard', and other operating systems providers have provided equivalent facilities. Older (legacy) systems which may not have a separate database generally do not have the ability to access the data using ODBC, which means that extracting information from these systems can be difficult. However, software can be written to access this data provided there is sufficient demand.

There are hundreds of tools that use the techniques described above to produce information, and many suppliers have more than one tool. To reiterate what has already been said, the use of these tools is no small task and requires significant training, expertise and knowledge if meaningful and useful reports are to be produced. Some of the better-known tools are listed in Table 6.1. Each supplier may provide many tools, which are optimised to present and analyse data in a specific way,

Table 6.1 Reporting tools

ODBC-compliant query tools

Crystal Reports
Access, Query Excel
Impromptu, Power Play
Business Objects

and this should be seen as an indicator that the analysis of data is no small task.

Developing and designing reporting information

The quotation 'knowledge is power' (Francis Bacon) is particularly relevant to the data collected by all organisations in that it can, if properly analysed, give the knowledge and hence the power to make informed decisions. The design and development of reports from stored data is one of the most neglected areas of IT when applied to smaller businesses and organisations. Larger organisations such as supermarkets and banks have vast volumes of data relating to millions of customers and have teams of personnel dedicated to providing and analysing this, which helps them to make business decisions. The same principles apply to pharmacy organisations, and managers must recognise that sufficient resources need to be allocated to the generation of information on which informed decisions can be made. Managers need to think about the information and indicators that are required on a regular basis to meet the goals of the business. These indicators, often referred to as 'key performance indicators' (KPI), should be measurable. For example, in a dispensary the number of 'owing' prescriptions can be used to indicate the level of service given to customers, and corrective action taken if the levels are unacceptable. In addition, they need to think about other indicators that will show exceptions from the norm, and the way this information is presented so that it can be interpreted easily. For example, in hospital pharmacies it is usual to provide a monthly report detailing the issues of drugs in descending order of value. These reports typically list every single product dispensed, and are very long. What is more useful is the top 20 by value and volume compared with the previous 3–6 months, so that any trends can be seen and the reasons investigated. If a report is more than a few pages long it is quite likely that it will never be read, or that somebody will have to go through it to summarise the data, which defeats the objective of having a system that provides information as a byproduct of the business process. As stated earlier, the production of reports can require considerable resources and time. The effort required to create and test reports needs to be balanced against the number of times a report will be required. If a report is only required once then it may be that it will take less time for somebody to summarise the data manually than to produce the report electronically. However, if the report is required routinely, say weekly or monthly, then it is likely that the effort required will be far less than summarising the data on a routine basis. This is a principle that should be applied to all computer systems development, not just reports, i.e. the effort required to design, program and test a system should be balanced against the effort it will save over a period of time.

Many software reporting tools allow the reports to be stored so that they can be run at the click of a button. This means that the person who runs the report does not have to have the skills to create it. In many tools the reports can be scheduled to be run on a periodic basis, such as weekly or monthly. When the reports are run many tools allow parameters to be input by prompting the user. For example, a report on drug usage may be designed to prompt for the name of the drug or therapeutic category so that the contents of the report are restricted. Obviously prompts cannot be used for scheduled reports.

Designing and producing reports

In common with any software project, before starting to design any report it is essential to define and document the objectives of the report, which clearly states why it is required. A certain amount of background information as to why the report is required is useful as there may be more than one way of providing the information and determining the approach to be taken. Once the objectives have been understood the requirements for documentation can be produced.

Requirements

The requirements need to be considered systematically and should detail the information required, how often it will be produced and, if possible, a sample of the expected output.

Many reports require that the information displayed is for a specific period in time. This will be the case in most drug usage reports, especially when trying to compare the usage from one period to another so that trends can be spotted. If data from a specific period is required the requirements should also detail whether the report needs to be run retrospectively, i.e. can it be run at any time in the future for the specified period? Whether this is possible will depend on the underlying structure of the database being used.

Selection criteria

Consideration needs to be given to the selection criteria that will be used and possibly input. There can be many different selection criteria, which will not always be obvious from the data presented in the report. It is therefore essential that these criteria are included as part of the overall report, as part of the title and header information, as this defines the context of the report. This should also include the date and time when the report was created. Selection criteria can sometimes be variable and may be input by the user when the report is run, e.g. Drug usage between two specified dates. If this is the case then the header information needs to show these variable criteria.

Sort criteria

The majority of reports will need to be sorted in a particular order. This will be determined by the objectives of the report, for example in alphabetical order of drug name. In many cases the report will need to be sorted by multiple criteria, for example by therapeutic category and then by drug name within category. The sort criteria need to be given careful consideration, as they may be crucial to the usefulness of the report. Some reports will need to be sorted by summary information, such as the total spend on a particular drug.

Output criteria

Output refers to the data to be presented in the reports. Most reports are constructed in the form of tables, with vertical columns and horizontal rows. The columns will have headings that determine the data elements that will appear in each row, such as drug name, value, etc. The sample layout of the report will define the different data elements to be included in the report.

Output modifiers

Output modifiers will determine whether the information output will be at a detail or a summary level, or both. For example, in drug usage reports it is unlikely that each individual issue of a drug will be required. Much more likely is a summary of each drug over a period of time, with the total value or quantity for each. In some cases both the detail and summary data will be required, and that totals are shown when groupings change, i.e. when a specific data element such as therapeutic category changes. Summary totals are usually referred to as subtotals, totals and grand totals. An example would be a drug usage report sorted by therapeutic category and drug within each category. At each change of drug a subtotal would be shown and at each change of therapeutic category a total of all the drugs in that category. A grand total would give the total of all drugs in all therapeutic categories.

Once the requirements have been defined the next stage is to determine whether the data is collected as part of the business process, and if so where it is stored and whether it is accessible. This means that whoever is going to create the report needs a detailed knowledge of how and where the data is stored, and just as importantly, how it is collected. It may be that after investigation the data is not available to provide the report as defined in the original requirements. The requirements documentation will give a reference point as to what is achievable based on the data available. If the data is stored in multiple sources or databases there must be some mechanism of 'joining' it together. For example, if a report is required of a patient's complete dispensing record which is stored in two separate systems, the normal pharmacy system and a TPN system, there must be some method of linking the patient record on one system to the same patient record on the other. This is usually achieved by using a unique patient identifier or number and is dependent on the functionality of the systems where the data is stored. This is a key issue for many organisations that have disparate systems and do not use a single unique identifier, such as a hospital number, to identify a patient. It then becomes very difficult to provide a complete patient record, as there is no way of linking the data for the same patient.

Once the source of the data has been located then a tool needs to be selected to create the report and the report produced. This can be quite time-consuming and is dependent on the accessibility of the data and the complexity of the report.

The last stage, and one that is often neglected, is to QA the report and make sure it is producing the results expected. The details of the report should be validated, and wherever possible reconciled against the information produced from sources independent of those used to produce the report.

7

Procurement, project management and implementation of systems

Procuring systems – introduction

Information technology (IT) is used by almost every type of business. It is inconceivable to imagine any pharmacy 'business', be it community or hospital, being able to operate without computers. However, computers and software are merely tools to fulfil a business requirement. For example, the production of dispensary labels using computer technology is only one part of the business process that leads to the patient receiving their medicine. The business process can be defined as a collection of related structural activities that produce a specific outcome for a particular customer or patient. All pharmacies in Great Britain were required by January 2005 to set up standard operating procedures (SOPs) detailing the activities that take place in the dispensing process. Standard operating procedures specify in writing what should be done, when, where, and by whom. There is a great deal of similarity and overlap between the documentation required to produce an SOP and that required to document the business process. The business process documentation will concentrate on the design of the systems that lead to the procedures required. The business process rarely operates in isolation: other processes will depend on it and it will depend on other processes. A business process will employ different resources to enable that process to be completed. In the dispensing of a medication it involves staff, IT technology, stockholding of medicines, etc. When purchasing IT systems or solutions it is essential to understand how the technology will affect the business process. The aims should be to make the process more efficient and ultimately meet the goals of the organisation. It is not uncommon for IT to be seen as the panacea for all business problems – i.e. IT will solve any problem – but the impact of the IT solution on the business process must be fully assessed if the implementation is to be successful. For example, there is a significant difference in terms of cost and impact between procuring a piece of software that must integrate fully with business processes and procuring one that does not. Take, for example, a word processor and dispensary system used in community pharmacy. The word processor is a tool for producing documents. If the computer on which the word processor is running fails, it may be inconvenient but it is quite likely that the document will be able to be produced on another PC. However, a dispensary system will, as a minimum, be required to produce labels and reorder drugs dispensed. If this system fails it can cause significant problems unless there is a second system, as the production of labels is a fundamental part of the business process of dispensing medications. In addition, the dispensary system must be designed and programmed in such a way as to integrate with the way prescriptions are processed. In hospitals, the systems and business processes are even more complex, as there are usually more users and workstations all accessing a central database. There are usually multiple dispensaries and a pharmacy store, which all have their own stock, adding to the complexity of interrelationships between the different processes.

Thus, when procuring or purchasing software, it is essential to clearly understand and define the objectives and reasons for introducing the new technology. Even the purchase of a word processor has implications for a certain business process, as presumably that is why it was purchased in the first place. If the person who is going to use the word processor does not know how to do so, say because of inadequate training, this will affect the production of documents, which will ultimately affect the business process.

Clearly, identifying both the reason why the software is required and the benefits is equally as important for personal purchases as it is for business. In common with many of the processes involved in the practice of pharmacy, a systematic approach to procuring and implementing software should be taken irrespective of the final cost of the solution.

The resources required to implement IT solutions are often totally underestimated, usually because of a lack of appreciation of the complexity and interrelationships between the business processes, staff and the technology. It is for these reasons that most IT solutions should be set up as discrete projects.

The definition of what is a project and what is not can be difficult, but essentially it can be defined as the production of a solution which has a business need as its driving force. The project will have a finite lifespan and result in the delivery of a defined set of products, which will constitute the solution. Project management is the application of knowledge, skills, tools and techniques to a broad range of activities to meet the requirements of the particular project.

There are many different project methodologies, which are essentially frameworks for ensuring that a structured approach is taken to project management so that there is a better chance of achieving a successful outcome. That is not to say that using project management techniques will guarantee success, but it does mean that a systematic approach is applied. The major aims of any project should be to ensure the solution meets clearly stated objectives, is to the specified quality, keeps within the budget, and is delivered on time.

Thus when procuring systems and solutions, it is advisable in the first instance to consider the impact the potential solution will have on the organisation. In the majority of cases this will be such that a project needs to be initiated and managed using a tried and tested methodology.

Procurement

When purchasing or procuring any IT solution, a system requirements specification should be produced which clearly states the objectives and requirements of the system. It could be argued that this should take place for any software purchased, even a word processor. However, because of the relatively low cost of this type of software and the standard features included in most commercial word processors, this is usually considered unnecessary, but it is still important to understand the objectives and how they will be met. However, for community systems costing several thousand pounds and hospital systems costing many tens of thousands a requirements specification is essential if the risks of purchasing inappropriate systems are to be avoided.

It is not untypical for the requirements for a hospital pharmacy system to be several hundred pages long. The requirements of one hospital pharmacy will be much the same as those of another, as they basically provide the same service. This results in a requirements specification from one organisation being passed on to another. The small differences in requirements from one hospital to another are added to the original document, and eventually the requirements specification ends up being a list of what would be nice, rather than what the organisation needs. Thus it is essential that the detail in the specification be considered with reference to the overall business processes of the individual organisation, which might be slightly different from those of other organisations. There are many different methodologies for procuring systems. In the NHS the official methodology used for IT projects is POISE, which was developed principally by NHS Purchasing and Supply Agency. The guidance sets out the best practice to be adopted by all NHS bodies when procuring IM&T equipment and services. Understanding the methodology and producing the outputs required can be a bigger task than the work involved in the procurement itself. The introduction to the POISE manual is over 100 pages long. Just reading and understanding this can be overwhelming and potentially conflicts with the prime requirement, which is to procure the IT solution. This is where a commonsense approach is essential, a principle that should be adopted wherever methodologies and frameworks are used. The methodology is essentially a framework to ensure that all the necessary elements have been considered. Use the parts of the framework that are relevant to the size of the procurement involved. The size of the procurement will determine how much detail is required to ensure that all requirements and objectives are met. The following list can be used as a basic framework.

- Identify the business need.
- Define the objectives.
- Produce requirements specification.
- Select the product.
- Implement the solution.

When considering each of the above steps it is essential to consult and communicate with those who will ultimately be using the solution, and any others who have expertise and knowledge that might be relevant.

The budget available to deliver the solution needs to be identified and estimated at an early stage. It is no good putting effort and resources – which themselves cost money – into making a business case if the funds are unlikely to be available. In estimating the costs it is essential that all elements of the proposed solution are costed and accounted for. Many people make the mistake of assuming that the costs involved in procuring a system are just the cost of purchasing the software and/or hardware and any ongoing support costs from the supplier. This could not be further from the truth, unless the system has little impact on the business processes. A significant amount will be associated with the implementation and the ongoing use of the system.

Some of these 'hidden' costs are:

- Procurement costs
- Project managements cost – internal and external
- Implementation cost
- Training
- Documentation costs – procedures, training
- Contingency
- Ongoing system costs – staff time to maintain the system
- Training of new starters.

Timescales need to be kept in mind when procuring a system or solution. All of the above will take time and resources. It is not uncommon for the procurement of a hospital system to take several years, during which time many business processes can and will change, and consequently the requirements may need to be reviewed. Wherever possible, timescales, from defining the business need to implementation, should be as short as possible.

The current trend is for the requirements specification to be defined in terms of the outputs; this is known as an output-based specification and focuses on the outputs required, rather than how they are provided. However, in many instances the way the output is provided is very important. Take, for example, the production of dispensing labels. In an output-based specification the requirement would be to produce labels with the appropriate information. However, the ease and speed with which these labels can be produced is critical to any pharmacy system. It is therefore essential, where circumstances dictate, to specify the detail of how the requirements should be provided.

The way the requirements specification is structured will depend on what is being procured, but as a minimum will have the following sections:

- **Introduction**   This section should outline the reasons why the solution is being sought and the objectives to be satisfied.
- **Background**   This should give an overview of the organisation in relation to the required solution.
- **Requirements overview**   This should give an overall description of what is required, so that the detailed functionality can be put into perspective.
- **Detailed requirements**   This section should contain the details of the outputs required. It is often useful to categorise the outputs into those that are mandatory and those that are optional.
- **Additional requirements**   This section should contain details of requirements that are service related. This includes items such as assistance with implementation, training and ongoing support.

Once the requirements specification has been written it is usual for it to be sent out to suppliers with an invitation to tender. The invitation to tender should outline the criteria by which the responses will be evaluated. An example of some of the suggested criteria is given below.

- **Initial support**
  Project management
  Installation team
  Quality
  System testing

Scope of responsibility
Training
- **Ongoing support**
Reliability
Profile of support team
Approach to system changes and upgrades
- **System**
Product features
Upgrade paths
- **Commercial**
Initial cost
Ongoing cost of ownership
Contractual conditions
- **Other**
Reference sites.

It may be that, having produced the requirements specification, it becomes obvious that a ready-made solution does not exist. The options available then need to be carefully considered. The development of bespoke applications can be an expensive and time-consuming task requiring detailed system specifications, programming, documentation and quality assurance. It may also be possible to use a combination of software tools to provide a solution. Whichever way is chosen it is essential to re-evaluate the costs and ensure that the project is properly controlled, as the risk becomes far greater with unproven systems and solutions.

Once all bids have been received they can be assessed against the requirements specification. It is usual to produce a shortlist of suppliers, who are invited to give demonstrations. Preparation for these is essential. Scripts should be prepared that reflect the essential business processes, and the supplier should be asked to demonstrate how their system will cope with these activities. All key personnel who will be affected by the solution should be invited to the demonstration and asked to score and comment on the functionality demonstrated. This ensures that a level of objectivity is applied to the selection of the system. The majority of suppliers will concentrate on the visual look and feel of the software, rather than its ability to integrate with the business processes, which in the author's view is one of the prime considerations. Take, for example, the production of dispensary labels, which is essentially a data input task given the volumes that must be processed. Data input tasks usually require the user to navigate the software using a pre-defined route. Windows interfaces are generally constructed so that the user can navigate in any sequence required, usually involving the use of a mouse. Although this is very useful in many types of application it is not appropriate for data input tasks where speed is of the essence. It is easy to forget this in a demonstration situation, where real-life environments are difficult to recreate. This is why it is very useful to see the system or solution at an existing customer's site if possible.

Although price is an important consideration it is by no means the governing factor. Just as important is developing a good relationship with the supplier. Implementing systems requires good project management and teamwork from both the supplier and the customer. Views should be sought from existing customers of the supplier.

Once the choice of system has been made it is essential to ensure that the contract negotiated covers all aspects of the implementation and the associated costs. A project plan with timescales and milestones should form part of the contract. Payments to the supplier should be staged, based on predefined milestones being reached. It may also be necessary to consider including financial penalties if these milestones are not met.

Once the contract has been signed the implementation can begin. The quality and implementation of any system will ultimately determine whether the project is a success or not. This requires good project management from both the supplier and the customer. From the author's viewpoint it is essential that both customer and supplier identify project managers who will meet on a regular basis throughout the implementation period. This ensures that the supplier is kept aware of the requirements and constraints of the customer, and vice versa. Good project management ensures that the implementation is controlled and that everybody affected is fully aware of progress and how it affects them. The quality and depth of training usually has a significant impact on the ultimate success of the project. The system may do exactly what is required, but if insufficient effort has been allocated to developing the procedures to be used and the training required the implementation can still fail.

Project management

Project management is a term the use of which has significantly increased over the last 20 years. Although there are many different types of project management methodology, applying project management techniques is really about using common sense and taking a structured approach to what one would do instinctively. Most people use project management techniques every day without actually calling it project management. Project management methodologies are basically frameworks that can be used to try to ensure that projects are completed successfully. As a project becomes more and more complex it is essential that it is controlled, so that all affected parties are aware of the progress and potential problems that may arise. The project should be controlled and directed by representatives of the management, who must be fully aware of the objectives and the impact on the overall business. Those who control the project are responsible for taking key decisions and the commitment of resources, such as staff and money. In one of the most used and proven methodologies, PRINCE, the project is controlled by a project board, a small group of senior people who have the authority to make key decisions. The board is kept informed of the progress of the project at regular intervals by the project manager. The project manager is responsible for day-to-day control and should have a detailed understanding of all the subsystems required to deliver the overall project, while keeping in mind the overall objectives and goals. The project manager needs to understand the interrelationships between the different tasks, so that the impact of any changes or delays can be assessed and appropriate action taken.

What is a project?

There are many definitions of project, but to all intents and purposes it is about non-routine tasks, i.e. change. It is particularly significant to the IT industry because of the impact that IT solutions have on business processes, but can be applied to any sector. It is the principles that are used which are important. In deciding whether to set up a project the following question should be considered.

Does the work in question have a business need as its driving force? If the answer is yes, then a project needs to be initiated with the objective of providing the solution. The project will deliver end products that can be used to fulfil the business need. The decision to initiate a project needs to be made by those in the organisation's management who have the authority to commit the resources required.

The major aims of any project should be:

- To deliver a solution that meets the clearly stated objectives
- To meet the specified quality
- To keep within the budget allocated to the project
- To deliver the solution on time.

The project manager is responsible for creating a plan that meets the defined objectives of the project, and also to ensure that the other aims of timeliness, quality and cost are controlled. The plan will normally be broken down into small manageable tasks that can be managed in their own right.

Some of the most important reasons for producing a plan are:

- It is a means of controlling the project.
- It can be used as a benchmark to monitor progress.
- Relevant parts can and must be communicated to the people involved.
- The relationships between the different tasks can be seen.
- If there is a delay in the completion of the task then the impact can be assessed and corrective action taken.
- The plan should identify who is responsible for each task.

There are many software tools that can be purchased to help to document the project plan, e.g. Microsoft Project. Although these can be valuable in large projects they are not usually necessary. Any documentation can be produced using a word processor or spreadsheet. The most important aspect of any plan is that the relevance and impact of any single task and its relationship to the overall plan is fully understood.

In addition to the obvious skills of planning, an effective project manager needs to be able to think strategically. It is very easy to get bogged down in the detail and forget about the overall objectives of the project and the business value it will produce. A good project manager needs good communication skills that can be adapted to the different types of audience likely to be encountered, such as executives, team members, technical specialists, line managers and end-users. It is the project manager's job to ensure that the team members allocated specific tasks understand the importance of completing those tasks according to the timetable, and the impact on the project if the timescales are not met.

Initiating a project and using a project methodology is no guarantee of success. It is an often-quoted statistic that 70% of software projects fail, and it is worth considering some of the main reasons why.

- The objectives of the project are not properly defined and so it is impossible to identify the goals.
- Failure to involve all the relevant personnel throughout the life of the project.
- Lack of communication between all parties involved.
- The goal of the project is defined properly but then changes to it are not controlled.
- The project is planned properly but then it is not resourced as planned.
- The project is planned such that there is no contingency plan.
- The project is not planned properly.
- The project is not led properly.
- The expectations of participants are not managed. People often say 'in our company, deadlines are imposed on us'.

- The project is planned properly but then progress against the plan is not monitored and controlled properly.
- Project reporting is inadequate or non-existent.
- When projects get into trouble, people believe the problem can be solved by some simple action, e.g. work harder, extend the deadline, add more resources.

Ultimately, successful projects are a result of effective planning, communication and teamwork.

8

Training

Introduction

The importance of training in relation to information technology cannot be overestimated. Lack of training is one of the most common reasons why systems fail or do not provide the benefits that were intended. Computer systems are merely tools to aid and enhance some process that fulfils an organisation's business objectives. Users need to be trained to use the tools, but also need to understand the impact of their use on the overall business process. For example, when using a dispensary labelling system, not only does the user need to be trained to navigate the system so that they can produce labels quickly and efficiently, they also need to be trained on how the system fits into the business process and its impact if the correct procedures are not followed. Recording of a patient's demographic information on a dispensary system is a classic example. A patient's name and date of birth are usually enough to uniquely identify a person, whereas the name alone is not. Therefore, this information should be confirmed with the patient when the prescription is handed in, so that the details on the system are recorded correctly. Incorrect input of the patient's name and the absence of data such as date of birth will mean that the name on the labels will be incorrect and that it will not be possible to identify the patient easily on subsequent visits, resulting in duplicate records for the same person. This means the patient's record is split between two records, and functions that rely on a complete record, such as interaction checking against previous medications, will be incomplete. Examples such as this illustrate why clear policies and procedures should be developed for the use of all IT systems, and that staff are trained in their use. These policies and procedures can be seen as an extension of the standard operating procedures but covering in more detail the collection, use and input of data into the system. One of the most neglected areas of training is the procedures to be followed when errors are made. If users are not trained in these it will result in misleading and inaccurate information. For example, when a dispensing label is produced incorrectly, it is important that the correct procedure is followed to produce a rectified label. If users just produce another label, this will result in incorrect usage data, stock control data and patient medication records. It is quite common for the computer to be blamed for inaccuracies in the information it provides, but more often than not it is usually the result of poorly trained users and is the derivation of the term 'garbage in, garbage out' (GIGO), i.e. the input of incorrect data will result in the output of inaccurate information.

IT systems are merely tools to aid and achieve an objective, and contrary to popular belief do not work by 'magic'. All tools have to be designed to fulfil a specific objective, and computer systems and applications are no different. Each tool must be used appropriately, and the users need to be fully trained in order to get the best out of it. It is essential that the managers of the organisation have an understanding of the relationships between the different business processes and the impact of the tools being employed. If they do not, they will be ignorant or unaware of the training required to ensure the objectives of the organisation are met.

Training costs are often omitted when computer systems and applications are purchased. The costs of purchasing computer systems should take into account the costs associated with training, not just the costs of hardware and software. It is a common mistake to forget or underestimate the costs of training. In large multiuser systems such as hospital pharmacy systems the resources required for training can be considerable. Before the users are trained, the policies and procedures on the use of the whole system (i.e. the business process), not just the computer system, should be discussed and documented. Only when these have been produced can training courses and guides be designed which can be used to train all the relevant staff. The written procedures and training guides should also act as a point of reference in the future for anybody unfamiliar with the system, such as new starters. Training costs should also take into account any temporary staff required to cover for the staff being trained.

Users should not be trained on a 'live' system as this will result in the data being 'corrupted'. A system can be considered as two distinct parts: (a) the application and (b) the data. In the case of applications such as word processors, the data is stored in separate files, one for each document. Thus documents used for training can easily be discarded because they are quite discrete. However, in systems designed to collect data to be stored in a database this can be a problem. A database contains many tables, which are all related and used to store information. If the 'live' system database is used for training, the tables will contain

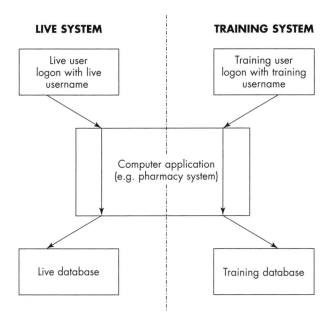

Figure 8.1   Schematic of example duplicate live and training systems.

data created as a result of the training and lead to misleading and incorrect information. Although it may be possible to delete these training entries it is not the ideal solution. A far better solution is to have a duplicate system or database, so that users can use the training system without any impact on the live data (Figure 8.1).

This can normally be facilitated by simply logging on to the system with a different username that routes the user to the training database, but there are other ways of achieving the same objective. Having a training database also has the benefit of being able to test how a system works in particular circumstances without affecting the live data.

Training requirements

Training related in IT can be classed into two broad categories, general and specific.

General training

General training covers the basic skills required to use and interface with computer technology. Whereas most people will learn these skills at school, there are many who have never had any formal training in the use of computers because of the amazing pace at which IT has developed in the last 20 years. Although many get by and manage to use the technology, they certainly do not use the systems efficiently. In addition, they start to become dependent on the technology without realising the implications if things go wrong. For example, many people do not understand why it is important to have backups of data, which can be likened to owning a house and not having any insurance. Hopefully it will never be needed, but if there is an untoward event, such as a fire, and it is not available the implications can be catastrophic. The same is true of backups.

It is essential that all people who use IT regularly should be trained in the basic skills, and this should be as much a part of continuing professional development as any other subject.

Many organisations require an employee to have basic competency in using a personal computer and popular applications such as a word processor. One of the ways in which competency can be achieved is by obtaining European computer driving licence (ECDL) (www.ecdl.com), which covers seven modules:

- Basic concepts of IT
- Using the computer and managing files
- Word processing
- Spreadsheets
- Databases
- Presentation
- Information and communication.

No prior knowledge of IT or computer skills is required to study for the ECDL.

There is also a more basic course called 'equalskills', which is designed to address the needs of those who feel intimidated by computers. The programme covers four main topics, after which students are encouraged to move on to the ECDL programme:

- **Computer basics**
  Parts of the computer
  Getting started
  The keyboard
  Using the mouse
- **Introduction to the desktop**
  Desktop
  Windows
  Creating a document
  File types

- **The World Wide Web**
  The WWW
  Web browser
  Searching
- **Email**
  Email accounts
  Messages.

There are many more advanced programmes sponsored by the European Computer Driving Licence Foundation (ECDLF). In the UK the British Computer Society (BCS) manages and promotes the ECDL on behalf of the ECDLF (www.ecdl.co.uk).

User interface

The ways in which users interface with computers tend to become standardised, and this is the reason why a particular operating system dominates the market. There are two main types of interface, character based and graphics based, and the way a user interacts and navigates with the two types is completely different.

One of the fundamental training needs is to acquire the basic skills necessary to interact with the different types of interface. The Windows operating system is by far the most common interface used at home and in businesses, and users need to understand its basic principles. It is amazing how few people have actually had formal training and are consequently unaware of many basic concepts required to use it efficiently. If a different operating system is to be used, then the user will need to be trained in the specifics of that particular system. For example, although many of the principles of Windows and MacOS are the same, there are sufficient differences in navigation and presentation to warrant additional training.

Touch typing

Considering how many people use computers, it is very surprising but understandable how few have learned to touch type. Most people start to use the keyboard using the index finger of each hand. This is very inefficient and invariably leads to errors, as the majority of people have to look at the keyboard as they type. If they look at the screen they are much less likely to make errors or to correct them as soon as they are made. Many people think that learning to touch type is primarily about increasing speed, which it is, but one of the other key reasons is that it can dramatically reduce the number of errors.

Typing with two fingers is like reading by looking at each letter of a word. Being able to touch type allows text to be entered into the computer subconsciously, without needing to look where the letters are on the keyboard. This means that the user can concentrate on what needs to be input, rather than the mechanics of getting the letters into the computer. Learning to touch type is like riding a bicycle, i.e. a person becomes more proficient once they have acquired the basic skill of balancing the bike. Ten fingers are obviously more efficient than two. It is quite difficult to learn to touch type when one has been used to typing with two fingers, but worth the effort in the long run when one considers the amount of time spent using the computer.

One of the misconceptions that prevents people from learning to touch type is the notion that it is time-consuming and difficult, particularly for two-finger typists. Many people have an image in their mind of sitting at a manual typewriter doing boring and repetitive drills for hours and waiting months to see results. However, the introduction of the personal computer has made learning to type quick and easy. People can now learn on their own computers, either at work or at home, in 10–20 hours. Computer-based training offers many advantages. It is generally cheap, self-paced, and recognises the needs of the individual. A speed of 20 words per minute is enough for the user to type faster than they can write and to feel comfortable at the keyboard.

There are many touch-typing applications available, some free from the internet. These applications start with simple exercises and give feedback on the accuracy and speed of typing.

Specific training

There are hundreds of thousands of software applications, all designed as tools to perform some function. Some of these are general-purpose tools such as word processors or spreadsheets, and others are specific to a particular sector, e.g. a community dispensary system. The majority of these applications will use a familiar user interface such as Windows. It is often said that the use of Windows applications is 'intuitive', i.e. once a person has learned to use one Windows application they can use any Windows application. This could not be further from the truth, and is generally used to sell the product. Although the interaction and navigation round these applications will for the most part be the same as for any Windows application, the menu options in each will be different and will depend on what the application is designed to do. It is quite likely that there will be common menu options, such as printing, but for the most part the options will be different and specific to the application. Because of this perception that Windows is intuitive, users click on menu options and see what will happen. This is analogous to trying to drive a lorry when all that the person has been used to driving is a car, i.e. the user interface is very similar but the effects are completely different. The driver of a lorry needs specific training that takes into account the differences between the car and the lorry. So it is with software applications, in that although the interface may look similar, the end results of the application will be completely different.

It is probably true to say that the majority of the facilities built into common applications such as word processors and spreadsheets are never used because users are inadequately trained and unaware that they exist. Therefore, training should be specific and cover topics that are relevant to how the user will use the application in practice. Even though a spreadsheet is a general-purpose tool and can be used by many different types of organisation, the way it is used will depend on the outputs required. In pharmacy, for example, it can be used as a tool to display and maintain lists of drugs, or alternatively it can be used to summarise drug usage. In the first case the user will need to know about the basic facilities of spreadsheets, but to summarise drug usage without the need to rekey data the user will need to be able to use advanced techniques, such as referencing data from different spreadsheets, and creating subtotals and pivot tables. On numerous occasions the author has seen the inappropriate use of applications resulting in many hours of unnecessary work, simply because the user was not aware of some functionality and had not been properly trained. To a certain extent this is a case of 'you don't know what you don't know'. However, it is a good rule of thumb to ascertain whether anyone else would want to perform the same or a similar task. If the answer is yes, then there is a good chance that the facility exists. Talk to an 'expert user' if one is available, or try searching the internet using specific keywords related to the task. There are many web sites dedicated to the use of common applications such as Excel and Word, and many can point the user in the direction of the training required.

It is also important that the training is not just limited to the actual mechanics of using an application, but also the context to the business process in which it is used. This is particularly important when the application is specific to a particular type of business. For example, training in the use of a pharmacy dispensary system should not only cover the mechanics of performing a function such as producing a label, but should also cover what effect it has on the business process. In most systems producing a label will update the patient medication records, change the stock levels and reorder if necessary. If an incorrect label is produced then the training should include the rationale and procedures to be followed to rectify the mistakes. If users simply create another label the information in the system will be incorrect, thereby causing problems in the future. Incorrect information is due to poor system design or inadequate training, and a common reason why users blame the computer when things go wrong.

The complexity and vast amount of functionality included in most applications is such that no one can be expected to grasp all the concepts in a short period of time. Learning to use computer applications efficiently and effectively requires the user to build on existing knowledge and experience.

9

Support

Introduction

Even though computer hardware and software is very reliable there are times when it malfunctions and will not work. One of the major problems with computers is that when something stops working it is often difficult to determine why. Some faults will be glaringly obvious, i.e. that it is a hardware or a software problem. However, in many IT situations it is very difficult to ascertain what has gone wrong. Take as an example a computer linked to the internet which is used to browse the World Wide Web. To enable this to function many different components of hardware and software are required, which must all work together. If this functionality has previously been working and then suddenly fails, where does the problem lie? It could be the internet service provider, the telephone line, or a faulty piece of equipment such as a modem or configuration setting, to name but a few. If a car breaks down a mechanic will be called who will try to isolate the problem based on their knowledge of how a car works. Although there are many different models of car, fundamentally they all work in the same way. The same principle applies to IT systems, in that if something goes wrong the person trying to fix it must understand how the system functions before they can isolate the problem. Therein lies the problem, in that there are thousands of IT systems and solutions which have all been individually configured. The only people who understand how these solutions work are those who design and build them. This is why it is essential to have a contract with the supplier that covers all aspects of support. If an organisation is dependent on these IT solutions to operate their business, for example a pharmacy system, and the system fails, then it is essential that problems are fixed promptly. A service-level agreement (SLA) should form part of the contract and detail the levels of service expected, such as response times.

Many 'systems' are developed by employees to fulfil a particular requirement or need. These 'systems' can be built using readily available tools such as spreadsheets (e.g. Excel) and database management systems (e.g. Access), which are part of a typical office suite of applications. In many cases these systems have been developed without any formal methodology and documentation, and all the knowledge of how the system works lies solely with the employee. If the employee is no longer available or leaves, then this can result in the organisation being at serious risk if it becomes dependent on the system to perform its normal business. These types of 'systems' need to be identified and the risks assessed so that if anything should happen to the employee, the impact is known and can be managed.

Individual PC users have many different applications and facilities that they use on a routine basis. If they belong to a large organisation then it is likely that there will be an IT department who will provide a certain level of support when problems occur. For small organisations and individual users it is just as important to have access to support when needed. There are companies that will provide hardware support contracts, usually at a fixed cost on an annual or monthly basis. Software and configuration problems can take a great deal of time to diagnose and resolve, and require knowledge and experience of the underlying systems. Some companies provide telephone support lines for software problems, but the cost of calls can be very high (e.g. £1 per minute) and can become very expensive, with no guarantee that the problem will be solved.

As time passes people are becoming more and more dependent on IT for both business and pleasure, and need to ensure that they have service agreements in place should problems arise. This is no different from having a service agreement with the AA or RAC for when a car breaks down, or with the utilities companies should there be a problem with one their services.

Software maintenance

When software is made available publicly it is said to be 'released'. Each release of a particular software product will have a certain level of functionality. As time passes, the developers will include additional functionality and release a new version. In order to keep track of the functionality included in a software product, each release is given a version number. For example Word, a popular word processor developed by Microsoft, is available in many different versions, e.g. '97, 2000, 2003. In this example the versions are indicated by adding the year of release as a suffix. There is no standard way of allocating version numbers and each developer will use their own particular method. In many cases it is not obvious which version of a product is being purchased, so it is important to understand which is being obtained and the functionality it includes.

All released software will potentially have many faults, known as bugs. A bug is an error or unintended action in a program. Although testing and quality assurance should ensure that bugs are kept to a minimum, owing to the complexity of software and the number of different permutations that may be encountered when using it, the elimination of bugs is almost impossible. The majority will be found as part of the QA process. However, there will always be cases where bugs are found as a result of particular circumstances occurring. The effects of these can vary enormously, and can range from minor irritations to preventing a system functioning. If the problem is in the latter category then the problem will need to be fixed immediately, once it has been identified. The time taken to identify a problem will vary depending on the circumstances.

Bugs are corrected by creating a new version of the software which has changes that fix the fault. This is often known as a software patch, and will be given a version number. All software needs to have some element of version control, otherwise it is impossible to keep track of the bugs fixed in a particular version. Each version of software is normally given a number for each major release of new functionality, e.g. 1.0. When a bug fix is released the version number will be updated by '.1' for each minor release, e.g. '1.1'. This example is very simple and developers will have many different ways of numbering their versions, many of which can be quite complex.

The developer should issue documentation with each release, detailing all the changes in functionality and bug fixes included, so that an assessment can be made regarding the impact on the end users.

Upgrading systems

The updating of new versions and bug fix releases on to a computer system needs to be given careful consideration and will depend on the individual circumstance and its impact. For instance, take the upgrade of a word processor on a single PC from one version to a later version. The training implications and any problems occurring as a result of the upgrade will generally only affect that user. Contrast this with a multi-user system such as a hospital pharmacy system, which has many users and uses a central database. The training implications are much greater, in that all users will need to have been trained on the changes before the upgrade can take place. If there are any problems with the upgrade it will affect many people and may significantly affect the ability of the organisation to function. The risk in the first example is relatively low, whereas in the second it is potentially fairly high. The risk will determine the approach that should be taken to upgrading software.

Where the risk is high, the upgrade needs to be planned, controlled and managed. A separate environment should exist which can be used as test system which has no impact on the live system. This allows the upgrade to be installed initially into the test environment without affecting the live system and hence the normal business. Users can be trained on the new releases and any impact of the software on the organisation assessed. Once the system has been tested the upgrade of the live system can be scheduled. Even though a 'bug fix' release may not have any training implications that users will see when using the application, it should still be tested in the test environment as configuration problems can occur when upgrading software.

10

Business disaster and recovery

Introduction

Although the title of this chapter may be very intimidating, it is essential that if IT tools are used in business the impact of losing them is fully understood. This chapter is not intended as a complete guide to disaster and recovery: its main purpose is to stimulate thought, so that managers and individuals understand their vulnerability should IT systems fail.

One of the problems with using computers is that it is very easy to become totally dependent on them without actually realising the impact if there is a failure. For example, in a community pharmacy if the labelling system develops a fault and cannot be used, the dispensing process effectively stops. There are numerous reasons why the labelling system might fail, e.g. hardware failure, software failure, data corruption, to name but a few. As systems have more functionality added and become more complex the impact can become even greater. Take for example the electronic transmission of prescriptions (ETP), which is due to be introduced into community pharmacies in the near future. Failure of a labelling system which incorporates the functionality of ETP will have far greater impact than at present, because it is likely that there will be no paper prescription and payment will be based on an electronic submission. Loss of data may result in loss of payment, and it is essential to have a recovery strategy that takes account of the risks associated with failure. These risks need to be balanced against the costs associated with managing them. Careful consideration needs to be given to the problems that may arise as a result of IT tools being used, whether for personal or business use. For example, many people become so dependent on email that if they lose access for a few hours it can severely disrupt their productivity. Failure to access email can occur for many different reasons, e.g. inability to connect to the mail server by the normal method, mail server fails and is unavailable, or the PC has a hardware failure. Many users store text documents, spreadsheets and old emails for future reference. The devices on which these are stored must be regularly backed up on to some other device or medium, so that if something untoward happens to the original device then the files can be recovered and accessed on another machine. Untoward events are manifold, such as fire, theft, device failure, file corruption, etc., and the backup strategy must take this into account. For example, a person may back up their key files on to a CD and store that in the same place as the PC. Although this will accommodate events such as disk failure or file corruption, it will be of no use if a fire destroys both the original copy and the backup. This is the reason why most organisations store backup data off site, such as in a bank. Backup strategies should be thought of as a chain, in that they are only as strong as their weakest link.

Backup and business recovery should be viewed like insurance, in that it will permit recovery if some untoward event occurs.

In the same way that the premiums for insurance are calculated based on the risks of an event happening, so do the risks need to be assessed in relation to the failure of the IT tools. The time taken to restore and recover the system back to its original state also needs to be considered. In large systems where significant amounts of data are held, the recovery from backup tapes can take many hours, and while the system is being recovered it cannot be used.

Planning for disaster is therefore about making sure that if any part of a system fails there is a plan detailing the steps that need to be taken. Recovery planning needs to take into account all aspects of the business process, not just the IT elements, especially where specialist skills and knowledge are required. It is quite common for businesses to use IT and be dependent on the skills and knowledge of a single person. If that person leaves or cannot work for any reason, it can cause significant problems unless another member of staff is adequately trained. These plans need to be documented and tested, which is analogous to the plans and testing that take place in case of fire.

Assessing business risk

Disaster recovery is the ability to restore business-critical systems. The first task is to identify:

- The critical business functions
- The risks associated with those functions
- The financial impact if the functions are lost.

Once the critical functions have been identified the IT systems used in those functions can be assessed.

The number of hours or days that the business can function without the system should be estimated. If necessary, the systems may then be broken down further into different elements of functionality and the number of days or hours estimated for each element. For example in a community pharmacy business the IT system provides labelling functionality and ordering functionality. The business could not operate without the labelling system for more than a few minutes, but could function without the ordering function for a few hours or days (fallback would be to write down the drugs used and give the order verbally over the phone). The list of systems can then be prioritised into those that will cause the biggest impact if unavailable. Each system or element of the system should then be assessed to determine the associated risk and the steps that need to be taken to cover that risk.

When this has been done processes and procedures need to be developed detailing the actions that need to be taken to ensure that the business can continue to operate should problems arise with the critical functions.

Once the recovery plans have been formulated they need to be tested with the full involvement of staff, so that they are clear about the procedures to be undertaken. The procedures need to be tested regularly, in the same way as fire drills.

Backup and recovery strategies

Backup of the data stored on any electronic device is essential in case of system failure or disruption.

The data consists of software and the files created by the software. Although software does need to be backed up in the event of a major problem with the computer, it can usually be obtained from another source, e.g. the original software disks. However, data created by the software applications is unique in that it is specific to the user who created it, and so is irreplaceable. Many people never stop to think about the amount of irreplaceable data stored on the various computing devices they use, but it is essential if a problem arises with the data. The main reasons why data is lost are:

- Hardware error, e.g. hard disk crash
- Human error, e.g. accidental deletion of files
- Theft, e.g. device stolen
- Software corruption, e.g. software bugs and viruses
- Hardware destruction, e.g. fire.

Backing up is an essential process which must be given considerable thought. Although many people are aware that they need to back up data, they give no thought to the strategy that should be used to do so. Backup is required for all devices that hold data in an electronic form if the loss of that data would disrupt their normal way of working. The details of which files and how they are backed up are very important, otherwise it may be assumed that files are being backed up when in fact they are not. It is common for people to assume that data is being backed up, especially in a business environment. Assume nothing: check that data on all systems is being backed up regularly.

Before a backup strategy can be formulated it is necessary to understand where and how the data is stored.

Backing up personal data on a PC

A PC consists of an operating system and applications stored on a hard disk. The operating system is loaded from CDs. In the majority of cases the PC will be purchased with the operating system already loaded on the hard disk. Many systems also come preloaded with a variety of applications. If there is a problem with corruption of the hard disk the computer may need to be rebuilt. If this is the case, the original software disks will be needed to load the operating system and applications. When purchasing a computer make sure that the supplier provides copies of the original disks, which should be kept in a safe place. Any additional applications which are purchased or downloaded from the internet should also be kept in a safe place and be readily available. It is very easy to use and become dependent on numerous applications, all of which will need to be reinstalled in the event that a computer needs to be rebuilt. However, the most important data that needs to be backed up is that created by the user. Whereas software can eventually be obtained from alternative sources, possibly resulting in inconvenience and extra expense, personal data can never be recreated. Personal data is any information such as documents, spreadsheets, digital photographs, emails, etc. that is unique to a user or organisation. It also includes 'collections' of files or data that may not have been created by the user but which would require a significant amount of work to recreate if it was lost, for example music collections and reference material. The size of data files will also have a bearing on how the data is backed up. Files such as music, photographs and documents with lots of graphics tend to be fairly large, of the order of several megabytes (Mb). Floppy disks, which only have a capacity of 1.44 Mb, would be impractical for storing these types of files, even though it is possible by using compression programs such as Winzip, whereby data can be stored across multiple floppy disks. As time goes by the number of files, and hence their total size, increases.

The total size (i.e. the sum of the size of the individual files) of the data will determine how it is backed up and how it should be organised. Backing up an image (i.e. all the files and its directory structure) of the whole hard disk on to a removable hard disk that connects to the computer by a USB2 port is an option. These disks have a capacity of many gigabytes and can be purchased for less than £150. However, because of the size it can take some time to back up all the data, but the advantage is that in the event of hard disk failure, theft or loss of the computer, a new machine could be purchased and the computer restored back to the state of the last backup. The backup data should be stored in a separate geographical location from the original to eliminate the possibility of both being destroyed at the same time, e.g. by fire.

It is important to understand where the data is stored on the hard disk. Files are stored in folders, and these folders can have subfolders. This results in a folder structure known as a tree structure, because it has many separate dividing branches originating from a single root folder.

Most applications store the data by default in a particular folder specifically created by the application. These defaults will be different for each application, resulting in the data being stored in many different folders and in different branches. This makes it difficult to back up the data, as it will be scattered all over the disk. Thus it is essential to understand where and how data is stored by each application. It is better for the user to create specific folders, rather than accept the defaults suggested by the applications, so that the data can be organised in a structure that is easily backed up. It is very easy to forget applications such as email clients, where the data is not usually 'saved' but moved into different folders. These applications will have data files to hold the emails and must be backed up if the data is not to be lost. If the user creates their own folder structure, in much the same way that they would organise a filing cabinet, then it becomes easy to back up the folder structure with a single copy command that backs up the root directory and all branches off the root. All modern operating systems provide copy functions that allow folders to be copied on to some external medium such as a CD-ROM (capacity 650 Mb) or DVD (capacity approximately 4.5 Gb).

If the user has access to a network hard disk drive it is possible to back up data to this. This has the advantage that the two computers are in completely separate locations and so both copies of the data are unlikely to be destroyed by the same event. However, it is still essential to ensure that the network drive is being backed up on a regular basis. The newer operating systems such as Windows 2000 and Windows XP include software that helps manage the backup of files to an offline disk by keeping a track of all files modified, created and deleted in specific folders. It is particularly useful for users of laptops that may be used away from the office. When the user reconnects to the network the software automatically detects the files that have been changed and copies them to the relevant disk.

Pen drives are useful for making temporary copies of data which may contain many hours of work and cannot be backed up using the normal strategy until some time later, for example if the user is away from the office. These devices plug into a USB port and have capacities of between 250 Mb and 2 Gb.

In summary, there are many different ways of ensuring that data is backed up and available in the event of some mishap. Each has its strengths and weaknesses, which must be carefully considered and reassessed as circumstances change. It is essential to think through the process of recovering the data from backup copies should the originals be destroyed, and to ensure that process is robust.

11

Internet (World Wide Web) and information sources

The internet and its beginnings

The internet had its beginnings in 1966 as a result of the US government's requirement to provide a decentralised, highly resilient communications network that could not be destroyed by nuclear attack. Originally the computers allowed to connect to the network were limited to government defence bodies, but this was then expanded to include other public bodies such as universities, and eventually opened up to commercial organisations and the public. The internet is therefore an international computer network made up of smaller networks, all of which have the potential to communicate with each other. One of the key features of the internet is its robustness, which means it is usable even if part of the network fails or is destroyed. The public nature and the robustness are two of the main reasons why the internet has flourished. The ability of computers to communicate with each other is not very useful *per se*: it is only when they can provide services or facilities that they become useful. Some of the main services provided by servers on the internet are:

- Electronic mail (email)
- Telnet or remote login. This allows one computer to log on to another computer and use its resources
- File transfer protocol (FTP). This allows the transfer of files from one computer to another
- Web pages, often referred to as the World Wide Web.

The growth of the internet is due mainly to the World Wide Web, a set of standards and protocols that allow documents (which may contain images, sound and video) to be read by anyone who has access to a web browser and is connected to the internet. Computers are connected to the internet via routers (also known as gateways). Large organisations connect directly to these routers, but smaller organisations and individuals connect via telephone lines or optical cables to organisations known as internet service providers (ISPs). There are hundreds of ISPs, many of which provide limited free services, although the cost of the telephone connection is paid to the telephone company. Many ISPs incorporate the charge for the telephone line in a fixed monthly fee, which usually permits unlimited access. In addition to the connection to the internet, the ISPs also provide additional services such as email and an amount of web space on a server, so that users or organisations can create their own web site.

The main feature of World Wide Web is that it allows hypertext links to be embedded in pages which, when clicked, take the user to another page. These pages can be located on any computer attached to the internet, which is why the system is referred to as a web.

The World Wide Web relies for its operation on three main software components:

- Hypertext markup language (HTML), which describes the syntax of how pages should be created so that they can be read by a web browser.
- Hypertext transfer protocol, which allows a web browser to send a request for HTML pages to computers attached to the internet and to return the content of those pages.

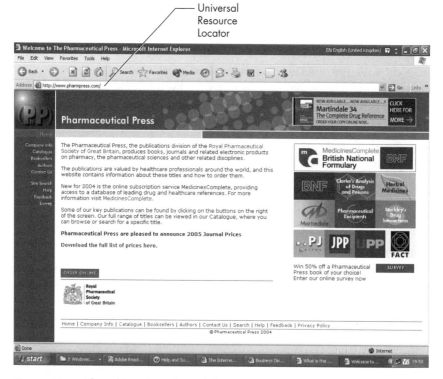

Figure 11.1 The address bar of a web browser.

- Pages are identified by a unique address known as a universal resource locator (URL). This can be seen in the address bar of a browser, e.g. http:://www. pharmpress.com (Figure 11.1).

The robustness of the internet and the ease with which pages can be referenced has led to the World Wide Web becoming a universal tool for disseminating information, and more recently for conducting electronic commerce.

Basics of web sites

Web pages are located on computers running server software whose job is to accept requests from computers running software known as web browsers. When the web server receives a request for a page it will send back an HTML document according to HTTP protocols across a TCP/IP network. HTML documents are simply documents written to a particular standard called hypertext markup language (HTML), which is essentially a plain text document that web browser software can read to produce the pages displayed. Most browsers have an option to view the source, which displays the HTML document as it is stored, not how it is displayed (see Applications for samples of HTML pages). This looks very complicated, but is essentially a series of instructions, each starting and ending with a 'tag' to instruct the browser what text and images to display and how to display them. Each image displayed in a web page has to be downloaded from the server. An image is stored as a separate file and can be very large. This is the reason why a page with lots of graphics takes longer to load and display than one made up mainly of text. In addition to text and images there are many other functions supported by the HTML format that allow access to external programs. This is how many complex functions, such as placing orders or searching databases, are achieved through a web page where interaction with the user is required.

Web pages are essentially a hierarchy of links to other pages on the same computer or others connected to the internet. Each page has a unique address known as a universal resource locator (URL), which is a string of characters used to identify a resource such as a computer, a file or a web page. A URL can be thought of as the exact 'address' of a resource. On most web browsers the URL of the page being viewed can be seen in the 'address bar'. On many occasions the address will be filled in automatically by the browser when a hyperlink is clicked. A hyperlink is any object (e.g. text or image) within a web page which, when clicked, displays the web page or resource of the URL associated with that hyperlink. The URL will normally contain not only the web site address but also the actual page on the server.

A URL is made up of several parts. For example, the URL http://www.rpsgb.org.uk/members/registration/index.html accesses the Registers page of the Royal Pharmaceutical Society of Great Britain web site. The first part of the address is the protocol, which tells the web browser what sort of server it will be talking to in order to retrieve the resources associated with the URL. In the case of a browser accessing a web page, the protocol will be 'http', which stands for hypertext transmission protocol. The second part of the example URL between the '//' and the first '/' is the domain name of the web site to connect to. In the example, the domain name is www.rpsgb.org.uk. Domain names are the unique names used to conveniently contact an internet site or email address. Without a domain name, the user would be required to enter the unique internet protocol (IP) address of that site. An IP address consists of four numbers (e.g. 165.123.125.24), which are difficult for humans to remember. As domain names are unique they have to be registered with a central registry before they can be used, for which there is a small fee. In the UK the registry for '.uk' names is maintained by Nominet.uk (www.nominet.org.uk). Many ISPs will register a domain name on behalf of a customer when setting up a web server. The third part of the example URL is the path at which this particular web page is located on the server. In this case, the path is 'members/registration/index.html'. Similar to a file name, a path usually indicates where the page is located within the web site; in this case it is located in the basic subfolder of the 'registration' folder, which is in the folder 'members'. The 'members' folder is located in the top-level web page directory of the RPSGB web site.

Creating a web site

Creating a simple web site is relatively straightforward once the basics are understood.

Creating pages for the web site

As described above, a web site consists of any number of HTML pages all linked together in a hierarchical structure. Since HTML pages are made up of basic text it is possible to use a simple text editor to create a web site. Most are created by using software authoring tools. These are referred to as WYSIWYG (what you see is what you get) applications, which have graphical interfaces and allow the user to create a page as it will appear on the final web browser. Once the pages are finished they are saved and the authoring tool creates the HTML pages, which are put on to a computer running server software. Two of the most popular authoring tools used to create web sites are Macromedia's Dreamweaver and Microsoft's Frontpage.

Hosting the web site

Once the pages that make up the web site have been created they need to be transferred to a computer that is running web server software. This will normally be provided by an internet service provider (ISP). Two of the most common web server software applications are Apache and Internet Information Server. Many ISPs will provide customers with sufficient space on a server to create a web site. The domain name used to access the site will be that of the ISP, e.g. 'home.btconnect.com/folder', where 'folder' is replaced by a unique name to identify the customer, e.g. 'home.btconnect.com/abcpharmacy'. The pages that make up the web site are then copied to this directory. The ISP will give instructions on how this can be achieved, but it is essentially just copying the files to the new location using the 'ftp' protocol.

Web browsers

Anyone wishing to access the content of the web site enters the domain, e.g. home.btconnect.com/abcpharmacy, into the address bar of a web browser and the pages are displayed. There are many different types of web browser, but two of the most common are Internet Explorer and Netscape Navigator. It is important that the pages are designed and constructed so that the user can navigate easily round the web site. If it is not obvious how to get to another page on the site the visitor will go elsewhere.

ISPs usually provide a service whereby a customer can register their own domain name, but it must be unique and cannot already have been registered by someone else. This means that the URL will be more personalised and not have the name of the ISP in the address. Domain names can usually be transferred from one ISP to another for a small fee. The advantage of using an ISP is that the computer will always be connected to the internet and thus always available. Now that ADSL lines are available which are 'always on' and permanently connected to the internet, it is feasible to host the web site on a home or business computer. However, a fixed IP address is required and it is essential that the rest of the computers on the network are protected from unauthorised access.

Designing, testing and maintenance

Although it is relatively easy to create a simple web site there can be a significant amount of work involved in design, testing and maintenance if the site is to be kept current. It is also essential, as with any system, to design the pages so that it is easy for the visitor to navigate through the site easily. The site needs to be tested by using different web browsers to ensure that the pages are displayed as expected, as different browsers can display the same pages differently.

More complex sites

Many ISPs offer facilities to access data stored in databases, so that visitors to the site can search through catalogues. Others offer the ability to create online shops, with payment being taken electronically on a web page. Pages can be created which can communicate with other programs and allow all sorts of facilities, such as music and videos, to be accessed and downloaded.

Information sources

The World Wide Web has had a huge impact on the dissemination of information. Most organisations take it for granted that customers will have access to a web browser. One of the problems with the internet, however, is that there is an overwhelming volume of information easily accessible through search engines. Once information is located it is essential to validate the source, as the internet is uncensored and any individual or organisation is able to create web pages, which may represent their views, biases, etc. and which may not be factually accurate. One of the advantages of the internet over traditional dissemination methods is that it can be quickly updated. There are many organisations providing medical information for use by healthcare professionals. The UK Medicines Information (ukmi.nhs.uk) service provides a web site that supplies information according to evidenced-based principles. This is a network of 16 regional centres and smaller local centres. Most sites of this type enable the user to search for all articles on a specific topic, and it is not unusual for a search on a single word to produce many hundred of matches. Searches can therefore be refined and additional parameters added to make the search more specific, thereby reducing the number of matches. Each match is presented as a hyperlink which, when clicked, will take the user to the relevant article. Many articles are presented as PDF files, which is a standard method for reading documents produced by different software packages. PDF is an acronym for portable document format, which was invented by a company called Adobe. PDF documents must be read with Adobe Reader, which is free and can be downloaded from the Adobe site (www.adobe.com). A link to download the software is usually provided on sites that use the PDF format. Some pharmacy information sites provide a daily summary of news articles from a variety of sources relevant to healthcare professionals. These can be viewed by connecting to sites in the normal way. Alternatively, the user can register with the site to receive the headlines by email on a daily basis. This has the advantage that the information is pushed to the user rather than pulled, i.e. the user is automatically updated rather than having to remember to go and look at the site. Two sites that offer this service are www.druginfozone.nhs.uk (Guys and St Thomas Regional Information Centre) and www.npc.co.uk (National Prescribing Centre).

The *BNF* is also available online at www.bnf.org. This is provided from a central site, but it is also possible to obtain versions which are located on intranets and can be tailored to meet a hospital's own requirements in terms of formularies.

The Royal Pharmaceutical Society's web site www.rpsgb.org.uk has many resources related to the practice of pharmacy. Almost all documents published by the society are available online and can be downloaded. A links page contains hyperlinks to the home pages of many pharmacy- and healthcare-related sites. The Library and Information Centre of the RPSGB provides information on a whole range of topics, and much of this is available online. Search facilities exists which allow the library catalogue to be viewed online. In addition, the RPS e-PIC is available online. This covers all aspects of pharmacy, its practice and current research, particularly in relation to the United Kingdom. The subject coverage includes drugs and therapeutics, pharmacy practice and management (particularly hospital and community), pharmacy ethics and professionalism, interprofessional relationships, Society matters and its pronouncements. The *Pharmaceutical Journal* is covered in detail (www.rpsgb.org.uk).

The *Pharmaceutical Journal* is also available online (www. pjonline.com) and the site can be searched for any articles that have appeared in the journal since 1999.

Learning on the internet and continuing professional development

Many sites, such as the Centre for Pharmacy Postgraduate Education (CPPE) provide online training courses. With the advent of high-speed ADSL lines online learning becomes far more practical and can be completed from any PC with access to the internet. Recording of continuing professional development online is being rolled out to all pharmacists on the RPSGB register.

General information sites

There are many sites dedicated to providing information normally found in paper directories and have many of the advantages of traditional methods. For example, Yellow Pages is available online at www.yell.co.uk. In addition to the telephone numbers of organisations they can also give a map of their location via a hyperlink. BT provides the same facilities for private telephone numbers. Both use the facilities of Multi-Map (uk2.multimap.com), which can be used independently to find the location of any organisation.

There are many other sites offering travel information, and the list is endless. The internet is quickly becoming the de facto standard for providing all sorts of information.

Summary

The information available via the internet is infinite, so much so that it can lead to information overload. The challenge is to find efficient mechanisms for locating information quickly and effectively, as such information can be a major benefit for both business and personal use. As wireless links to PDAs become faster and more efficient it is easy to envisage information being available wherever the user may be. This will have major benefits for pharmacy professionals, who may want to look up information on a particular topic or access patient records when a PC is not available, for example on a ward drug round.

12

Primary and secondary care systems

Introduction

The use of IT in both the primary and the secondary care sectors of pharmacy has until recently centred on the supply function of pharmacists, and as such is not clinically based. Although both hospital and community pharmacy systems have the facility to record information on the patient's medication record, this is only a byproduct of the dispensing process, i.e. the supply function. In hospitals, the supply of drugs is very different from that in the community. Many drugs in hospital are supplied in bulk to the ward rather than on an individual basis, as is the case in community pharmacy. This difference is reflected in the fact that the IT systems used in hospitals are generally not the same as those used in community pharmacies. The role of pharmacists in both primary and secondary care is changing and becoming more clinically oriented and focused. To carry out this role pharmacists require access to a patient's medical history and laboratory results. Much of this information is available in the paper notes or in many disparate computer systems, but can be time-consuming to obtain and requires access to GP systems and notes. One of the government's key programmes is the National Programme for Information Technology (NPfIT) (www.npfit.nhs.uk), which consists of many separate projects and will enable new ways of working by utilising the benefits of IT. The programme has been rebranded as Connecting for Health (www.connectingforhealth.nhs.uk). Some of the projects that are significant to pharmacy are the new National Network, the electronic transmission of prescriptions (ETP) and the NHS Care Records Service. The National Network, which is also referred to as N3, is a technical infrastructure project and will provide fast broadband network services that will be required by many of the other projects of NPfIT. The ETP project will be a new service that will transfer prescriptions electronically from GP systems to community pharmacy systems and on to the PPA for payment, and can be seen as an extension of the supply function of the pharmacist. The NHS Care Records Service, in contrast, is a project that will give healthcare professionals access to patient information where and when it is needed. A summary of care and clinical history will be held on a national database known as the 'spine', so that important patient information is always accessible and available. In view of the fact that the role of pharmacists is changing and becoming clinically focused it is essential that they have access to the information on the spine. It is important that pharmacists are aware of how and when they will access this information, and the implications for their current and future practices. The computer systems of the future need to be designed around the new working practices and business processes pharmacists will provide in their changing role.

Another important enabling technology is the Dictionary of Medicines and Devices (dm+d). The computer systems currently in use use different coding systems to describe and identify medicines and drugs. These different systems have been created to fulfil a specific requirement for the different functions carried out. For example, hospital and community pharmacies use the PIP code system (among others, such as LINK and PROSPER) to order drugs, while using other codes and descriptions to dispense the drugs. Clinical information systems use still different codes and descriptions, such as Read codes. This is significant when trying to integrate disparate computer systems, especially when exchange of data is required. Although it is possible to produce maps from one coding system to another there is the potential for mapping errors. Improving patient safety is at the heart of all the NHS IT initiatives, and the National Patient Safety Agency (NPSA) (www.npsa.nhs.uk) has emphasised the importance of designing systems that prevent harm. With all these issues in mind the NHS Information Authority commissioned a programme called the United Kingdom Clinical Products Reference System (UKCPRS) to create a coding system for medical products and devices which would address all the above issues and be used by all computer systems used in the NHS. The coding system has had various names throughout its development and is now known as the Dictionary of Medicines and Devices (dm+d). Essentially, the dm+d provides a database of unique codes for each medicine and device along with an unambiguous textual description. Both the ETP and the NHCRS projects, which are part of the NPfIT (Connecting for Health) programme, mandate that the dm+d will be used as the method of coding drugs. In hospitals the pharmacy computer systems and the electronic prescribing systems being developed will also need to ensure that they use the dm+d as the method for displaying and coding drugs, so that they will be compatible with the NHS systems being developed. It can be seen from the above that the dm+d is a key enabling technology for many future IT computer projects.

Hospital and community systems

Although some of the requirements of hospital and community IT systems are the same, e.g. the labelling of dispensed medicines, the majority of the requirements are totally different. This is reflected in the fact that the business processes operating in hospital and community are completely different. Whereas community pharmacies for the most part have only one dispensary and one pharmacist, in contrast, hospitals have multiple dispensaries, a main pharmacy store and many pharmacists and technicians. This means that the systems developed and used in community pharmacies are very rarely used in hospitals, and vice versa. In hospitals, the systems need to be able to cope with the variable number of dispensaries and stores and the movement of stock between them. Whereas at present community pharmacy is fundamentally about dispensing drugs to individuals, hospitals dispense drugs to individual patients and also issue a substantial amount to wards to top up the ward drugs cupboard. In the past many hospitals have tried to implement pharmacy software developed for the American market, with little success. In America the business processes used in hospitals are totally different from those used in the UK. This highlights the fundamental requirement that computer systems must be designed to work with the business processes and not the other way round.

In hospitals, pharmacy is only one aspect of the overall service provided to patients. There are many other departments which have IT systems to assist in the management of patients, such as medical records, pathology and radiology, to name but a few. The business processes of all these departments overlap at some point, making a hospital one of the most complex organisations that exist. This means the hospital computer systems must be designed to meet the specific requirements of each department, but also to satisfy the overall objectives of the hospital in the treatment of patients. There have been many initiatives in hospitals attempting to produce computer systems that cover the majority of departments, with varying degrees of success. These systems have had various names, depending on the thinking at the time, such as resource management, hospital information support system (HISS) and electronic patient record system. The requirements specification for a complete hospital information system can run into many hundreds of pages and the cost many millions of pounds, reflecting the functionality that needs to be provided if the majority of disciplines are to be covered. These types of system tend to be provided by a single supplier, where the applications to support each department are tightly integrated and work with a central database. At the heart of these systems is the electronic patient record (EPR), which seeks to cover a patient's treatment by any department in the hospital. Many hospitals have chosen to try to create an EPR by interfacing the existing (sometimes referred to as legacy) departmental systems. This approach requires interfaces to be built which transfer the relevant information from one system to another. Many hospital pharmacy systems are interfaced to the hospital patient administration system, which provides the basic demographic information about a patient, such as hospital record number, name and address. The majority of hospital departmental systems require access to the patient's demographic information. Usually the departmental systems are provided by different suppliers, and each will store the demographic data in its own database, meaning that there are multiple copies of the same or similar information. This not only results in duplicated effort in collecting and recording this information, but also goes against the fundamental principle of holding data once wherever possible; otherwise, when this information changes, it will have to be changed in every system and becomes very difficult to manage. This highlights the difference between systems that are integrated as opposed to those that are interfaced. Integrated systems will actually store the data only once, and it can be used by all departmental systems. When the information is changed as a result of contact with one department all departments accessing the integrated record will be using the current, up-to-date information. Interfaced systems, on the other hand, will store the same information on their separate databases. Any updates will need to be sent through an electronic interface to all the other systems, which is not always practical, bearing in mind the complexity and cost of an interface between two systems. It is therefore usual to nominate one of the systems as a 'master' (usually the patient administration system) and build interfaces to this system.

The electronic patient record is one of the most important developments to affect both the hospital and the community pharmacy sectors in the future and is encompassed in the National Program for Information Technology (NPfIT; www.npfit.nhs.uk). Also known as Connecting for Health (www.connectingforhealth.nhs.uk) this program has many different projects and the government has set aside £2.3 billion over the next 3 years to fund it. One of the key projects is the NHS Care Records Service, whose main aim is to provide a central electronic record of a patient's medical care that can be accessed by healthcare professionals. An individual is likely to be treated by a variety of care professionals in a range of locations throughout their life. The

NHS Care Record is a means of ensuring that the details of their care and treatment are held in a single, easily accessible electronic record. Initially this will hold patient demographic information based on a single unique number allocated to the patient, i.e. their NHS number, and eventually their health and care history. This project has many implications with regard to the way information is recorded, and there are many smaller projects that will address these issues. One of the most important aspects is the confidentiality of the patient record and the control of access to specific parts of the record. Each healthcare professional will need to be accredited with the service before they will be allowed to access a patient's record. These projects will have significant impact on pharmacy and the way in which IT systems are developed and used in the future.

One of the most important projects as far as pharmacy is concerned is the Dictionary of Medicines and Devices (dm+d; www.dmd.nhs.uk). The objective of this project is to provide a unique unambiguous identifier and associated textual description for medicines and medical devices, and it was instigated to address the problem of many different coding systems for identifying drugs. Electronic systems need to use codes rather than textual descriptions to reference drugs, and the dm+d will do this. This is one of the prime reasons why the NPfIT has mandated that the dm+d will be used as the prime reference to drugs recorded in the NHS Care Records service. The dm+d will also be used in the Electronic Transmission of Prescriptions project, which is one of the key projects in the NPfIT. This project will allow GPs to transmit prescriptions to community pharmacies electronically.

It is clear that many of the initiatives and projects of the NPfIT are interrelated and will have a big impact on the future of pharmacy.

Enabling technologies for NPfIT (Connecting for Health)

As mentioned in the introduction, in order to produce a coherent system there must be enabling work allowing data to be shared in a consistent and coherent way. Two projects that will enable the data to be exchanged and shared efficiently are the N3 and the dm+d. N3 is essentially a secure network of connections between the different computers with the capacity to cope with the volumes of data that will be transferred.

Dictionary of Medicines and Devices (dm+d)

The dm+d (www.dm+d.nhs.uk) is a dictionary containing unique identifiers and associated textual descriptions for medicines and medical devices. It has been developed for use throughout the NHS (in hospitals, primary care and the community) as a means of uniquely identifying the specific medicines or devices used in the diagnosis or treatment of patients.

The dm+d is part of the United Kingdom Clinical Products Reference Source (UKCPRS) project instigated by the NHS Information Authority (NHSIA) in 1999. The objective of the project was to bring together the initiatives associated with the coding of drugs in electronic systems. Initially there was an urgent need for a primary care drug dictionary (PCDD) to support the GP primary care prescribing system Prodigy (an NHS-sponsored knowledge management system). Later it was used to re-engineer the Prescription Pricing Authority's (PPA) in-house systems and will be used to underpin the electronic transmission of prescriptions (ETP). Although the PCDD meets the requirements of primary care it does not meet those for secondary care and medical devices. Phase 2 of the UKCPRS project was to develop dictionaries for secondary care (Secondary Care Drug Dictionary; SCDD) and medical devices (Medical Devices Dictionary; MDD). The PCDD model was assessed for its applicability to these two dictionaries and found to be acceptable with relatively minor modifications. A reconciliation process resulted in a harmonised model that meets the need of all sectors of pharmacy and resulted in the complete UKCPRS dictionary. The complete dictionary was renamed the Dictionary of Medicines and Devices (dm+d).

The dm+d will be used in the NHS Care Records service as the NHS standard for naming and coding medicines and medical devices. It will enable interoperability between diverse clinical systems by ensuring the safe and reliable exchange of information on medicines and devices, and allow effective decision support. It is anticipated that the dm+d will play a major part in improving patient safety, which will be achieved by the use of consistent textual descriptors and codes for prescribing and dispensing, leading to safer systems (i.e. fewer errors).

The population of the dm+d is nearly complete. The next challenge is to ensure that computer system suppliers adopt the dm+d and incorporate it into their systems. The fact that the NHS Care Records Service and the Electronic Transmission of Prescriptions project have mandated that the dm+d be used should ensure its adoption. The distribution and update of the dm+d is a key issue for all system suppliers, and must be robust and timely if suppliers are to invest in the considerable expense of changing their systems to use it. New drugs will have to be added to the dm+d and distributed to suppliers and then on to end-user systems well before a drug becomes available for prescribing and dispensing. The maintenance and distribution of the dm+d is no small task, bearing in mind the number of systems that will need to be updated.

N3 – the National Network

One of the core projects of the NPfIT (Connecting for Health) is the replacement of the existing NHSnet. This will be known as N3, the National Network (www.n3.nhs.uk), and will provide sufficient connectivity and broadband capacity to meet the current and future demands of the NHS. The National Network is part of the technical infrastructure which is required to enable other projects, such as the NHS Care Records service and electronic transmission of prescriptions. N3 is a secure wide-area network developed exclusively for the NHS. Only authorised users will be able to access it, to ensure that information, particularly patient records, is secure. Approximately 18 000 NHS locations will be connected to N3. In addition, 12 000 community pharmacists will need to be connected as part of the Electronic Transmission of Prescription project, as N3 will be part of the infrastructure required. The mechanism by which this is achieved has yet to be determined, as no system connected to N3 can also be connected to other networks. Community pharmacies, being businesses, need to connect to other networks in order to carry out their normal business, such as ordering drugs from wholesalers. Pharmacies will also need access to the National Care Records service to view patient records, which will be delivered over N3. The N3 network provides many other services, such as email, access to NHSweb, and access to the internet.

Electronic transmission of prescriptions

Electronic transmission of prescriptions (ETP) (www.npfit.nhs.uk/programmes/etp/) is a term used to describe the process of sending prescriptions electronically from a doctor to a pharmacy. In the UK the ETP project enables prescriptions to be sent electronically to community pharmacies directly from the GP. These prescriptions can then be sent electronically to the Prescription Pricing Authority (PPA), which reimburses the pharmacist for the drugs dispensed.

An ETP pilot was set up and closed at the end of June 2003, having served its intended purpose of proving the feasibility of transmitting prescriptions electronically. It has been demonstrated that ETP is technically viable and could provide a range of benefits, including improved patient choice and safety. ETP is one of the core projects of the NPfIT (Connecting for Health) and will be introduced from the beginning of 2005. The new community pharmacy contract includes money to fund the connection of all community pharmacies to the National Network (N3). The electronic prescription will be sent from the prescribing system, such as a GP practice system, to a central ETP service, which is part of the NHS Care Records Service, and is then available for dispensing. If the patient has nominated a particular pharmacy from which to receive their medication a copy of the prescription is also sent straight to the pharmacy, so that the medicine can be dispensed. If the patient does not nominate a specific pharmacy they will be given an ePrescription token to present at the pharmacy of their choice. It is anticipated that this will look like a normal prescription but with a barcode printed on it containing a unique number. This will then enable the pharmacist to obtain the details of the prescription from the central ETP service so that it can be dispensed. The implementation of ETP by community pharmacies has many implications: for example, the systems will have to be timely, robust, and always available during business hours, otherwise patients may be inconvenienced. In addition, the processes to rectify errors and mistakes will need to be clearly defined if incorrect information is not to be transmitted to other systems, such as the PPA and the NHS Care Records Service. Additional services such as repeat dispensing and electronic reimbursement will be incorporated into the service as it evolves. As can be seen, there is a considerable amount of work to be done before ETP becomes routine in the primary care environment.

NHS Care Records Service

The National Care Records Service (www.npfit.nhs.uk/programmes/nhscrs) is intended to address the current deficiencies related to the sharing of health records which are at present held on a mixture of computer and paper records. At the centre of the system will be a national database of patient records known as the 'spine', which will allow information to be safely shared across the NHS by healthcare professionals. An individual is treated by a variety of healthcare professionals throughout their life and in many different locations. The NHS Care Record is intended to keep the details of care and treatment in a central, easily accessible electronic record. This will store the individual's unique identifier, their NHS number, and demographic details such as address and date of birth. As the patient receives treatment, the record will be updated with that treatment. It will include information that might affect a patient's future treatment, such as allergies and medical conditions, e.g. diabetes. As the pharmacist's role becomes more clinically oriented they will need access to the patient information held on the 'spine' if they are to carry out their role efficiently. In addition, they will also contribute to the information held on the 'spine', for example medication reviews. The clinical role will mean that the processes related to patient contact will change and result in modifications to the computer systems currently used. It is essential that these changes take into account the bigger picture of the NHS and the pharmacist's evolving role.

The National Care Records Service has been developed because of the complexity in the way that healthcare is delivered. A patient will be seen by many different healthcare professionals in many different locations, but primarily by their GP. They may also be seen by specialists in hospital, and may have other medical events, such as visits to an A&E department, all of whom need access to the patient's medical record in order to give appropriate treatment. In addition, diagnosis and treatment of a patient's conditions is becoming increasingly specialised and can involve organisations and healthcare professionals working in cooperation. For example, medication reviews by pharmacists will require cooperation between them and the GPs. All these organisations and individuals will use computer systems that can access the information on the 'spine'. The GP's computer system, for example, will update the 'spine' with the summary details of any encounters. More in-depth details will be held on the local systems where the care is delivered. This will include detailed personal health information, such as a record of conditions, medications, operations, tests, X-rays, scans and other results. Links to local information will be available from the summary record of the spine (Figure 12.1).

NHS Care Record

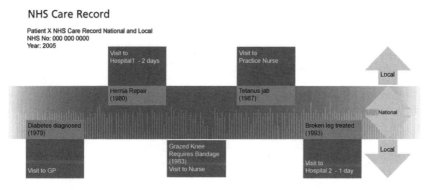

Figure 12.1 NHS Care Record (reproduced with the permission of NpfIT).

All computer systems that access the 'spine' will need to be modified so that they are compliant with the NPfIT requirements and standards. GP system suppliers who have been awarded contracts by NPfIT have already begun the process of modifying their systems. There is a considerable amount of development, implementation and training to be done before the NHS Care Records Service will be fully available. The implementation is to split into four phases: phase 1 is due to be completed by the summer of 2005, with phase 4 due for completion in 2010. Implementation plans and details are available on the NPfIT website (www.npfit.nhs.uk) or Connecting for Health (www.connecting forhealth.nhs.uk).

Glossary

10BaseT   A cabling system used for networking computers using ethernet protocols, which employs twisted pairs of wires (normally Category 5). The 10 refers to the maximum transfer rate of 10 megabits per second (Mbps). Computers can be placed a maximum of 100 metres from each other before hardware repeaters are required to boost the signal.

100BaseT   Same standard as 10baseT except that the maximum transfer rate is 100 Mbps.

802.11   A family of specifications developed by the IEEE for wireless LAN technology. 802.11 specifies an over-the-air interface between a wireless client and a wireless base station, or between two wireless clients. Each variation to the original specification is given a letter suffix.

802.11b and 802.11g are the most commonly found specifications associated with wireless equipment.

802.11b (also referred to as Wi-Fi) is an extension to 802.11 that applies to wireless LANs and provides 11 Mbps transmission rates and wireless functionality comparable to that of cable-based ethernet. 802.11g supports higher transfer rate of 20 Mbps and is compatible with 802.11b equipment.

Accelerator key   A key or combination of keys that perform specific actions in an application without the need to navigate through menus. For example, in Microsoft Windows pressing the 'Ctrl' and 'C' keys has the same action as selecting the 'Copy' function from a menu. The name derives from the fact that for a touch typist the use of keys is much quicker, as the hands do not need to leave the keyboard and grasp the mouse. Also called Keyboard shortcuts.

Access   Access is a relational database and is one of the applications that make up the Microsoft Office suite of software. Access is a database management system (DBMS) and enables users to create tables and forms to collect data. The data stored in the database can be queried using tools provided as part of the application. Many applications use an Access database to store and manage the data created by the application.

Acrobat Reader   A software application which is used to view PDF files and is available free from Adobe Systems. It has recently been renamed Adobe Reader. The PDF format is becoming one of the de facto standards for reading documents over the internet.

Acoustic hood   A special cabinet designed to fit round a dot matrix printer to reduce the noise produced when printing.

Adobe   Adobe Systems is a software company that invented the Postscript page description language, used to print highly formatted documents on laser printers and typesetting equipment used by professional printers. It also invented the PDF document format, which is widely used to capture any document in its original format. The reading of a PDF document requires Acrobat Reader or Adobe Reader, which are available free and can be downloaded from the Adobe web site. PDF documents can be protected so that they cannot be altered using a word processor. www.adobe.com

Adobe Reader   The new name for Acrobat Reader, which is used to read PDF files. It is available free and can be downloaded from the Adobe web site. The PDF document format is becoming one of the de facto standards for reading documents over the internet. Adobe Reader is also available for PDAs, which enables PDF documents to be read on a handheld device. www.adobe.com

ADSL   Asymmetric digital subscriber line. A special type of telephone line that allows voice and data to use the existing telephone system. Data and voice can use the line at the same time, allowing a home computer to use the internet at the same time as somebody is using the telephone for a voice call. The term asymmetric is used because the speed of data transfer differs in each direction. Downstream is normally twice the speed of the upstream rate. This is perfectly acceptable in practice, as the majority of data flows downstream, i.e. from the internet to the home computer. Cable modems provide roughly equivalent speeds for households having access to cable TV.

Adware   Adware are programs that have the same effect as web browser pop-ups, which are displayed when surfing the internet. Pop-ups are usually displayed intentionally by the developer of the web page being viewed, whereas adware are programs located on the user's PC and contact specific sites to advertise something which is totally unrelated to the site being viewed. Adware is usually unwittingly installed on a computer by the user clicking a web site link and the program being downloaded and installed in the backbround without the user being aware. Both pop-ups and adware can become very annoying, and it is difficult to distinguish between them. Pop-ups can be blocked by configuring the web browser to prevent their display (or only to allow pop-ups from certain sites). Adware, on the other hand, must be removed from the computer using a program to detect their presence, in much the same way as a virus scanner.

AMD   Advanced Micro Devices is a company that manufactures microprocessors, the Athlon and K6 series, which are used as alternatives to the Intel Pentium microprocessor in personal computers. AMD microprocessors tend to be less expensive than the equivalent Intel chip.

Analogue modem   Frequently abbreviated to the term modem, these are used to allow digital computers to communicate with each other over a standard telephone line. Analogue modems have a maximum speed of 56 000 bits per second (bps) owing to the physical limitations imposed by the signals used to transmit the data. They are built to strict standards so that any modem can communicate with any another modem. They have many additional facilities, such as the ability to be used as a fax when used with additional fax software.

ANSI   American National Standards Institute, which facilitates the adoption of standards by accrediting the procedures of standards-developing organisations. Standards are crucial in IT, as it is possible to program computers in numerous ways to achieve the same result. One example of a fundamental standard, used since the early days of computing, is ASCII (American

Standard Code for Information Interchange), in which each alphabetic, numeric or special character is represented by a seven-bit binary number (a combination of seven 0s or 1s). It is the most common format used to code text files in computers and on the internet. www.ansi.org

API Application program interface. A standardised method of allowing applications to interface with other programs, such as an operating system. The operating system designers and programmers will provide functions that can be used by the application programmers to perform specfic tasks, such as printing a document. The designer of the API will define the standard for communicating with their system via external programs or applications. An analogy would be the use of the domestic electricity supply. Manufacturers of equipment who wish to use the standard electricity supply must conform to various standards, e.g. the connector must be a three-pin plug and be able to accept 240 volts.

AppleMac See Macintosh.

Application software Software written to perform a specific set of functions or tasks, such as a word processor or spreadsheet.

ASCII American Standard Code for Information Interchange, the most common character set used to represent text characters on a computer. Each character is given a unique binary number, which will always represent that character, e.g. the character 'a' is represented by the binary number 01100001, which is equivalent to decimal 97; 'b' is represented by 01100010 or decimal 98. The binary number will always fit within one byte, i.e. it is never greater than decimal 255. The ASCII standard was certified by the ANSI in 1977 and ISO adopted an almost identical code as ISO646.

Athlon A CPU (central processing unit) manufactured by AMD which is used in many personal computers.

Audio port The audio port is located on a PC's soundcard and enables the computer to play music and sounds. Stereo speakers can be plugged into the audio port.

Authentication A process of identifying a user, computer or software process by comparing information supplied with that already saved on the target system. This is usually in the form of a username and password, but can be a digitally encrypted file.

Background task A software process that continues to run without any user interaction and any visible display while other programs are being used. A multitasking operating system is required to achieve this type of functionality. In the Windows operating system printing of a large document is an example of a background task.

Bandwidth Bandwidth is used in analogue communication to signify the difference between the highest and lowest frequencies a transmission channel can carry. It has been adopted in digital communications to indicate the speed at which a communications channel can operate, e.g. the maximum bandwidth of a standard telephone line is 56 000 bps.

Bar code A pattern of vertical black stripes of variable thickness which can be read by a reader or scanner. There are different methods of coding the stripes, but essentially the bar code will represent a number or alphanumeric text. The stripes can be read instantaneously by a bar code scanner, alleviating the need to input the numbers manually via a keyboard, thus increasing the speed of processing. The bar codes can be printed on product labels and lists, such as ward top-up sheets, and are often used to increase the speed of input. There are different encoding systems (known as symbologies, e.g. Code 39, Code 128) that determine the number and width of the stripes for each character.

There are two-dimensional bar codes that overcome the limitations of conventional bar codes, which restrict the amount of information that can be stored to the space available. Two-dimensional bar codes can store the information contained on an A4 sheet of paper in the space of a conventional bar code. PDF417 is an encoding symbology for two-dimensional bar codes, the PDF standing for portable data file.

BASIC   Beginners All-purpose Symbolic Instruction Code, a simple programming language used on the early versions of the IBM PC to create applications.

Bit   The lowest level of information used in digital computing and data communications. A bit can have one of two values – 0 and 1 – representing one of two states, on or off. In contrast, analogue devices store values between 0 and infinity. Bits are then grouped together in series of eight to form a byte. A byte represents the decimal numbers 0–255. Each number is then used to represent an alphabetic, numeric or punctuation character, which can be displayed as text. The number used for each character is governed by different standards, the most common of which is the American Standard Code for Information Interchange (ASCII), defined by the American National Standards Institute (ANSI).

Bit map   Bit map is a term applied to images which are stored in a computer's memory or file. An image can be represented as series of rows and columns of dots. In its simplest form, each dot is represented by a bit, which can be set to 1 or 0 signifying black or white. When viewed from a distance the dots create an image to the human eye. Colour images use more bits to define the colour of each dot. The quality of the image is determined by the number of dots in a given space and the number of colours used. The greater the number of dots per inch the better the resolution (quality) of the picture.

Blackberry   A range of radio-based PDAs that allow connection to networks using GRPS technology and which are used primarily to send and receive email while on the move. Email is integrated with the user's PC-based email account and is 'pushed' to the device, so that the user is alerted to any new messages, which can be read while they are out of the office. Emails can also be sent from the device. The devices also have the usual PDA functionality of appointment diary, contacts, to-do list and note taker, as well as having an integrated phone.

Bluetooth   A method of connecting portable devices to other mobile devices, such as phones, PDAs and other Bluetooth-enabled devices. Bluetooth uses radio waves to communicate between the sending and receiving devices, but does not need to be within line of sight to establish a connection. It is only intended to be used over short distances, i.e. the devices must be within 10–30 metres of each other.

Boolean logic   Boolean logic is derived from Boolean algebra and is the basis on which all computers are based.

Boot   Term used to describe the actions are taken by the computer when it is switched on. These are usually in the form of a set of instructions stored in permanent memory and are carried out when the power is applied.

bps   Bits per second. The units used to measure the speed of data transfer between computer devices.

Broadband   Term used to describe a high-speed link between a home computer and the internet. ADSL telephone lines and cable TV lines are examples of broadband links. Typical download speeds are 512 kilobits per second.

Bug   A term used to describe an error or unintended action in a software program. Although testing and quality assurance should ensure that bugs are kept to a minimum, because of the complexity of software and the number of different permutations that may be encountered, the elimination of bugs is almost impossible. Software testing is thus an essential part of software development.

Business intelligence   A term used to describe the processes and technologies used to interrogate data, usually stored in databases, with a view to making informed business decisions.

Business objects   A company that provides a range of products used to interrogate and analyse the data stored in databases. The use of these tools requires considerable skill and knowledge. The terms business intelligence and online analytical processing (OLAP) are often used in conjunction with the solutions provided by these products. www.businessobject.com

Business process   A term which encompasses the processes that need to be carried out to achieve the basic aims of a business. For example, in a community pharmacy one of the prime business processes is to dispense prescriptions. To fulfil this function, many separate interlinking tasks must be performed, many of which involve the use of computer systems, e.g. to produce a dispensary label and order drugs. The computer systems must interface with the business tasks in a way that improves, rather than hinders, the efficiency of the process. The system should be designed around the business process and not the other way round.

Byte   A group of eight bits representing the binary numbers 00000000–11111111, which are equivalent to the decimal numbers 0–255. The byte is a fundamental unit of memory measurement (kilobytes and megabytes) and data transfer (kilobytes per second).

C   A programming language used to develop software applications and operating systems. The Unix operating system was developed using C.

Cable modem   Cable modems are used to connect computers to the internet where the household already has cable TV installed. These modems are much faster than the analogue modems used on a standard telephone line, operating at speeds equivalent to those of ADSL modems, which work on specialised telephone lines and are described as broadband links.

Case   A font type which is used to display text on a screen or printer contains two sets of alphabetic characters, lower case and upper case (capitals). Text is often referred to as upper or lower case.

Case sensitive   Many systems are programmed to distinguish between capital alphabetic characters (upper case) and small alphabetic characters (lower case). These systems are said to be case sensitive. Passwords are frequently case sensitive, i.e. 'pharmacy' is not the same as 'PHARMACY', and such errors are common when entering passwords.

Cat 5   Category 5 describes network cabling that consists of four twisted pairs of copper wire terminated by RJ45 connectors. Cat-5 cabling supports frequencies up to 100 MHz and speeds up to 1000 Mbps. It can be used for 1000Base-T, 100Base-T and 10Base-T networking, which is based on the ethernet standard.

CBT   Computer-based training. A method of learning which requires the user to interact with a computer to complete various lessons on a subject. Typically lessons are provided on a CD-ROM, but it is becoming more common to complete them via a network or over the internet. CBT is particularly suited to training in computer applications, as the lessons can be integrated so that the student can practise while actually using the application.

CD   A compact disk is a plastic optical disk which was originally developed to distribute digital music but which has been adapted to store programs, videos and computer data. The first CDs to be produced were CD-ROM (read-only memory) and could only be read, hence the name. However, CDs are now available on which data can be written. There are different types of writable drives and disks. CD-R (compact disk recordable write once) drives allow data to be written to a CD-R disk. Data can only be added to free space on the disk, i.e. when it is full no more data can be written to it, in contrast to CD-RW (compact disk read–write), on which data can be overwritten. The drives use different technologies to write the data, therefore the correct type of CD must be purchased. CD-RW disks are more expensive than CD-R. However, most modern CD-ROM drives can read CDs recorded from both CD-R and CD-RW drives. Drives can now be purchased which combine the functionality of all types into one drive.

CD-R   Compact disk recordable. This is a CD which allows data to be written to free space, i.e. when the disk is full no more data can be written to the device. Has a capacity of 650 Mb.

CD-ROM   Compact disk read-only memory, a compact disk which can only be read by a CD drive. Normally used to distribute music or commercial software. Has a capacity of 650 megabytes (Mb).

CD-RW   Compact disk read–write (or CD ReWritable) allows data to be overwritten and can be used many times. Has a capacity of 650 Mb.

CCTA   The Central Computer and Telecommunications Agency.

Cell   The location in a spreadsheet where a row and a column intersect. The cell stores and displays a piece of data or a formula.

Check digit   A check digit is a digit added to a number either at the end or the beginning, and is used to validate the authenticity of the number. A simple algorithm is applied to the other digits of the number, which yields a check digit. By running the algorithm and comparing the check digit generated against that encoded within the original number, the system can verify that all of the digits have been read correctly. It is used by computer programs and systems to ensure that a number has not been read or input incorrectly. For example, a simple algorithm may be to multiply each digit by 2, add all the products of the multiplication and use the unit value as the check digit. It is possible that an incorrectly input number could produce the same check digit, but the more complex the algorithm the less likelihood of the invalid number producing the same check digit. A PIP code consists of seven digits, the last one being the check digit.

Click   The term used to describe the clicking of a mouse button to select an object or icon on a computer screen, such as a menu option or a button. This use of a mouse to select objects is a fundamental method of interacting with a graphical user interface.

Client–server   Programs are generally designed to work on a single computer, for example a word processor such as Word will use the resources, such as the CPU, memory and file storage, located on the PC on which they are running. In a client–server arrangement, one part of the software will run on the client and the other part on the server. The two programs will communicate with each other by exchanging messages in an agreed protocol. The advantage of this arrangement is that the work of the program is shared between the client and the server computers. In addition, the server can deal with the requests of many clients. The client and the server do not necessarily have to run on the same CPU and operating systems. The fact that there is communication between the two implies that some sort of networking technology must be in place to permit this. A classic example of a client–server relationship is a web browser accessing information from a web site on the internet.

Clinical terminology   Clinical terminology is a structured list of terms for use in clinical practice by healthcare professionals. The terms cover areas such as diseases, operations, treatments, drugs, administrative items and so on. This allows the detailed recording of treatment using consistent terms. For example, in the dm+d, which uses SNOWMED CT terms, the identifier (or code) '323509004' will always mean 'Amoxicillin 250 mg capsules'.

Clipboard   A special area of memory where data is stored temporarily before being pasted to another location. Many applications, such as word processors, use a clipboard for copying and pasting. The text to be copied is highlighted and the copy command issued. The software then copies the text to the clipboard, from where it can be pasted into its final destination. In Windows and MacOS the clipboard can be used to copy data from one application to another. This can include objects such as pictures as well as text.

Cognos   A company which provides a range of products, notably Impromptu and Powerplay, which are used to interrogate and analyse the data stored in databases. The use of these tools requires considerable skill and knowledge. The terms business intelligence and online analytical processing (OLAP) are often used in conjunction with the solutions provided by these products. www.cognos.com

Column   A column is the vertical component of a table in a database or spreadsheet. It represents a single data item in a record, often referred to as a field or attribute. For example, in a table of drugs the Drug Name, Strength and Form are all columns and identify the type of data stored in that field:

Drug Name	Strength	Form
Amoxicillin	250 mg	Capsules
Paracetamol	500 mg	Tablets

The column heading names are used in the database schema.

Command An instruction to a computer or device to perform a specific task. Commands can take different forms, depending on the interface being used. When a command line interface is used the commands will be in the form of special keywords that the operating system understands. The command may also be in the form of a menu option provided by an application. In a graphical interface, a command may be executed by clicking a picture icon or button. In many applications pressing a combination of special keys will issue a command.

Command line interface An interface in which the user interacts with the computer by entering text only. The system displays text only and the user is restricted in the way that they can interact with the computer. Typically there is a series of hierarchical menus or specific commands. This type of interface is generally much more difficult for inexperienced users to use than a graphical user interface, as they have to learn and understand the commands before they can use the system.

Communications port A communications port is an electronic interface which enables a computer to use peripheral devices such as printers and disk drives. The communications ports are also used to communicate with other computers and equipment directly or via telecommunications equipment such as a modem. In a personal computer the term normally refers to the serial, parallel and USB ports built into the motherboard.

Compiler Programs are written in high-level programming languages such as C or BASIC, which are easily read by the trained user. The instructions and commands that make up a program are known as source code. However, these instructions cannot be understood by the processor. Another computer program, called a compiler, translates the source code into machine code, which can be run and understood by the processor. A compiler differs from an interpreter, which analyses each line of source code in succession without looking at the entire program. The advantage of interpreters is that they can execute a program immediately, whereas compilers require some time before an executable program emerges. However, programs produced by compilers run much faster than the same programs executed by an interpreter. C is an example of a compiled programming language. BASIC is an example of an interpreted programming language.

Compound key A column key in a database system is used to identify a unique record and is called a primary key. Normally this is a single column name. However, sometimes a record can only be uniquely identified by using more than one column. In this case the key is said to be a compound key.

Connecting for Health The new branding given to the National Programme for Information Technology (NPfIT).

Context sensitive Any property that changes depending on the context of current state. For example, in Windows, when an application is in a particular state, certain menu options cannot be used. The menu option is usually 'greyed out' if it cannot be used. An example is the Copy and Paste function. The 'Paste' menu option cannot be used unless the 'Copy' menu option has previously been used in the same or a different application.

Control characters One of the ASCII characters between 0 and 31 which are not printed or displayed but are used to control the way computer programs carry out certain actions, hence their name.

Cookies   Some web sites store information in a small text file on a user's computer after they have accessed the web site. This file is called a cookie. It is a file created by an internet site to store information on the user's computer, such as their preferences when visiting that site. Cookies can also store personally identifiable information, i.e. information that can be used to identify or contact a user, such as their name, email address, home or work address, or telephone number. However, a web site only has access to the personally identifiable information provided by the user. For example, a site cannot determine a user's email name unless they provide it. A persistent cookie is one stored as a file on your computer, and it remains there when the web browser is closed. The cookie can be read by the web site that created it when the page is accessed in the future. This is how some web pages are able to identify the user when they access a page in the future.

There are several types of cookie, and a user can choose to allow some, none or all of them to be saved. If a user does not allow cookies at all, it may not be possible to view the content of some web sites or take advantage of customisation features (such as local news and weather, or stock market quotes).

Copy and paste   A function supplied with graphical user interfaces which allows the user to highlight a region in a window containing text and pictures and use the 'Copy' menu option to store it in a temporary area called the clipboard. The user can then use the 'Paste' menu option to paste the contents of the clipboard into a different region of the same or a different window.

CPU   The central processing unit is the most important part of a modern computer and is responsible for executing programs and moving data from volatile memory to permanent memory such as disk drives. There are CPUs in many devices other than computers, such as mobile phones, but these are usually much smaller. Examples of CPUs made for PCs are the Pentium processor manufactured by Intel, and the Athlon made by AMD.

CSV   A comma-separated values (CSV) file is a text file, frequently used to import and export data between databases and spreadsheets. Each record occupies a new line and is separated by a newline character (which is not displayed), and each field within the record is separated by a comma. As text may contain commas, the text is either surrounded by quotes or another *delimiter* is used, but this is still referred to as a CSV file.

> 'Amoxicillin', '250 mg', 'Capsules','500'
> 'Paracetamol', '500 mg','Tablets','1000'
> 'Chorpheniramine', 4 mg/10 ml, 'Syrup','150ML'

or, using the ' | ' (vertical bar) character:

> 'Amoxicillin | 250 mg', 'Capsules | 500'
> 'Paracetamol | 500 mg | Tablets | 1000'
> 'Chorpheniramine', 4 mg/10 ml, 'Syrup | 150 ml'

Data type   Each column in a database table is given a data type, which determines the type of data that can be stored there. For example, a column defined as data type 'Integer' can only store whole numbers, e.g. 37, whereas a column defined as data type 'Character' can store text. This is necessary as a computer needs to know what is a legitimate computation for different columns. For example, it is legitimate to add two numbers stored in a column defined as integer data types, but not to add two values stored in a 'character' data type as text. Storing the text characters '3' and '7' in character data type is allowed. However, in this form they could not be added to another number. The character data type would first have to be converted into an integer before the computation could proceed. There are many different data types, which can be classified as follows:

- Numerics, e.g. integer, real
- Strings, e.g. character
- Booleans, e.g. true, false or null
- Datetimes, e.g. date, time.

Data type is also used in programming when defining the type of data a variable is going to hold, e.g. a string or a number. A variable is given a name which identifies the memory location where the data is stored.

Database administrator (DBA)   A person responsible for maintaining the functionality, integrity and security of a database. In very large database systems the role is full-time and highly responsible. In some organisations there will be teams of DBAs, highlighting the complexity of some database systems.

Database management system (DBMS)   A database management system is a set of programs used to define, administer and manage data stored in a database. These programs have the facility to add, delete and update records in the database and to interface with application programs. Most modern applications will use a separate DBMS to store the data. There are many companies which supply DBMS systems, the most notable and common of which are Access, SQL Server, Oracle, Ingres, Informix, IBM BD2 and Sybase.

D connector   A type of electrical connector used on small computers to connect serial, parallel and monitor cables. When viewed end-on the shape is an outline of a D, which prevents it being plugged in the wrong way. There are different sizes with a varying number of pins (or holes).

Decision support system   Decision support system is the term used to describe a computer application that analyses knowledge bases. An example of a decision support system used in medical applications is Prodigy, used by GPs as an aid to diagnosis. The GP inputs the symptoms and the system guides the doctor to the correct diagnosis based on the data stored in its knowledge base.

Default   A term used in computing to describe the value a parameter takes unless changed by the user. For example, in Windows, if there is more than one printer available to the computer the system will select one of them as a default. All documents will be sent to the default printer unless the user intervenes and selects a different one. Default settings can usually be changed by the user.

Delimiter   A non-alphanumeric character used to mark the end of records and fields in a text file. This allows computer programs to determine the beginning and end of records, so that they can be imported into databases such as Access and Oracle. When a comma is used as the delimiter the files are often called comma-separated values (CSV) files. In the early days of computing a comma was used, but because text sometimes contains commas other characters were used that did not appear in the text, but the file is still referred to as CSV and given the extension .csv.

Demographic   The information stored about people, e.g. address, ethnic origin, gender, age, etc.

Developer A developer is any person or organisation who writes computer software to fulfil a particular function.

Device driver A program used by the operating system to access a hardware device connected to the computer. Also known as a driver, it is written by the manufacturer of the hardware to standards defined by the developer of the operating system. A different driver is required for each different type of operating system. A driver written for Windows will not work with MacOS, and vice versa.

DHCP Dynamic host configuration protocol was developed by Microsoft to dynamically allocate IP addresses to computers attached to a local area network. The addresses are all in the same address range, so that the computers can communicate with each other. The IP addresses are allocated by a computer or device which acts as a DHCP server, i.e. it is responsible for allocating the IP addresses. The IP addresses are only allocated for a certain period, known as a lease. When the lease expires a new IP address is allocated.

DIMM Dual inline memory module. This is a small printed circuit board which has memory chips soldered on each side. The modules are supplied in different sizes, e.g. 128 or 256 Mb, and plug into the main PC motherboard. This memory is used by the CPU as temporary storage and is referred to as volatile memory, i.e. the contents are lost when the power is switched off. In general, the more memory of this type that a PC has, and the faster the speed of the CPU, the better the performance.

Directory A structure which enables files to be grouped together in an organised manner. A directory can then be split into subdirectories ad infinitum, and is analogous to an office filing cabinet, which is split into drawers into which are then placed folders.

dm+d Dictionary of Medicines and Devices. This is a dictionary containing unique identifiers and associated textual descriptions for medicines and medical devices. The identifiers and terms used are based on SNOWMED CT. clinical terminology. It has been developed for use throughout the NHS (in hospitals, primary care and the community) as a means of uniquely identifying the specific medicines or devices used in the diagnosis or treatment of patients. It is intended that dm+d will become the NHS standard for medicines and device identification, enabling interoperability between diverse clinical systems, thus ensuring the safe and reliable exchange of information on medicines and devices and allowing effective decision support through linkage of data. www.dmd.nhs.uk

DNS Domain Name Service (System) is an internet system of computers that communicate with each other and maintain lists of domain names and their associated IP addresses. When a domain name such as www.google.co.uk is first entered into a web browser the computer requests the IP address from a computer that holds a list of domain names. If this computer does not have the name in its list it will make requests to other servers until it finds one that does. It will then update its own list and pass the IP address back to the original computer. This mechanism avoids the need for a centrally maintained list of domain names and IP addresses, which would be impractical given the number of domain names in existence and the volume of requests.

Domain Domain names are the unique names used to conveniently contact an internet site or email address, e.g. www.google.com. Without domain names, contacting an internet site would require the user to enter the unique internet protocol (IP) address of that site. An IP address consists of four numbers (e.g. 165.123.125.24) and is difficult for humans to remember. Domain names have to be registered with a central registry before they can be used, for which there is a small registration fee. In the UK the registry for .uk names is maintained by Nominet.uk (www.nominet.org.uk). Many ISPs will register a domain name on behalf of a customer when setting up a web server.

A system called the Domain Name Service (DNS) translates the easy to remember domain names into the less friendly IP addresses required to connect to a site.

DOS shell A DOS shell is a window in which applications developed for the MS DOS operating system can run on a Microsoft Windows system. These applications are character based, which is obvious when the display is compared to any normal Windows application. There can be several DOS shells open at the same time. This means that any program written for MS DOS can be loaded and run on Windows.

Dot matrix printer Dot matrix printers are impact printers that form characters by firing a series of pins against an inked ribbon in front of the paper. The number of pins used in the print head varies from 9 to 24. The more pins, the better the resolution or quality of the print. However, dot matrix printers cannot achieve the quality achieved by inkjet and laser printers. They are cheap to buy and run, but tend to be noisy and need an acoustic hood if used for large-volume printing.

Double-click The action of clicking the left button twice in rapid succession on a mouse used with a graphical user interface such as Windows. Double-clicking is used to select an option or command. When users first start to try double-clicking they usually end up performing two single clicks, which have totally different actions. This is because the time between the two clicks is not short enough. However, with practice the skill is quickly learned.

Download Refers to the copying of a file from one computer to another. It is normally used with reference to files located on the World Wide Web that are to be transferred to another computer via a web browser.

Drag and drop A term used to describe the interaction with computer programs that have a graphical user interface. The user is able to select an object and 'drag' it to another location, where it is 'dropped' and carries out some action. For example, when copying files from one folder to another the user usually uses menu options. However, using 'drag and drop' the user can copy a file by selecting that file, holding down the mouse button and at the same time dragging the file to another folder. Other common uses of drag and drop are to rearrange columns in a table or spreadsheet.

Driver A program designed to communicate between the operating system and other programs or hardware. The program needs intimate knowledge of the device or program so that it can translate requests by the operating system into commands that can be actioned. All hardware used with a PC requires a driver so that it can communicate with the operating system.

DVD Digital versatile disks are visually the same size as CDs but have a much greater storage capacity of at least 4.7 Gb. They were originally used to store movies (and were called digital video disks), but like CDs have been adapted for use with computers. There are three writeable versions of DVD: DVD-R, which can only be written to once, and DVD+RW/–RW, DVD-RAM, which can be written to many times. Combination drives are available which can write and read both CDs and DVDs. Owing to their enormous capacities, DVDs are useful for backing up large volumes of data. As with CDs it is important to obtain the correct type of DVD for the DVD writer installed in the computer.

DVD-R DVD recordable – DVDs that can be written in the same way as DVD-RAM, but with the limitation that they can only be written on to free space, i.e. parts of the disk that have not already had data written to them.

DVD-RAM DVD-RAM provides the capabilities of a rewriteable CD-RW which allow users to run programs from the disks, copy files to them and rewrite or delete them. The capacity of the disks is between 4.7 and 9.4 Gb, thus making them very useful for backing up a hard disk drive and large volumes of data.

DVD+RW/DVD–RW DVD rewritable. DVDs that can be written to many times in the same way as DVD-RAM. There are two formats, + and –, which are incompatible.

EAN code European Article Numbering. European version of UPC, the UPC encoding symbology for bar-coding products such as drugs. EAN-8 encodes eight numeric digits consisting of two country code digits, five data digits and one check digit. EAN-13 is the European version of UPC-A. EAN bar-code numbers are assigned to specific products and manufacturers by an organisation called ICOF located in Brussels, Belgium.

ECDL Electronic Computer Driving Licence, an online learning scheme that aims to equip staff with the right IT skills for their job. In the UK the British Computer Society manages and promotes the ECDL on behalf of the European Computer Driving Licence Foundation (www.ecdl.co.uk). The National Health Service has adopted the ECDL user skills as a standard for its staff. For more information visit the NHS Information Authority web site at www.ecdl.nhs.uk.

Eighty–twenty rule A rule of thumb for computer projects which states that the last 20% of the functionality takes 80% of the time to develop. Also known as Pareto's law.

email Electronic mail is text messages which are transferred electronically between computers. The messages are sent from one computer to another utilising network technology, and therefore a prerequisite is that the computer must have access to a network. The basis of an electronic mailing system is fairly simple and works in much the same way as the postal service. In the conventional postal system each household has a unique address. The person writes a letter and puts it in an envelope with the name and address of the addressee on the front. This is then placed in a postbox, collected by the postal service and taken to the sorting office. The address is scanned and the best route for the letter determined. It may go to several sorting offices before it is delivered to the final one that can deliver the letter to the actual address.

In an email system, a mailserver is the equivalent of the sorting office. The mailserver is located on a particular computer with a unique domain name and has a mailbox for each user registered with that mailbox. The format of an email address is always the same and has two main parts separated by the symbol @. The first part of the address is the name of the mailbox. The second is the domain name of the mailserver on which the mailbox is located. Emails are sent and received in the mailbox, and are created and read using an email application. Files can be attached to the text messages, thus allowing all sorts of different documents, such as pictures, to be easily and quickly transferred between users.

Embedded Where a hardware or software system relies heavily on another sub-system in order to operate. For example, a dispensing system will generally rely on a database management system (DBMS) to store all the data, such as drugs and dosages. The DBMS is embedded within the dispensing system software, which cannot function without its presence.

Entity An entity is something that has an independent existence. It is used in data-base terminology to describe the columns (fields) in a table. For example, in a table of drugs the full description of a drug could be stored in one column called Drug Description, e.g. Atenolol 100 mg Tablets. However, Drug Description can be broken down into three entities (or columns): Drug Name, Strength and Drug Form, as these can exist independently. Entities have relationships with other entities. These are usually shown as an entity–relationship model, which is usually a graphical representation of the relationships.

Error correction A process used to detect and repair errors in digital data streams, i.e. when digital data is moved from one location to another, such as from a CD-ROM to the computer memory, or from one computer to another over a network. Data detection methods all work by adding extra bits to the actual data. These are known as redundant bits, as they are not part of the data. A single redundant bit added to a data stream will allow detection of the error but not its correction. Adding more redundant bits allows the system receiving the data to actually correct the errors.

Ethernet Ethernet is one of the most popular network protocols and is the industry standard for smaller networks. All ethernet devices are connected to the same piece of wire and must contend (compete) with each other to send signals over it. Conflicts are resolved by forcing the devices to resend the data at different intervals until the conflicts are resolved. Ethernet has a transmission rate of 10 Mbps and is a very cheap method of connecting devices via a network. A second-generation ethernet standard allows transmission speeds of up to 100 Mbps.

ETP Electronic transmission of prescriptions, the process of sending prescriptions electronically from a doctor to a pharmacy. In the UK the term is used to describe a system that enables prescriptions to be sent electronically directly from the GP's system to a community pharmacy. They can then be sent electronically to the Prescription Pricing Authority (PPA), which pays pharmacists for the drugs dispensed. An ETP pilot was set up to prove the concept and closed at the end of June 2003, having served its intended purpose. It has been demonstrated that ETP is technically viable and could provide a range of benefits, including improved patient choice and safety. The implementation of ETP is one of the core aspects of the National Programme for NHS IT (NpfIT). The government has stated that by 2005 electronic prescriptions will be routine in the community.

Many people use the terms ETP and electronic prescribing to mean the same thing, when in fact one is related to the prescribing of drugs and the other relates to the supply of the drugs once the prescription has been created. http://www.ppa.org.uk/news/etp.htm; http://www.schin.ncl.ac.uk/ETP/

Excel Excel is a spreadsheet which is part of the Microsoft Office suite of applications. Office's popularity stems from the fact that several of the applications in the suite, one of which is Excel, are the best in their market.

FAQ Frequently asked questions. The FAQ or list of frequently asked questions (and answers) has become a feature of the internet and is used to answer commonly asked questions about a specific topic. The FAQ list for a topic is maintained by someone with an interest in the subject who publishes the questions and answers on a web site. Entering 'FAQ' and a topic of interest into a search engine will list the URLs of sites that maintain FAQs. For example enter 'ETP' and 'FAQ' into a search engine such as Google and the URL for commonly asked questions on electronic transmission of prescriptions will be displayed. Note: There will be many subjects that do not have any FAQs.

Field A field is a single unit of data stored as part of a database record. Each record is made up of one or more fields, which correspond to the columns in a table. Fields are often referred to as attributes, and in spreadsheets are called cells.

File A file is a structure used to store data on storage devices such as hard disks and CDs. Software applications (which are themselves stored as files) create files that store related data in separate files. Each file is given a file name which uniquely identifies it. On a PC there will be thousands of files grouped together into directories or folders, in much the same way that a filing cabinet is used to organise related documents. A file name cannot be used more than once in the same directory or folder.

File name The file name is an identifier by which a computer file is distinguished from others. The operating system will limit the characters that can be used in file names, and in many older systems there are limits to the length of the name.

File name extension An identifier which is added to the end of a file name and which is typically three characters long. The extension is separated from the filename by a dot. Extensions are used by many operating systems to indicate the type of file, and in many cases the application that created it. Although there are no strict rules relating to the naming of extensions there are many common ones, such as '.txt', which is used to indicate a text file, e.g. Readme.txt. Many operating systems such as Windows associate the extension with an application, so that when the file is double-clicked with a mouse pointer in Windows Explorer, for example, it will automatically open the correct application provided it has been loaded on the PC.

File specification A document which details how data in a file is organised so that it can be interpreted by some computer application or program. There are many different ways of storing data, and the file specification should explain how the data is stored and organised.

File system All computers need to store data in files, which is the responsibility of the operating system. The mechanism by which these files are maintained is known as the file system. The majority of operating systems allow files with a common purpose or function to be stored together in a directory or folders, which is analogous to common paper files being stored in the same folder of a filing cabinet.

Firewall A special type of device or piece of software that monitors all data traffic passing between a LAN and the outside world, such as the internet, to prevent security breaches. The firewall allows LAN traffic to pass to the outside world, so that users can browse the World Wide Web or send emails, but prevents malicious users from outside from accessing the computers on the LAN.

Firewire   Also known as IEEE 1394. This is a high-speed serial bus which can support transfer rates of 400 Mbps. It also supports plug and play and hot swapping. This has led to its being used to connect peripheral devices that transfer large amounts of data, such as camcorders and external CD-ROM drives used with notebook computers. It is very similar in its use to USB, but can transfer data nearly 400 times faster than USB 1.1. However, with the introduction of USB 2.0, which supports 480 Mbps, there is not much difference between USB and Firewire. The connection required will depend on the type of connection supplied on the peripheral device.

Flat file database   A relatively simple database where the data is stored in a single file. In contrast, relational databases use multiple tables to store information, and each table can have a different data structure.

Floppy disk   Floppy disks (removable memory storage devices) consist of a disk of flexible plastic coated with a magnetic oxide and are protected by a rigid plastic outer cover (originally these were flexible, hence the name floppy). Because the disk is removable it is used to store copies of data, e.g. documents and programs, stored as files, which need to be transferred to another computer. The capacity of a floppy disk is relatively small by today's standards – 1.44 Mb. It has a small switch which can prevent the data on the disk from being overwritten.

Focus   In a Windows-based user interface the window that appears in front of all the windows and receives user input, such as typing text or mouse clicks, is said to 'have the focus'. One of the controls within the window, such as a button or field, will have the focus. The focus can be changed by moving the mouse pointer over a control or window and clicking the mouse button.

Folder   Also known as a directory. A folder is a 'container' for a number of related files stored on a memory device such as a hard or floppy disk. It is analogous to the cardboard folders used in physical filing cabinets.

Font   Font refers to the characteristics of a set of characters that can be displayed on screen or printed. These characteristics include the typeface (i.e. its shape), size, pitch (i.e. its width) and spacing. There are many hundreds of fonts that can be used with computer systems, each with its own name, such as Courier or Times Roman. In graphical systems such as Windows they are a fundamental part of the operating system.

The height of a font is measured in points, a point being 1/72 inch. The width is measured by the pitch, which refers to how many characters will fit into an inch. Fonts can be fixed pitch (e.g. Courier), in which each character has the same width, or proportional (e.g. Times Roman), where the width varies depending on the shape of the character. Proportional fonts do not have a pitch because the number of characters per inch will vary depending on the characters printed. In word processors the font size refers to the point size, i.e. its height, not the pitch size. The choice of font has programming implications where there is limited space available, such as on dispensary labels.

Foreign key   A foreign key is a field (column) in a relational table that is used to match the primary key column of another table. The foreign key can be used to cross-reference or to join tables.

Free software Free software is software that is free from copyright and licensing restrictions and the source code is available to the end user. The Unix operating system is the most significant example of this type of software and was part of the GNU project, which is sponsored by the Free Software Foundation.

Freeware Software that is offered at no cost to the user. Freeware may be subject to copyright, which may prevent modification or resale. Compare this with shareware, which is normally offered for trial with a request for payment should it be used regularly.

FTP File transfer protocol. A protocol which is used to transfer files between networked computers. FTP is commonly used on the internet to download and upload files.

Function keys These are special keys labelled with 'F' and a number, e.g. F5. They are usually found on PC keyboards and have different actions depending on the application that is running.

Gateway A gateway is a piece of equipment which connects two separate networks. The equipment may be specifically designed for the job and is then known as a router, or it may be a computer that runs networking software.

Gigabyte A unit of computer memory equal to 1024 Mb (1 048 576 bytes). (In decimal notation 'kilo' means 1000.) As computers use the binary system (base of 2), kilo refers to 2^{10}, i.e. 1024. 1 Gb is therefore equivalent to 1 073 741 824 bytes (1024 × 1 048 576). Gigabyte is often shortened to Gig and is the unit of measure used to define the size of a hard disk drive.

GIGO Garbage in, garbage out, a phrase used to describe the fact that if the quality of the data which is collected is poor then the reports based on this data will also be poor.

GNU GNU is a recursive acronym for 'GNU's Not Unix'. The GNU Project was started in 1984 to develop a Unix-style operating system which is 'free software' and now encompasses all variants, such as Linux. The principal sponsor of the GNU project is the Free Software Foundation, whose aim is preserve, protect and promote the freedom to use, study, copy, modify and redistribute computer software. This is analogous to free speech, rather than free from payment. www.gnu.org

Google One of the most popular search engines available on the internet.

GPRS General packet radio system, a method of connecting portable devices such as mobile phones and PDAs to the internet using radio technology for GSM networks. Data transmission rates are between 20 and 30 kbps, with a theoretical maximum of 172.2 kbps. Devices that connect using GPRS must have special hardware and software installed and a telephone provider who supports GPRS. The service is said to be 'always on' and is charged on the basis of the volume of data transmitted rather than time connected.

Graphical user interface A graphical user interface (GUI) is the most common form of interface between the user and the computer, in which text and images are displayed on the computer screen. Images represent real-life objects such as buttons, which can be pressed by using a pointing device such as a mouse. The most common GUI is the Windows operating system. The mouse has two buttons which can be clicked or double-clicked to select a particular action. These types of interface use far more computer resources than do character-based interfaces.

Greyed-out   A visual method of indicating in a Windows user interface that a menu item is unavailable for use by changing the text from black to grey.

GSM   Global System for Mobile Communications is an international communications network that joins together various mobile networks in different countries. It is used to connect mobile phones and PDAs to the GSM network. The fastest data transfer rate that can be achieved with GSM is 9600 bps.

GUI   Graphical user interface.

Hard disk   Hard disks consist of multiple platters (metal disks) of rotating (10 000 revolutions per minute) magnetic material. A moveable recording head moves forwards and backwards along the radius of each platter, writing or reading data. The capacity of modern PC drives is measured in gigabytes, and capacities range from 20 to 200 Gb. The hard disk drive is one of the most fundamental components of the modern PC, storing the operating system, programs and data.

    Hard disk drives work to very high tolerances. The read/write head floats above the platter and must not come into contact with the surface. If it does, it will result in a 'head crash', leading to loss of all data and rendering the drive useless. As a result hard disk drives are manufactured as sealed units, which prevents particles entering the unit.

Help   Most modern applications have the facility to provide explanatory or reference information about the application. Help buttons are provided at various points in the user interface, and at its simplest the help consists of short paragraphs of text with an index and table of contents, which describe how to use the application. The help text associated with many applications is 'context sensitive'. When a help button is pressed the help text displayed is relevant to the action or operation the user is currently engaged in.

    The help text should supplement the user documentation, although in many applications it is the only way a user can learn how to use the software.

Hexadecimal   Hexadecimal is a method of numbering that uses 16 as its base instead of 10, as in decimal. In decimal the notation is positional, for example the number 318217:

3	1	8	2	1 7

hundred thousands; ten thousands; thousands; hundreds; tens; units.

    Hexadecimal uses the characters 0, 1, 2, 3, 4, 5, 6, 7, 8, 9, A, B, C, D, E, F which can be stored in four binary digits (bits):

1	1	1	1

eight four two units.

Which is equivalent to decimal 15. Thus the decimal number 12 is represented in hexadecimal by the characters '0C', 25 by '16', and 29 by '1D'. Therefore in hexadecimal the number FF can be stored in one byte:

F	F

sixteen units

Home page   The home page is the first page of a web site to which visitors are initially directed and from which other pages can be accessed. The URL, e.g. www.google.com, will direct the visitor to the site's home page.

Hotspot   Hotspot is the name given to a wireless access point in a public location such as a railway station, airport, hotel, etc. Some train operators also provide hotspots on trains. Any Wi-Fi-enabled device such as a laptop or PDA can connect to these hotspots and have high-speed access to the internet and hence access to any facilities normally provided by a telephone link. There are many providers, with different payment plans, as with mobile phones. Most locations will indicate that they are a hotspot provider. However, hotspots can also be found by entering the name of a town into hotspot finder web pages, such as http://intel.jiwire.com/ or http://www.wi-fihotspotlist.com/. The UK has the most hotspots of any country outside the USA.

Hot swapping   Refers to the ability to disconnect peripheral devices, such as CD-ROM drives, from a computer without having to switch it off.

HTML   HTML is short for Hypertext Markup Language, which is a protocol used to describe how the pages and documents published on the World Wide Web should be displayed. This is a series of instructions written in plain ASCII text which is interpreted by the web browser and creates the page as designed by its author. The instructions are contained as separate elements in the plain text called tags, which control how the browser creates and displays the page. The instructions for each element are usually contained between two tags, one that switches on the effect and another that switches it off. A tag shows as two angled brackets < > which contain the instructions. An end tag has the same instructions as a start tag but is preceded by a slash (/). For example:

Information Technology <i>for Pharmacists</i>

will italicise the 'for Pharmacists', giving the result: Information Technology *for Pharmacists*.

HTTP   Hypertext transfer protocol, the protocol by which a web browser requests information from a web server. Every web page has a unique address, known as the URL, which is used to locate the page and transfer the details to the web browser. The protocol and the URL appear within the address bar of the browser.

Hyperlink   A hyperlink allows text or an object (such as a logo) in a document to be linked to some other text or object in the same or another document. This is achieved by storing the URL of the target text in the hyperlink object. Clicking a hyperlink with a mouse will result in the linked page being displayed. Hyperlinks are the reason that the World Wide Web has been so successful, because it is easy to navigate from page to page using them.

Icon   An icon is a small graphical picture displayed on a screen to represent a particular type of object such as a file or folder. When the mouse pointer is passed over the icon and clicked, the object is activated. For example, clicking on a file with a 'Word' icon next to it will start the 'Word' word processing application and display the contents of the file. There are hundred of icons used in graphical user interfaces, which leads to the problem of knowing what each icon represents.

Index   In order to retrieve information from databases in a timely manner, a computer will use an index to access key pieces of information. If an index did not exist the computer would have to look at each piece of data to see if it matched the search criteria. All modern databases use indexes to enable quick access to data.

Infrared   Infrared devices use infra wavelengths to enable infrared-enabled devices to be connected together. These devices must have line of sight between the transmitter and the receiver. They are generally used to connect portable devices to PCs wirelessly, but can be used to connect networks in different buildings where there is line of sight.

Inkjet printer Inkjet is the most commonly used type of printer for printing good-quality documents and will print in both black and colour. It does not take continuous stationery and so cannot be used to print dispensary labels in an efficient manner. Inkjet printers have separate cartridges for black and the coloured inks. The colour cartridge is composed of three primary colours, which combine to give any other colour. The image is formed on the paper by spraying the ink (which is liquid) at the paper. The ink needs to dry, otherwise it will smudge, which makes inkjet slower than laser printers. Although inkjet printers are relatively cheap, the cost of the ink cartridge can make them expensive to run.

Inner join When two tables in a relational database are joined on a common field it results in a new table where the rows in both tables have the same value. Any rows that do not have corresponding rows based on the source tables are discarded and not displayed. This is the normal or default type of join used in relational databases.

Integer An integer refers to a whole number, e.g. 1, 2, 3, as opposed to real numbers, which are fractional, e.g. 0.35, 7.1. Computers store real numbers and integers in different ways.

Integration An integrated application system is one in which the different software components are seamlessly combined together. This usually manifests itself in the user interface, in which all aspects of the system are the same. The same supplier usually supplies all parts of the system. For example, in an integrated hospital system all modules, e.g. patient administration, pharmacy, X-ray etc., will be supplied by the same supplier. If separate suppliers supply each module the consequence will be a different look and feel for each module. Where common details are needed, such as patient name, date of birth, etc., an interface that transfers the data from one system to another would be needed. Generally, integrated systems are much easier to upgrade and maintain than interfaced systems.

Intel Intel Corporation is the largest manufacturer of microprocessor chips in the world. The company manufactures the Pentium family of processors, which are used in the majority of personal computers.

Interfacing An interface is a boundary where two different systems can be joined. It is used in IT to describe the mechanism by which two different software systems can exchange common data, and can apply to both operating systems and application systems. For example, many hospital pharmacy systems are interfaced to the Patient Administration system so that patient details do not need to be rekeyed. There is a significant amount of design, programming, testing and maintenance involved in creating such an interface.

Internet This is an international computer network made up of smaller networks, all of which have the potential to communicate with each other. One of the key features of the internet is its robustness, which means it is usable even if part of the network fails or is destroyed. The public nature and robustness are two of the main reasons why the internet has flourished. The ability of computers to communicate with each other is not very useful *per se* – it is only when they can provide services or facilities that they become useful. Some of the main services provided by servers on the internet are:

- Electronic mail (email)
- Telnet or remote login. This allows one computer to log on to another computer and use its resources.
- File transfer protocol (FTP). Allows the transfer of files from one computer to another.
- Web pages, often referred to as the World Wide Web.

The growth of the internet is due mainly to the World Wide Web, a set of standards and protocols that allow documents (which may contain images, sound and video) to be read by anyone who has access to a web browser. Computers are connected to the internet via routers (also known as gateways). Large organisations connect directly to these routers, but smaller ones and individuals connect via telephone lines or optical cables to organisations known as internet service providers (ISPs).

Internet Explorer Internet Explorer (developed by Microsoft) and Netscape Navigator (developed by Netscape Communications) are the two most popular web browsers used on PCs. Internet Explorer is only available for the Windows and Macintosh operating systems, whereas Netscape is also available for Unix.

Internet information services (IIS) IIS are software used on web servers that support web site creation, configuration and management, along with other internet functions. Their main function is to service requests for web pages stored on the server.

Interpreter Programs are written in a programming language such as C or BASIC. The instructions and commands that make up a program are known as source code. However, these instructions cannot be understood by the processor. Another computer program called an interpreter translates the source code into machine code, which can be run by the processor. When the program is run the interpreter looks at each line of source code. Interpreters can execute a program immediately, unlike compilers, which require some time before an executable program emerges. However, programs produced by compilers run much faster than the same programs executed by an interpreter. C is an example of a compiled programming language. BASIC is an example of an interpreted programming language.

Intranet A network within an organisation which uses internet technologies and protocols but is private (rather than public, i.e. the internet) and available only to the employees of the organisation.

IrDA The Infrared Device Association is the organisation that defines the standard for infrared communication links between devices. The term IrDA is used to indicate that a device can communicate with other infrared-enabled devices. In general, IrDA has been superseded by WiFi and Bluetooth.

ISDN Integrated services digital network. ISDN lines carry digital signals over the telephone network. They are designed for home use and typically have a speed of 64 kbps. Two channels can be combined together to provide a speed of 128 kbps, but two charges are incurred, one for each line. For home use these lines are being superseded by ADSL and cable modems, which have a higher transfer rate and are much more cost effective.

ISO International Organisation for Standardisation. www.iso.ch

ISP Internet service provider, an organisation that provides access points to the internet via dial-up telephone lines, ADSL lines or cable modems. They will also offer other facilities, such as email and web hosting services. The cost of providing these services will vary depending on the type of access being used, and there are various pricing options, ranging from those based on the time connected via the telephone line to unlimited access for a fixed monthly fee.

Join A join is a method of combining the data from two tables in a relational database based on a common field (attribute). The join results in a new (virtual) table that combines the contents of all rows having the same value in the common field. The mechanism for creating a join is performed by writing a query that interrogates the data. There are different types of join, giving different resulting tables. The main types are an *inner join* and an *outer join*.

Keyboard The keyboard is the basic input device for the majority of computers. The standard layout of letters, numbers and punctuation is known as QWERTY, because the first six keys on the top row of letters form the word QWERTY. The QWERTY keyboard was designed in the 1800s for mechanical typewriters and was actually designed to slow typists down to avoid jamming the keys. Although this is no longer a consideration, attempts to redesign the keyboard have failed. Although many people start to use the keyboard using one finger on each hand, it is well worth the effort to learn to touch type, as speed and accuracy of input can be improved dramatically. Computer keyboards have additional keys, such as function keys, which can be used under program control to execute common tasks.

Keyboard shortcut A combination of keystrokes that can be used instead of a menu option or button, which avoids the need to keep switching between keyboard and mouse. For example, in Windows, to close an active window press the ALT and F4 keys together.

Kilobyte (kb) A unit of computer memory equal to 1024 bytes. Kilo in decimal notion refers to 1000. As computers use the binary system (base of 2), kilo refers to 2^{10}, i.e. 1024.

Knowledge base A knowledge base is a collection of facts about a subject which is usually structured and accessed by application software to provide information to the user. In most pharmacy systems there is a knowledge base of drugs and their characteristics, such as indications, doses and interactions. A combination of the software and data from the knowledge base is used to produce warnings and advice regarding drug interactions.

LAN Local area network. A system for connecting computers together so that they may exchange and share data, and also share other resources such as printers. The computers are usually all in the same building or in close proximity to each other. LANs can be connected to the internet or other local area networks via telephone lines. When local area networks are connected to each other by telephone lines they are referred to as wide area networks. The most popular technology for LANs is ethernet, and the most popular protocols are TCP/IP and IPX.

Laptop computer Another name for a notebook computer.

Laser printer Laser printers are high-speed printers that work in much the same way as photocopiers. The image is formed by transferring powder electrostatically from the toner cartridge on to the paper. The powder is then heated to set it. This is the reason why laser printers have to 'warm up' before they can start to print. They are the most expensive printers to buy, but produce high-quality print and can produce the pages much quicker than inkjet and dot matrix printers.

LED   Light-emitting diode: small lights that use very little power and which are used in computer equipment as power indicators. They are also used in modems and network equipment to indicate that data is being transferred. Usually red or green in colour.

Legacy system   This is a term used to describe systems developed in the past that are now using obsolete hardware and software which are no longer supported and maintained by suppliers. Replacing legacy systems can be a significant problem if the organisation has become dependent on the functionality and the data stored within the system. Migration to new systems can be complex and costly.

Link code   An alphanumeric ordering code used to identify all products supplied by the AAH wholesaler. The pharmacy computer will use these codes to send electronic orders to AAH (a pharmaceutical wholesaler) via a dial-up modem.

Login   A login screen (sometimes known as logon) is used to control access to a computer system or application. The user enters a username and password to access an account which has previously been set up by the system adminis-trator. Sometimes these usernames and passwords are stored so that the user does not have to enter them each time they access the system. For example, when a user connects to the internet via a telephone line they will connect to an ISP, who will allocate them a username and password. The system can be set up so that when the user requires access the system automatically dials the number and enters the stored username and password. This situation should not be encouraged, as it means an unauthorised user can access an account if for any reason the computer is left unattended. Although the username may be stored, the password should always be entered manually and the software configured to always prompt for it.

Look and feel   'Look and feel' is the term used to describe how a software appli-cation is displayed on a monitor and the way the user interacts with the application. The 'look and feel' of applications developed for the Windows operating system is an example, in that the menus and navigation are the same irrespective of the purpose and function of the application.

MAC address   Media access control address is a hardware address that uniquely identifies a device (or node) on a network. (A node is a device that connects many parts of a network and determines the route data traffic should take. It is analogous to the intersections (crossroads, roundabouts) of a road network.) Any device on a network must have a unique address in the same way that a postal address must be unique, otherwise data could be sent to the wrong recipient. The MAC address is allocated when the network card is manu-factured. Any device that connects to a network must have a network card installed or be connected to a network adapter.

Machine code   A program stored in the form of binary numbers representing instructions that can be executed directly by the computer's processor. The programmer writes instructions in a programming language, which must be translated by a compiler before it can be executed by the processor. For example, in Windows, files ending in the extension '.exe' are executable machine code files.

Macintosh A range of computers manufactured by the Apple Corporation which run the MacOS operating system. The Macintosh range were the first commercially available computers to use a graphical user interface, but never attracted enough software development to displace Windows-based IBM-compatible PCs. However, the Macintosh range is used extensively in the publishing and graphic design industries.

MacOS Proprietary operating system developed by the Apple Corporation for use on Macintosh computers manufactured by the company. It was the first commercially available operating system to use a graphical user interface. Although it was the first, and in the opinion of many the best, it has not been as popular as the Windows operating system but does have dominance in certain sectors, such as the publishing and printing industry, because of the superior desktop publishing applications that are available.

Mailbox A mailbox is an account on a mail server via which email messages can be sent and received. Each mailbox (equivalent to an email address) must have a unique address and consists of two parts, which are always separated by an '@' symbol, e.g. pharmpress@rpsgb.org. The second part is the domain name of the computer on which the mailserver is located. Domains are unique, that is, no two computers in the world can have the same domain name. This is the equivalent of a sorting office in the traditional postal service. The first part is the name of each mailbox which has been set up on the mail server. When someone wants to send an email message to another user they use the email address of the recipient to compose the message. They then connect to the mailbox on the server and place the message in the mailbox. The mailserver then sends the email to the computer identified by the domain part of the email address. The mailserver on the receiving computer places the message in the appropriate mailbox. The email stays in the mailbox until the recipient accesses it using their email application.

Maximise In a Windows interface a window can be sized so that it does not cover the whole of the display. Clicking the maximise button (usually located in the title bar) will expand the window to fill the whole of the screen. (See also Minimise and Resize.)

Megabyte (Mb) A unit of computer memory equal to 1024 kilobytes (kb). Kilo in decimal notion refers to 1000. As computers use the binary system (base of 2), kilo refers to 2^{10}, i.e. 1024. 1 Mb is therefore equivalent to 1 048 576 bytes (1024 × 1024). Megabyte is often shortened to meg.

Menu A menu is used in software applications to present a list of options on the screen. Each option performs a specific task. The type of interface will determine how the user selects a menu option. In character-based systems the user will enter the number placed next to each option or use the arrow keys on the keyboard to move up and down the menu. In a graphical interface the option is selected using a mouse pointer.

Metadata Metadata is literally 'data about data', i.e. information about data itself, for example the origin, size, formatting or other characteristics of a data item. The structure of a table in a database is an example of metadata.

Microfilter A microfilter/splitter is a small device used to connect ADSL modems to the telephone socket. It is sometimes called a 'line splitter' if the same telephone line is to be used for both internet connection and voice calls.

Microsoft Office Microsoft Office is a suite of software applications supplied by Microsoft. It consists of a word processor (Word), spreadsheet (Excel), database management system (Access), presentation software (Powerpoint) and email system (Outlook). Its popularity stems from the fact that some of its components, such as Word and Excel, are the best in their market and that all the programs have a similar user interface. A version of Microsoft Office is also produced for the Apple Macintosh. www.office.microsoft.com

Minimise In a Windows interface the window can be collapsed into a small icon, usually in the task bar, by clicking a 'Minimise' button, typically located in the title bar. This temporarily removes the window from the display but the application is still loaded into the computer's memory. The window can be restored to its original state by clicking the icon in the task bar. (See also Maximise and Resize.)

MMC Multimediacards weigh less than 2 g, are about the size of a postage stamp, and are the world's smallest ($24 \times 32 \times 1.4$ mm) removable solid-state memory solutions for mobile applications, such as MP3 music players, portable video games, laptop computers, personal digital assistants (PDAs), mobile telephones and digital cameras. These convenient, reliable, rugged and lightweight standardised data carriers can store up to 128 Mb and capacity is increasing every year. The eBNF and AHFS Drug Information are supplied on these cards for use in PDA devices such as the Palm and Pocket PC.

Modem Short for modulator–demodulator. A modem converts digital signals into analogue ones so that the telephone system can be used to allow computers to communicate with each other. There must be a modem at each end of the link so that the analogue signal can be converted back into digital for use by the computer. The modems communicate using two channels, one to send data (upstream) and one to receive data (downstream). The maximum speed at which data can be transmitted with a conventional analogue modem is 56 kbps. Faster speeds can be achieved using ADSL adapters, but this requires the use of additional equipment in the telephone exchange.

Monitor Monitors, also known as video display units (VDUs), come in many different sizes. The size is determined by measuring the distance diagonally from top left to bottom right of the screen. The quality of the picture is determined by the number of pixels on the screen and the software used to display the picture, but generally the more pixels per square inch the better the picture (resolution). For personal use, a minimum size of 14 inches is required; 17 inch and 19 inch are better if the computer is used frequently throughout the day. The bigger the screen, the more expensive the monitor.

Monitors are based on two major technologies, cathode ray tube (CRT) and liquid crystal display (LCD). Monitors based on CRT are much bulkier than those based on LCD, so if space is a consideration choose an LCD screen. However, LCD screens are roughly three times the price of CRT.

Motherboard The main printed circuit board of a PC which contains all the principal components required to enable the computer to function. The majority of the components, such as the CPU and memory, are supplied as modules and can be plugged into the motherboard. This enables a PC to be upgraded by replacing the relevant module with a higher specification one.

Mouse A mouse is a device used with a graphical user interface (GUI) to move and control a pointer on the display screen to select menus and icons. Its name is derived from its shape. The mouse usually has two buttons, which the user can 'click' to select a screen object, such as a menu. More recently a wheel has been added for use when scrolling through long documents. There are a number of different types of mouse. The original mechanical devices use switches to detect the direction of a ball on the underside of the mouse and move the pointer accordingly. A mouse mat is used to ensure that the surface on which the mouse is moved is smooth, as the sensors have a tendency to clog with dust and dirt. This can affect the movement of the pointer, but is easily remedied by removing the ball and cleaning the sensors. The other main types are optical devices that use a laser to detect the mouse's movement and have the advantage that they can be used on any flat surface and are not affected by dirt. They are, however, more expensive than mechanical mice.

Mice can be connected to the computer in a number of different ways. Originally they used either a PS/2 mouse connector on the back of the computer or a serial port. More recently, mice have been introduced which connect using a USB port. Cordless mice are also available which use the infrared port or radio waves, which are very useful for notebooks, where the cord can sometimes get in the way because of the limited space available. Cordless mice are more expensive than corded.

MS-DOS The operating system written by Microsoft for the original IBM PC and compatibles. MS-DOS was a single-user single-tasking operating system which allowed users to run single text-based programs.

Multitasking Multitasking is the ability of an operating system to execute more than one program at the same time. Windows is an example of a multitasking operating system, which allows the user to run different programs in separate windows at the same time. In a non-multiuser system such as MS-DOS only one program can be run at any one time and the user has to exit one program before starting another.

Multiuser Multiuser refers to the concurrent use of a single computer by more than one user, usually via remote terminals or PCs. Unix is an example of a multiuser operating system which can communicate with many different users at the same time. Multiuser is also applied to applications that allow multiple users to view and update a single shared file or record in a database. Multiuser systems will normally have some sort of control so that only authorised users can access the system. This is usually in the form of a username and password, which also enable audit trails to be created as long as this is designed into the system.

N3 N3 is the working name of a project to procure services for the delivery of IP data communications for the NHS in England and aims to provide continuity of NHSnet after the end of 2003, plus meeting future NHS increased bandwidth requirements. N3 is the latest version of the NHSnet, which is a secure wide area network developed exclusively for the NHS. It is also used to provide email services to the 1.2 million NHS staff in England. It is the largest virtual private network in Europe, providing a range of communication and information services similar to that of the internet; a dedicated NHS network with guaranteed service and availability; and a secure and controlled environment for healthcare information. www.nhsia.nhs.uk/nhsnet/pages/n3

NAT Network address translation. NAT is performed by software that allows a LAN to use one set of IP address for internal traffic and another set for external traffic to another network, such as the internet. It adds security by acting like a firewall, by hiding internal LAN addresses from the outside world.

Netscape Navigator Netscape Navigator (along with Internet Explorer) is one of the two most popular web browsers used on PCs. There are many different versions which run all the major operating systems, i.e. Windows, Macintosh and Unix.

New line character An ASCII character used to tell the computer to go to a new line. This character is not shown on any display or printed output and hence is known as a *control character*. In Windows the new line character is decimal 10, or hexadecimal 0A.

NHSNet See N3.

Node A network node is a device that connects many parts of a network and determines the route data traffic should take. It is analogous to the intersections (crossroads, roundabouts) of a road network.

Notebook computer Notebook or laptop computers are self-contained and generally have a footprint smaller than that of an A4 sheet of paper. All the components described for a PC – base unit, keyboard and screen – are built into one unit. The main advantage of these computers is that they are portable and can be used in any location, as they use internal batteries. To make them portable the components need to be small and light, which means that the cost of a laptop is generally more than that of a desktop/tower PC of the same specification.

Notebooks are generally 'clam-shelled' in design, i.e. they are hinged down one side. When opened up, the keyboard is built into the main body of the notebook and the monitor is built into the top part. In addition to the keyboard there is a touchpad and two buttons, which give the functionality of a mouse.

Notepad A basic text editor which is delivered as part of the Windows operating system. Text files contain only text characters. They do not contain any formatting, for example bold or underline characters, as would be the case with a file produced by a word processor. Text files can usually by identified by a three-letter file extension of .txt.

NPfIT The National Programme for Information focuses on changes to IT in the NHS that will improve the patient experience. The first phase of the programme has four particular goals: electronic appointment booking, an electronic care records service, electronic transmission of prescriptions, and a fast, reliable underlying IT infrastructure. http://www.dh.gov.uk/PolicyAndGuidance/InformationPolicy/NationalIT Programme/fs/en. The programme has been rebranded as Connecting for Health.

ODBC Open database connectivity is a standard mechanism by which applications programmed to run on the Microsoft Windows operating systems can gain access to data in many different types of database. The functionality is implemented by loading a program (driver) which is specific to the type of database being accessed. Thus an ODBC driver for an Access database will be able to access the tables in any Oracle database. There are also ODBC drivers that allow data from spreadsheet and text files to be accessed.

ODBC driver An ODBC driver is a piece of software which acts as a translator between an application and a database. The application requests the data through the translator software, which then communicates with the database. The results are then passed back to the application via the ODBC driver.

Offline A term used to describe when a device is unavailable, frequently applied to printers. The printer usually has a switch that puts it into an offline state and stops the printing. A printer will automatically be put into an offline state if certain conditions arise, e.g. it runs out of paper.

Online analytical processing (OLAP) A term used to describe the use of computers to extract trends from the data stored in databases. OLAP is usually applied to systems with many millions of records, such as those held by supermarkets, and consequently require significant processing power. The term is often used by salesmen to describe the analysis of any database, irrespective of the number of transactions.

Operating system The operating system is the software that controls all input and output from the computer. When the computer is switched on, the operating system is normally loaded from the hard disk and is responsible for making sure that all the different components of the computer, e.g. memory, disk drives, keyboards and other peripherals such as printers, can communicate with each other in an orderly manner. The operating system also loads the application software that fulfils specific functions, e.g. word processors and spreadsheets. Application software must be written for specific operating systems, such as Windows or Unix.

Optical character recognition (OCR) This is a process whereby text in a printed document can be converted into text which can then be edited and manipulated by a computer program such as a word processor. The process involves scanning the printed text using a scanner. This creates a bit-mapped image, which can be stored as a computer file. This file is then analysed by a sophisticated piece of software that can recognise the text characters in the bit-mapped image. There are many different fonts used in printed text, and the better software can recognise most of them. However, handwritten text is difficult to analyse because of its variability. OCR software for PCs is normally bundled as part of a scanner package.

Oracle Oracle is a software company whose major product is a powerful relational database management system that offers a large feature set, also referred to as Oracle. Along with Microsoft SQL Server, Oracle is widely regarded as one of the two most popular full-featured database systems on the market.

Outer join When two tables are joined the first one is called the left table and the second the right table. The left table may have rows that do not have matching rows in the right table based on the common field in both tables. If an *inner join* is performed on these tables the unmatched rows are excluded from the resultant table. Outer joins do not exclude the unmatched row and are of three types: left outer join, right outer join and full outer join.

A left outer join will result in a table which shows *all* rows in the left table, as well as any rows from the right table where the common field has the same values. Any rows which are in the left table but not in the right table will have null (blank) values in the fields from the right table.

A right outer join will result in a table that shows *all* rows in the right table as well as any rows from the left table where the common fields have the same values. Any rows which are in the right table but not in the left table will have null (blank) values in the fields from the left table.

A full outer join will display all rows from both left and right tables. Any rows that do not have corresponding rows in the other table will have null values in the fields from the other table.

Outlook   The personal organiser function of the Microsoft Office suite of applications, which includes email, diary, contact details, notes and to-do list. Not to be confused with Outlook Express, which is available with Internet Explorer. Outlook Express contains only the email and contacts functions of Outlook.

Outlook Express   An email application delivered with the Windows operating system. This is a cut-down version of the Microsoft application Outlook, which also has facilities to manage a diary, contacts, notes and to-do list.

Palm   Palm is the term used to refer the operating system and the original PDAs invented by the Palm company, founded in 1992, which led to the emergence of handheld computing. In 1999 PDAs based on the Palm operating system accounted for approximately 70% of the market. The company was acquired by US Robotics and subsequently by 3Com, who in addition to producing PDAs licensed the operating system to other companies such as Handspring and Sony. One of the reasons for the Palm's success was that Palm Inc. encouraged developers to produce application software for the operating system. There are hundreds of thousands of such developers, who generally distribute the software via the World Wide Web. The devices are small enough to fit in a shirt pocket and allow input using handwriting recognition software called Graffiti rather than a keyboard. They are intended to be used in conjunction with a desktop or notebook PC, and applications are synchronised using a process called hotsynching. This process ensures that changes made on either the PC or the PDA, for example to appointments, are reflected on both machines. PDAs based on the Palm and Pocket PC operating systems account for the major share of the PDA market. Many of the devices produced have expansion capabilities and can accept SD, MMC and Compact Flash cards, which can store applications and data.

Parallel port   Parallel ports are 25-pin D connectors and use eight wires to send data, rather than just one as in a serial port. This means that the parallel port can transfer data much more quickly. Cables also tend to be thicker than serial cables, as more wires are required. Normally used to connect printers to the computer, but as with serial ports this is being superseded by USB.

Pareto's law   Pareto's law, in its generalised form, states that 80% of the objectives – or more generally the effects – are achieved using 20% of the means – or more generally the causes or the agents. Subsequently, it takes 80% of the means to achieve the remaining 20% of the objectives. Pareto's law can be applied to many computer projects, in that 20% of the effort results in 80% of the functionality. The last 20% of the functionality takes 80% of the effort.

PAS   Patient administration system. In hospitals the PAS keeps the demographic information of all the patients who attend. The system is used by the Medical

Records department to identify patients by assigning them a unique number, which is used to track case notes. Additional modules allow outpatient appointments and inpatient attendances to be managed using the same information. These modules are usually provided by the same supplier and so are integrated with the PAS. Other hospital systems, for example the pharmacy system, may be provided by another supplier but wish to use the demographic data collected by the PAS system. In these situations an interface between the two systems will need to be specified, designed and tested. This avoids duplicate entering of data, and any changes only need to be made in one place. There is a significant difference between systems that are integrated and those that are interfaced.

Password A password is a series of characters known only to the end user which allows them to access a computer, software application or system. It is common for many systems to insist that the passord is of a minimum length and contains at least one number. Passwords are generally case sensitive, i.e. a password written in lower case letters is not the same as that written in upper case letters, and this leads to common mistakes when entering passwords.

Patch A patch is a program that fixes an error (bug) in an existing piece of software.

Path Path is the term used to describe the full route an operating system must take to locate a file when the filing system is based on a hierarchical system of folders (directories) and subfolders. For example, in Windows there might be a file called 'Sample.doc' stored on a floppy disk. If this is stored in a subfolder called 'Mydocs', located in the folder 'Alldocs', then the full path name to locate the file would be: A:\alldoc\mydocs\sample.doc. The A: represents the drive on which the file is stored.

PC A personal computer based on a specification designed by IBM in 1981. Many companies started to make copies of these machines, which were known as IBM-compatible PCs. These copies or clones led to the explosion seen in the uptake and use of PCs since the 1980s onwards. The term PC became synonymous with an IBM-compatible PC.

PCMCIA Personal Computer Memory Card International Association is the body responsible for developing PCMCIA cards (PC cards), which are roughly the same size as a credit card. PCMCIA cards are small expansion cards used in notebook computers. They are used to add devices such as modems and network cards to the notebook, which normally have two slots. These slots can take two type 1 or 2 PCMCIA cards or one double-thickness type 3 card. More and more devices are being incorporated into PCMCIA cards, such as hard disk drives and GPRS modems.

PDA Portable digital assistant. PDAs or Palmtop computers are designed, as the term suggests, to be used in the palm of the hand. Typically these computers are no more than 3 inches by 5 inches by 0.5 inches thick, weigh a few ounces, and will fit easily into a shirt pocket. Instead of using a keyboard (although versions exist that have very small keyboards) to input text a stylus is used in conjunction with handwriting recognition software. One of the fundamental design aspects of a PDA is that it is meant to be used in conjunction with a personal computer. They are designed to work with a desktop or notebook PC in that they are supplied with cables and software that enable them to be connected to the PC.

There are literally thousands of applications written specifically for the Palm device, many of them medical applications and databases. Recently the BNF was released as an electronic version on an SD card. The capacity of these devices has increased enormously over the last few years, enabling many reference texts to be stored on the same device. Adobe Reader is available for both platforms and allows any PDF document to be read on a PDA. The screens have benefited from colour and the resolution has improved significantly, thus making text much easier to read. It is anticipated that these devices will replace many paper-based reference books in the near future. http://www.palmone.com/us/products/compare/palmos-vs-pocketpc.html

PDF   Portable document format, a file format developed by Adobe Systems that is used to capture almost any kind of document with the formatting of the original. Viewing a PDF file requires Acrobat Reader, which is built into most browsers and can be downloaded from Adobe free of charge. (www.adobe.com).

Pen drive   Small memory device used to store and transfer files from one computer to another. The pen drive plugs into a USB port and is allocated a drive letter by the operating system. They are available in different storage capacities, typically 64 Mb to 2 Gb. Some devices can also be used as MP3 players, which allow music to be stored and played on the same device.

Pentium   A CPU manufactured by the Intel Corporation which is used in many personal computers.

Permission   Permission is a term used to signify the privilege granted to a user by the operating system or software application. The permission is managed by part of the software and may restrict access to certain files, folders or menu options, depending on the type of application. For example, later versions of Windows have different types of permission for each file. These are usually Read, Write and Execute. If a user has only been given Read permission they can read the file but not update it.

Personal information manager   Personal information management (PIM) applications are used to replace the functionality of a diary or Filofax. They store the information used by a person in everyday life, such as contacts, telephone numbers, appointments, to-do lists and notes in an electronic form. Frequently this functionality is integrated with other communication software, such as email. One of the most popular PIMs is Microsoft Outlook, which is one of the components of the Microsoft Office suite. It consists of five major elements: email, appointment diary, contacts list, to-do list and note taker. Obviously these elements can only be used while the user is sitting at the PC, and this limits their usefulness. This is why many PDAs, which are about the size of a diary, can be purchased with the elements of a PIM pre-installed and can be used in conjunction with a PC PIM such as Outlook. Changes made on the PC and independently on the PDA are updated by synchronisation software when the PDA is connected to the PC. Any changes made on the PC are automatically updated on the PDA and vice versa by the synchronisation software.

Peripheral   A device such as a mouse, keyboard, disk drive, printer or modem which is connected to the main computer via a dedicated port or communications port. For example, the keyboard has its own specific connector on the motherboard, whereas a printer is connected through a communications port, such as one of the serial, parallel or USB ports. Each peripheral needs a special piece of software known as a device driver, which allows the computer's operating system to control the device.

PIP code The Pharmaceutical Interface Products code was introduced in 1982 by Benn Publications, the publishers of *Chemist and Druggist*, in conjunction with the National Pharmaceutical Association. It is a unique number which has been allocated to and identifies each product distributed through the pharmacy supply chain. It is extensively used by retail pharmacies to order goods electronically from wholesalers and suppliers.

Pitch Pitch refers to the number of characters that can be printed in 1 inch. The term is only relevant to fixed-pitch fonts, where the width of each character is the same irrespective of its shape. The space taken up by characters in proportional fonts varies according to their shape, and so pitch is not relevant. Proportional fonts are measured by reference to the point size, i.e. the height.

Pixel A pixel is a single point in a graphic image. Graphics monitors display pictures by dividing the display into thousands (or millions) of pixels, arranged in rows and columns. The pixels are so close together that they appear connected. The number of bits used to represent each pixel determines how many colours can be displayed. In 8-bit colour mode, eight bits are used for each pixel, making it possible to display 256 different colours.

The quality (or resolution) of the video display is related to the number of pixels. The more pixels the better the quality (or resolution) of the display.

Plug and play Plug and play refers to an operating system's ability to automatically detect the peripherals connected to the computer and configure them for use without the need to go through a setup procedure. Only the later versions of the Windows operating system, e.g. '98 onwards, support plug and play.

Plug-in A plug-in is an application program added to a web browser which enables it to interact with special file types, such as video, sound, PDF document, Word document, etc. For example, when a hyperlink to a PDF document is clicked, the file is retrieved from the web server and if the Adobe Reader plug-in is installed within the computer's browser, the document is automatically displayed in the browser window with the Adobe Reader menus added.

Pocket PC Pocket PC is the term given to the hardware and operating system based on a cut-down version of Windows. The devices are classed as PDAs, compete in the same market as Palm-based PDAs, and are developed by many well-known hardware suppliers such as Toshiba, Hewlett Packard and Compaq. They are meant to be used in conjunction with a desktop or notebook PC. The Pocket PC also contains cut-down versions of Microsoft's Office application suite, e.g. Word, Excel, and has communications software such as a web browser and email. Some of the devices have expansion capabilities and can accept SD/MMC and Compact Flash cards. Comparisons between the Palm and the Pocket PC can be found at www.palmone.com/us/products/compare/palmos-vs-pocketpc.html

Point size Point size is used to measure the height of characters: 1 point is 1/72 inch. A proportional font is measured by reference to its point size, e.g. Times Roman 12 point.

POISE POISE (Procurement Of Information Solutions Effectively) is the official NHS IT procurement methodology. http://www.pasa.doh.gov.uk/computing/guidance/guidance.stm

Pop-ups Pop-ups refer to additional windows which are displayed when surfing the internet using a web browser. Pop-ups are displayed for different reasons, but the most common one is to display advertisements. They can become very annoying, and can be blocked by configuring the web browser to prevent their display (or only allow them from certain sites). Adware and spyware can create similar effects to pop-ups but work by installing programs on the PC.

Powerpoint Powerpoint is one of the components of the Microsoft Office suite of applications. It is used to create presentations incorporating text, graphics, sound and video, and operates like a slide-show on the computer. Each time the mouse is clicked the next slide is displayed. Very sophisticated presentations can be created which are typically viewed on a large screen by connecting a projector to the computer.

PPP Point-to-point security. A protocol used to communicate between two computers.

Primary key The primary key of a relational table uniquely identifies each record in that table, or it can be generated by the DBMS. The RPSGB Registration Number is an example of a reference that can be used as a primary key because it is unique to each pharmacist and never reused. It is possible for a primary key to consist of more than one column if the design of a table is such that there is no one column that uniquely identifies a row.

PRINCE PRINCE is a project management methodology which has been widely adopted by both the public and private sectors. It was established in 1989 by CCTA. The method was originally based on PROMPT, a project management method created by Simpact Systems Ltd in 1975. PROMPT was adopted by CCTA in 1979 as the standard to be used for all government information system projects. When PRINCE was launched in 1989, it effectively superseded PROMPT for government projects and is now widely used in both the public and the private sector. PRINCE remains in the public domain and copyright is retained by the Crown. PRINCE is a registered trademark of CCTA. www.prince2.com

Print Screen key A special key on PCs running Windows which, when pressed, copies the contents of the screen to the clipboard, which can then be manipulated by drawing and painting programs. Pressing the 'ALT' and 'Print Screen' keys together copies the top (or active) window to the clipboard.

Programming language A programming language is used to write computer programs which are more readable by humans than machine code instructions, which are ultimately used by the computer. There are hundreds of different languages, which all have their advantages and disadvantages. All ultimately produce software that performs some specific function. One of the easier languages to learn is BASIC, which is provided in many different dialects.

Prosper code A numeric ordering code used to identify all products supplied by the wholesaler Unichem. The pharmacy computer will use these codes to send electronic orders to Unichem via a dial-up modem.

Protocol A set of rules by which two communicating devices such as computers or modems can exchange data with each other. This is analogous to a conversation between two people. They must first decide on the language to be used for the conversation. They then need to agree on the rules when one can speak and the other listens, and vice versa. There are hundreds of different protocols currently in use, which are the foundations on which networks and communications devices operate. Two of the most important are TCP/IP and http, which are used extensively for communication via the internet.

PS2 port A type of communications port developed by IBM for connecting a mouse or keyboard to a PC. It accepts a mini plug containing just six pins. Often called the mouse port.

Query A request made against a computer database to retrieve and display selected records. Queries are typically written in a query language such as SQL, which allows selected records to be displayed. Many database management systems, such as Access, allow the user to create queries using wizards or dragging columns. This means that the user does not need to learn the syntax of the SQL language.

Radio button A visual component used in many Windows programs which acts as a switch that may be turned on or off by clicking with the mouse. If there is a group of radio buttons only one option can be active at any one time, which is analogous to the selection of a station on a car radio, hence the name.

RAM Random access memory. Memory that can be read and written to by a computing device. Most RAM is volatile, i.e. it loses its contents when the power is switched off. Programs and data must be stored on a non-volatile device such as a hard disk or CD-ROM and loaded into RAM by the processor when required. RAM is many hundreds of times faster to access than any non-volatile memory. Modern computers are designed to manipulate the data and programs loaded into RAM. Generally, the more RAM that is available to the computer the better the performance, as it reduces the number of times the computer has to access slow memory on a non-volatile device.

RDBMS A relational database management system is software used to create, administer, maintain and query relational databases. Almost all relational databases support the use of SQL to query and update information. The most common examples of commercially available relational databases are Microsoft Access, Oracle, Ingres, SQL Server, IBM DB2 and Informix.

Referential integrity Referential integrity is a term applied to relational databases. Relational databases have many tables, which are composed of various columns. Relationships may exist between columns in one table and columns in another. Take, for example, two tables in a pharmacy system, one of which holds details of drugs (DRUGS) and one holding details of drug orders (ORDERS). Each table will have a column which is common to both, known as a foreign key. This column will usually contain a short code that uniquely identifies the drug and which may be called DRUG_CODE; this will be included in each table. Rather than store the whole of the drug description in the ORDERS table every time a drug is ordered, the drug code from the DRUGS table will be stored in the DRUG_CODE column of the ORDERS table. When the system wishes to display details of the orders in the ORDERS table, it will use the drug code stored in the DRUG_CODE column to look up the details in the DRUG table and obtain the description of the appropriate drug. However, if the drug code and associated details had been deleted from the DRUGS table the ORDERS table would have no reference into the DRUGS table and hence would not be able to display the drug description.

The integrity of the system would therefore be compromised. The system designers should ensure that this can never happen, thereby ensuring the referential integrity of the system.

Release A version of a software product is made available as a release. Each major version of a product may contain different functionality, which is why each is given a different number to differentiate between them.

Resize In Windows the size of a window can be adjusted to suit the user's requirements. This is usually done by grabbing the border of the window with the mouse pointer and dragging it to the required position.

Resolution Resolution refers to the clarity and sharpness of an image. The term is applied to monitors and printers that use a large number of pixels to form an image. The more pixels in a given space, the better the resolution.

Restore window button A button included in a Windows user interface which restores the window to its original size if it has been maximised or minimised.

Rich text format A method of encoding text formatting and document structure using the ASCII character set. By convention, rich text files (RTF) have an .rtf file name extension. Documents are sometimes saved as RTF files so that they can be read by word processors other than the one that created the document. However, not all the formatting will be saved, so that the document may not look exactly like the original.

RJ45 A standard covering the connectors used to connect computers to each other and to other network equipment. There are two types, female and male. The male connector plugs into a female connector. Many organisations have a network infrastructure of Cat 5 cables terminating in female RJ45 connectors throughout their buildings. The cables terminate at convenient socket points, such as a floor or wall, in the same way as electrical sockets. Attaching a computer to the network is simply a matter of connecting the female RJ45 connector on the network card in the computer to the network infrastructure via a conveniently located female RJ45 wall socket, using a cable with male RJ45 connectors on both ends.

ROM Read-only memory, a type of memory whose contents, once written, cannot be erased. This type of memory is usually used to store programs. All PCs have a small amount of ROM, which contains a program (bootstrap) to start the computer and load the operating system for use. PDAs do not have disk drives and the whole operating system is held in ROM, which is why programs are immediately available when the device is switched on.

Router A piece of equipment which connects one or more networks together. Its job is to forward data packets from one network to another so that they arrive at the correct destination. A router is analogous to a post office sorting centre. The sorting office looks at the address on a letter and determines the most appropriate route for it to take. The router does the same thing with the data packets by looking at the address associated with each and determining the most appropriate route, based on routing tables stored in its memory. Routers are extremely sophisticated devices, even though for home or small business use they can be purchased for less than £100. They are often combined with other devices such as ADSL modems to provide multiple functionality in one device.

RS-232 port Another name used for a serial port on a computer which is used to connect to peripheral devices such as modems.

Scalable   A term used to describe applications that do not suffer degradation in performance due to increasing the number of users or increasing the volume of data stored. For example, a database management system such as Access may have perfectly acceptable performance for relatively small volumes of data and single users, but as the volumes of data and the number of users increase the performance decreases. This is mainly due to the underlying design and implementation of the system.

Scanner   A scanner is a device that can read text or illustrations printed on paper and translate the information into a form the computer can use using software known as optical character recognition software. This converts the text on a page into characters that can be manipulated by a word processor. The scanner works by digitising an image, that is, by dividing it into a grid of very small boxes called pixels. Each pixel is represented by one bit, which stores either a 0 or a 1, depending on whether the pixel is black or white. The resulting matrix of bits, called a bit map, can then be stored in a file and displayed on screen. Colour uses the same principle, but more bits are required to define the colour (up to 24). Scanners have a footprint which is slightly bigger than an A4 sheet of paper, as this is the most common size of document scanned. They have a glass screen on which the document is placed and are very similar to a photocopier. Most scanners can be purchased for less than £100. The most important aspects when considering the alternatives are the resolution and the speed at which the document can be scanned. The higher the resolution quoted in dots per inch (dpi), the better the quality of the scanned image.

Combined scanners and printers are available which can be used as photocopiers. Some also combine fax facilities.

Schema   A database schema describes the relationships between the data elements (columns) and tables in a database. A schema can be simply described as the 'layout' of a database that outlines the way data is organised into tables and the relationship between those tables.

Scrollbar   A component of the Windows interface which is displayed when the graphical object being displayed is bigger than the window. Word processors usually incorporate a vertical scrollbar on the left or right of the window so that the user can use the mouse to scroll through the document. Some applications, e.g. spreadsheets, also contain horizontal scrollbars.

SD card   Secure digital card. A solid-state memory card format used for compact devices such as PDAs, digital cameras, etc. They are about the size of a postage stamp and use a type of memory which is non-volatile, i.e. the contents are not lost when power is removed. The capacities range from 32 to 512 Mb and are frequently used to hold information databases, e.g. eBNF, which can be displayed on a PDA such as a Palm.

Search and replace   A function incorporated into many applications, particularly word processors, which allows the user to enter a word or part of a word into a dialogue box. The software then searches for that word in the document and allows the user to replace it with any other text. There is usually an option to automatically replace all occurrences of a word with another.

Search engine   A service offered on the World Wide Web which allows users to locate web pages based on their content by entering topics of interest into the search engine. There are numerous organisations offering search engines, the most popular of which are Google, Yahoo, Hotbot, Lycos and Alta Vista. All work by maintaining a massive index of words and their associated web sites. The user enters a topic into a search engine and it will return a list of all sites containing that topic. The number of matches is usually listed and can be in the millions. The number of matches can be reduced by entering additional words to make the search more specific, or by using the advanced search options.

Serial port A serial port (also known as an RS232) is either a 9- or a 25-pin D connector. On modern computers they are normally nine pins. Even though there are nine pins, only three wires are necessary to communicate with other peripherals, and data is sent as a stream of bits, which are then combined into bytes by the software on each device. These ports tend to be relatively slow and are being superseded by USB (see below), which are much faster and automatically configured on later versions of the Windows operating system. The serial port can be identified by a symbol of 0s and 1s (10101).

Server A computer that provides services and resources to other computers and electronic devices. Usually these are powerful computers that can deal with many concurrent requests for data or services. However, any computer can act as a server provided it has the necessary network connections and software.

Service-level agreement An agreement between a customer and a service provider that outlines the details of the service. In relation to IT the detail is usually related to the response times in which different types of software fault will be resolved and fixed.

Service pack The name given to a collection of patches used to fix errors (bugs) in software. It may also contain additional functionality. Microsoft identify the service packs for the Windows operating system with the prefix SP, e.g. SP-1. SP-2.

Shareware Shareware is software that is distributed free on a trial basis on the understanding that the user may need or want to pay for it later. Some software developers offer a shareware version of their program with a built-in expiry date (e.g. after 30 days the user can no longer access the program). Other shareware is offered with certain capabilities disabled as an enticement to buy the complete version.

SIM card Subscriber identity module card. This is a small printed circuitboard which is inserted into a device such as a mobile phone which accessed a network. The card stores data that identifies the caller to the network, and is used for both voice and data transmissions. Laptops equipped with a PCMCIA data card, which connects to the internet via the mobile phone network, use a SIM card.

SNOMED CT Systematised Nomenclature of Medicine Clinical Terms. A joint collaborative clinical terminology developed by the NHS and the College of American Pathologists with the aim of it becoming a de facto world standard. Snomed CT identifiers are used in the Dictionary of Medicines and Devices (dm+d). http://www.nhsia.nhs.uk/snomed/pages/default.asp

SOHO Small office/home office is a term used to describe the environment in which many users operate. As the role of pharmacists changes many are likely to work in a SOHO environment. Many companies aim their products at SOHO users.

Soundcard A type of expansion board on IBM PC-compatible computers that allows the playback and recording of sound. This allows the computer to play sound from WAV, MP3 or MIDI files, or music from a CD–ROM.

Source code Source code is the instructions written by computer programmers which is generally in a form that humans can read and understand, and is known as a programming language. Before it can be used by the computer this code must be converted into a binary format known as machine code. There are two main methods by which this is achieved. (1) The source code is compiled by running it through a program called a compiler, which produces an executable file. The time taken to compile source code can vary considerably and may take a few seconds to many minutes, depending on the size of the source code and the power of the computer compiling the code. The file produced can be executed by the operating system and results in the application being started. In Windows any file with the extension '.exe' is an executable file. For example, double-clicking the file 'excel.exe' will start the Microsoft Excel application. (2) The source code is processed through an interpreter when the program is run. This is much slower than using a compiler, and hence the programs tend to run a lot slower than compiled programs.

Spam Spam is the name given to unsolicited emails, usually sent by someone trying to advertise a product. Spam is also referred to as 'junk mail', and the volume of spam is becoming so significant that governments are considering legislation to outlaw the practice. There are many software tools available to filter out the spam from legitimate emails, with varying degrees of success.

Spooling A process in which a program sends output to a temporary disk file rather than directly to a device, so that it can be processed as a background task, thus allowing the first program to proceed as if the operation was complete. Usually related to printers, where the time taken to print a document can be quite lengthy if it is large. The operating system manages printing of the documents in the background while the user continues to use the application.

Spreadsheet A software application used primarily to manipulate numbers, which are arranged as a table of rows and columns. The intersection of a row and a column is known as a cell. The numbers can be manipulated by applying mathematical formulae to the cells, which can also contain text. This makes them useful for displaying and manipulating data that may have been taken from a database, e.g. drug usage information. The most commonly used spreadsheet is Microsoft Excel, which has many functions that allow data to be sorted, summarised and manipulated based on the user's requirements. Spreadsheets have so many facilities that formal training is essential so that the user can use them in the most appropriate way.

Spreadsheets are often used in their most basic form, e.g. to view lists of information such as a drug price list.

Spyware Spyware is software that is very similar to adware and is installed on the computer in the same way, without the knowledge of the user. Rather than pop-up windows, this type of software works entirely in the background to gather information about the user's activities when using the PC. The information thus gathered is relayed to advertisers or other interested parties. As with adware, spyware can be detected by special programs that identify and remove them.

SQL   Structured Query Language is a standardised query language for extracting and updating data stored in a relational database. It was originally developed by IBM in the 1970s, but is now subject to ISO and ANSI standards. Even though it is subject to standards it may be implemented (i.e. used) against relational databases in slightly different ways. For example, the syntax of a statement used to query an Oracle database may be slightly different from that used to query an SQL Server database. However, the majority of database products support SQL, which means that the principles can be applied to any other database. An example of a simple SQL statement would be:

> **SELECT** *DRUG_NAME, DRUG_STRENGTH, DRUG_FORM*
> **FROM** DRUGS **WHERE** DRUG_NAME = 'A%'

which would display a list of all drugs beginning with the character 'A' and their associated strength and form, which are stored in a table called DRUGS. The words in bold are SQL commands and the words in italics are columns in the table called DRUGS. www.sql.org

SQL Server   SQL Server is a database management system developed and supplied by Microsoft for use in large computing systems, as opposed to its other DBMS product, Access, which is part of the Microsoft Office suite of applications. SQL Server is much more scalable than Access and is generally used where many users access the same database. However, because it has more functionality and features than Access it is usually only used by computer professionals.

Standards   Standards are extremely important in all aspects of IT, as the ability to connect different hardware components and exchange data is one of its fundamental aspects. For this to occur hardware manufacturers and software developers must adhere to agreed standards. Such standards are developed by different organisations and can take many years to be agreed. Two of the most important organisations in relation to IT standards are ANSII and the ISO. There are also 'unofficial' standards. For example, although the format of a Word document is proprietary to the Microsoft Corporation, as Word is used by so many people worldwide other software developers will include functionality within their applications to read Word documents.

Symbology   Symbology is a way of encoding characters as a series of bars and spaces that can be read by scanners and barcode readers, in a similar way as Morse code encodes characters by dots and dashes. There are many different types of symbology, each with different rules for encoding the characters in wide and narrow bars and spaces.

Syntax   The rules governing how instructions should be written so that they can be interpreted by a computer program.

System administrator   An individual responsible for maintaining a multiuser computer system. One of the main duties of the administrator is to set up accounts that allow a user to log on and access the system by entering a username and password. In a multiuser system such as a hospital pharmacy system one of the pharmacy staff will fulfil this role. However, there will also be an administrator – more likely a team of administrators – who administer access to the hospital local area network.

System software Software written to manage all the basic functions of a computer and allow all the basic hardware components to communicate and interact. System software provides the basic building blocks on which application software can be built, and an analogy can be drawn between this and the basic amenities such as water, electricity and drainage required when building a house. Operating systems are very complex examples of system software.

Table The main structure that holds data in a relational database. It consists of horizontal rows representing records and vertical columns representing the fields (or attributes). The structure and content of each table are determined by the database designer.

Tag Tags are used in documents that use mark-up languages to control the display or printing of a document. The most common use of tags is in Hypertext Mark-up Language (HTML), used to display web pages which are actually plain text pages. The web browser software interprets the instructions signified by the tags to create the display in the browser window. The instructions are contained as separate elements in the plain text called tags, which control how the browser creates and displays the page. The instructions for each element are usually contained between two tags, one that switches the effect on and another that switches it off. A tag shows as two angled brackets < > that contain the instructions. An end tag has the same instructions as a start tag but is preceded by a slash (/). For example:

Information Technology <i>for Pharmacists</i>

will italicise the 'for Pharmacists' giving Information Technology *for Pharmacists*. The start tag also contain attributes that control other aspects of the instruction. For example, <Font SIZE=8 FACE='ARIAL'> will set the font of the text to Arial with a point size of 8. End tags do not contain attributes. There are numerous different instructions for displaying all sorts of objects, such as tables and buttons. The instructions that make up a page in a web browser can be viewed by clicking on a menu option in the browser window (usually View, Source). Although this may look unintelligible, it will follow the basic rules of tags described above (there may be other instructions that control the text, based on certain conditions).

Task bar A visual component of the Windows operating system which is usually located at the bottom of the screen and displays all currently running programs and tasks as icons. Clicking an icon with the mouse maximises the associated window. The task bar can be customised so that it is either permanently visible or automatically hidden when the mouse is moved away. It can also be moved to the top or side of the screen display. Other Windows user interfaces have a component which is equivalent to the task bar.

TCP/IP Transfer control protocol/internet protocol. The most common protocol used to communicate between computers.

Thermal printer Thermal printers, as the name suggests, use heat to form an image. They tend to be used for specialised printing such as labels and produce high-quality images. There are two different types: thermal and thermal transfer. Thermal printers work by heating up specially treated paper to form the image. One of the problems with this type of printer is that the image can fade with time, especially if placed in a fridge. Therefore, these printers should not be used for producing dispensary labels. Thermal transfer printers work by using special thermal ribbons. The print head transfers the pigment from the ribbon to the paper or label using heat. Special paper is not required for these printers and the image produced is of high quality and does not fade.

Title bar   A bar at the very top of a window which contains the name of the application and its current state. The title bar usually contains various control buttons that allow the window to be minimised and maximised. The arrangement of the title and buttons depends on the operating system being used. For example, Windows and MacOS have different arrangements and this contributes to the look and feel of the different systems. In most operating systems the window can be moved around the screen by clicking on the title bar and dragging to the required location.

TLA   Three-letter acronym. The computer industry is awash with acronyms, many of which are three characters long.

Toolbar   A series of buttons (icons) that perform frequent operations (as an alternative to selecting a menu option) and which are used in many Windows applications. The toolbar is typically placed under the menu bar, but in many systems is customisable by the user and placed in a location convenient for their use.

Tooltip   A message which is displayed when the mouse pointer is allowed to rest over a button (or icon) in a GUI interface. The message briefly describes the action that clicking the button will lead to.

Topology   The arrangement of connections between devices used to create a network. There are many possible arrangements or configurations, such as star, chain and ring.

Touch type   Touch typing is a technique in which the fingers are trained to hit particular keys while the typist is looking at the screen. Once the skill is learned the speed and accuracy of input are dramatically improved. Considering the time most people now spend using computers it should be considered an essential skill, and it is well worth the effort required to learn. There are many software applications that can be used to practice touch typing, many of them free.

Trojan horse   A Trojan horse is a malicious computer program similar to a virus that purports to be a normal program but which when executed causes damage to the computer, such as erasing the hard disk. A Trojan horse has no method of replicating itself. Most email viruses are Trojan horses, as they rely on the user opening them to execute the program.

Unix   Unix is an operating system that originated at Bell Laboratories in 1969 as an interactive time-sharing system. Ken Thompson and Dennis Ritchie are considered to be the inventors. Unix has evolved as a large freeware product, with many extensions and new ideas provided in a variety of versions by different companies, universities and individuals. Partly because Unix was not a proprietary operating system owned by any one of the leading computer companies and partly because it is written in a standard language and embraced many popular ideas, Unix became the first standard operating system that could be improved or enhanced by anyone. The majority of web servers making up the internet run on Unix. Linux is a Unix derivative which was developed to be used on PCs and is gaining in popularity.

UPS   Uninterruptible power supply. An auxiliary power supply which is usually connected to computer equipment so that in the event of a mains power cut, power to the computer is maintained. UPSs contain batteries that maintain the power for a defined period of time and are sufficient to cope with 'spikes' and brief cuts. They allow time for the computer to be shut down in a controlled manner if resumption of the mains power is delayed.

URL   Universal resource locator (URL) is a unique address that describes exactly where to locate a web page or other resource, such as a file or newsgroup on the World Wide Web. An example of a URL is http://www.pharmpress.co.uk/index.html. The first portion before the colon (:) is the protocol used to communicate with the web server. This will usually be http, to indicate that it is a web page. The portion following the double slashes and before the single slash is the domain name, which is translated into an IP address and uniquely identifies a machine. Further slashes then separate the folder paths on the web server. The text after the last slash will be the name of the target page. Other characters can be added after the target page name, which are known as parameters. These are used by programs on the server to determine how the page will react.

USB   USB is a standard that allows peripherals to communicate with the computer and was developed because of the limitations of serial and parallel ports. It is built into the motherboard of modern computers but can be provided on an expansion card for older computers. It is a relatively fast (12 Mbps) method of communicating. The cable can (but not always) supply power to low-power devices such as cameras, thereby removing the need for a separate power supply. Many new peripherals, such as printers, keyboards and mice, are manufactured to connect to the computer via a USB port. Peripherals can be daisy chained (if they have an input and output USB port), allowing multiple peripherals to be connected to one USB port on the computer. Some small devices such as cameras and phones have a smaller port known as USB Mini B, and are supplied with a cable which has a Mini B connector on one end and a normal-sized USB connector on the other.

One of the main advantages of USB is that when a device is plugged into the computer the operating system (on the latest versions of Windows, e.g. Windows XP) automatically detects the device that is connected and it can be used immediately. This is referred to as 'plug and play'. Pen drives use a USB connector to connect to the computer.

USB provides an expandable, hot-pluggable plug and play serial interface that ensures a standard, low-cost connection for peripheral devices. Devices suitable for USB range from simple input devices such as keyboards, mice and joysticks, to advanced devices such as printers, scanners, storage devices, modems and videoconferencing cameras. Migration to USB is recommended for all peripheral devices that use legacy ports such as the PS/2, serial and parallel ports.

USB 1.0/1.1 support data transfer at up to 1.5 Mbps for low-speed devices and up to 12 Mbps for full-speed devices. Microsoft, HP, Compaq, Intel, Agere, NEC and Philips are seven core members of USB-IF to have worked on USB 2.0 standardization. USB 2.0 will support up to 480 Mbps for high-speed devices. USB 2.0 is suitable for high-performance devices such as high-quality videoconferencing cameras, high-resolution scanners and high-density storage devices. In addition, USB 2.0 supports old USB 1.0/1.1 software and peripherals, offering customers impressive and even better compatibility. For more information on USB go to www.usb.org and click on the FAQ (frequently asked questions) link.

User interface   The method by which a user communicates with a computer. In a command line interface the user types in commands via the keyboard. The responses to the commands are normally displayed on the monitor as character-based text. In a graphical user interface the user uses the keyboard but also has a pointing device such as a mouse, which moves a pointer on the monitor display. The monitor displays windows, menus, buttons and icons, to which the user points with the mouse and then clicks the mouse buttons to action the commands.

Username   A username (sometimes called a user ID) identifies an end-user to a computer system or application where there are many users, such as in a hospital pharmacy system. A username is also required to log on to another computer, such as a network computer. The username is used in conjunction with a password to identify the user. Many systems use the username in audit trails to identify which user has performed a specific task or function, although this has to be specifically built into the application.

Vapourware   Vapourware is a term used to describe software that is talked about as though it is available but which does not actually exist.

Variable   A variable is the term given to a location that stores data. Each variable is given a unique name so that the contents of the location can easily be identified. Variables are used in programming languages so that data can be manipulated using the instructions, and can hold different values, hence the name. Variables are defined by a particular data type, depending on the type of data stored within them. For example, a variable called Number which is defined as an Integer data type can only store whole numbers. Variables defined as String data type can store text.

VDU   Visual display unit. A device that displays the output from a computer. Also called a monitor.

Version control   When software is made available publicly it is said to be 'released'. Each release of a particular software product will have a certain level of functionality. As time progresses software developers will include additional functionality and release a new version of the software. In order to keep track of the functionality included in software products, each release is given a version number. For example, Word, a popular word processor developed by Microsoft, is available in many different versions, e.g. '97, 2000, 2003. In this example the versions are indicated by adding the year as a suffix. There is no standard way of allocating version numbers, and each developer will use their own particular method. In many cases it is not obvious which version of a product is being purchased, so it is important to clarify this and to check the functionality it includes.

Virtual memory   Computers can address memory beyond that which is physically installed on the system. This non-physical memory is called virtual memory and is implemented by using part of the hard disk drive to emulate physical memory. This hard disk memory is usually stored in a single file called a page file. It is part of the operating system's task to determine when the virtual memory is used. If the size of the virtual memory is too small it can lead to degradation of the computer's performance.

Virus   A virus is a computer program that is capable of copying itself from one computer to another in the same way that a biological virus replicates itself in different hosts, hence the name. In the same way that a biological virus cannot exist in its own right and must use the DNA of a cell to replicate itself, so too does a computer virus by attaching itself to another program. Viruses are almost always written with malicious intent and for a specific operating system. The effects of a virus are dependent entirely on the aims of the programmer who created them, and can range from no noticeable impact to the total destruction of the machine by erasing the files on the hard disk drive. Many viruses remain dormant but replicate themselves on more and more computers until some event triggers their activation, such as a particular date in the future being reached.

Voice over IP (VoIP)   Voice over internet protocol refers to the use of computer networks to transfer voice telephone calls, rather than the standard telephone network. The voice data has to be digitised so that it can be sent as a data packet in the same way as any other network traffic. Software packages can be purchased which run on PCs and allow users to connect to other users with similar packages. This has the advantage that long-distance calls can be made at a fraction of the normal cost because they are not charged on distance or duration as with normal telephone calls.

VPN   Virtual private network. A mechanism of connecting to a private network via the internet which ensures that the data in the private network cannot be accessed by any computer in the public network. It has the advantage of connecting remote users to a LAN using standard internet connections.

WAN   Wide area network. A network that joins together computers or networks separated geographically by significant distances. These computers or net-works may be in different towns, countries or continents. The largest example of a WAN is the internet.

Web browser   An application program which is used to request and display information from the World Wide Web. The most widely used browsers are Microsoft's Internet Explorer, which is delivered as part of any new Windows operating system, and Netscape Navigator. The two main functions of a web browser are to request a web page from another computer whose URL has been typed in to the address field of the browser (if a hyperlink is clicked by the user this has the same effect); and to interpret the HTML page sent back by the web server and display it in the browser window.

Web browsers have many additional functions, such as the ability to download files, and can be enhanced with additional programs that allow video and sound to be played. Many applications, such as Adobe Reader, have functionality that allows documents to be viewed in the browser window with all the functions of the normal application. Clicking on a hyperlink that references an Adobe document, i.e. a PDF file, transfers the file from the web server and displays the document in the web browser window. If the PDF file is large this may take some time, and it sometimes appears as though the browser has stopped working.

Web server A computer networked to other computers running software that accepts requests for information from remote web browsers (e.g. Internet Explorer and Netscape Navigator). The information is displayed as a web page within the browser of the requesting computer.

Wi-Fi Short for **wireless fidelity**, and is meant to be used generically when referring to any type of 802.11 wireless network. Any products tested and approved as 'Wi-Fi Certified' are certified as interoperable with each other, even if they are from different manufacturers. Wi-Fi-enabled computers can connect with wireless access points, which allow them to access LANs. Their range is usually up to 100 metres.

Wildcard Wildcards are special characters used in search keywords that can represent any character or string of characters. For example, when searching for a file in Windows, the asterisk character is used as a substitute for zero or more characters. For example, if the file begins with something that is known, such as 'gloss', but the rest of the name cannot be remembered, type the following: **gloss***. This locates all files of any type that begin with 'gloss', including Glossary.txt, Glossary.doc and Glossy.doc. To narrow the search to a specific type of file, type: **gloss*.doc**. This locates all files that begin with 'gloss' but have the file name extension .doc, such as Glossary.doc and Glossy.doc.

Question mark (?) Use the question mark as a substitute for a single character in a name. For example, if you type **gloss?.doc**, you will locate the file Glossy.doc or Gloss1.doc but not Glossary.doc.

Windows The most commonly used operating system for PCs, developed by the Microsoft Corporation. Many versions of Windows have been released since the original in the early 1990s. These include Windows '95, Windows '98, Windows Millennium, Windows NT, and the latest version Windows XP. Each version has additional functionality packaged with it. Although strictly speaking the operating system is only concerned with controlling input and output, as outlined above, it will be delivered with various general-purpose applications, such as Notepad (a very basic word processor) and a calculator. Version naming, in Windows, is further complicated by the fact that different options are available for the same version. For example, Windows XP is available as the Home Version and the Professional Version.

Windows Explorer Windows Explorer is a fundamental part of the Windows operating system which allows the user to display and manage folders and files on the PC. When Explorer is started a window is displayed which consists of two panes. The left pane displays a view in a tree format of all the devices, such as hard disk drives, floppy disks, CD-ROM drives, network drives, and the different folders on each of the devices. Clicking a device or a folder in the left-hand pane expands the folder and shows its contents in the right-hand pane. The contents of each device or folder may have additional folders or files.

New folders can be created and files can be moved, copied or deleted. Double-clicking a file will usually result in the application that created the file being started and the contents of the file being displayed.

WinZip A widely used program which is used to compress files to make them smaller so that they take up less space. This means that they can be transferred over a network much more quickly than if they were uncompressed. The files have an extension of .zip.

Wireless access point A wireless access point is a piece of equipment that allows multiple users to connect to a wireless network or can act as point of interconnection to a fixed-wire LAN. This is useful for mobile workers who have notebook computers equipped with a wireless adapter. Many public places such as railway stations and hotels are starting to provide wireless access points, known as hotspots, so that users can access the internet. Wireless access points can also be purchased for the home environment and are relatively cheap (less than £100), thus enabling pharmacists with notebook computers to access the internet from home.

Wizard An interactive program which is used to guide the user through a complex configuration. The wizard will break the process down into a series of steps, which will be presented one at a time. Once the user has completed a step they usually click a 'Next' button to move through the steps until all are completed.

WMA Windows media audio. A streaming music file format developed by Microsoft which allows audio files to be played on PCs and WMA-enabled devices such PDAs. Other file formats that perform the same function are MP3 and RealAudio.

Word Word is a word processor which is part of the Microsoft Office suite of applications. Office's popularity stems from the fact that several of its applications are the best in their market. Word documents can be identified by the three-character file extension '.doc', which is automatically added to the end of any Word file name.

Word Pad A simple word processor that is delivered with the Windows operating system. It can be used to read documents created in Word with the '.doc' file extension.

Word processor A software application used to produce documents, e.g. reports, letters, etc. The word processor is probably the most widely used application on PCs. It allows all aspects of the document to be altered easily before saving and printing. If the document has mistakes or requires reformatting it can easily be recalled and modified and the changes saved and reprinted. The functions within word processors vary enormously. Notepad, which is included with the Windows operating system, is the simplest form of word processor, allowing the editing of text but very little formatting. Word Pad is also included with Windows and allows basic formatting of the text, whereas Word allows the creation of sophisticated documents that can include tables, graphics, table of contents, etc., but must be purchased separately.

Word wrap Used to describe the functionality in a word processor or text editor that automatically moves the cursor to the next line when one line of text is completely filled, so that the user does not need to keep track of line lengths and press the return key after each line. This means that if the text is moved to another location or the margins are altered, the word processor automatically takes care of the alignment.

World Wide Web This is a network of internet computers (servers) that support specially formatted pages known as web pages. The web pages can contain text, graphics, video and audio and support links to other web pages simply by clicking on a link, thus making it very easy to navigate and access other web pages. The pages are viewed through software applications called web browsers, e.g. Microsoft Internet Explorer and Netscape Navigator. The term World Wide Web and internet are often used interchangeably, but in fact are not the same. The internet is a massive network of computers which allows any computer connected to it to communicate with any other computer. This allows information to be exchanged in many different ways. The World Wide Web is only one of those ways: there are many others, such as email and FTP. Thus although the World Wide Web forms a significant portion of the internet, the two terms are not synonymous.

Worm A worm is very similar to a virus and is usually created with malicious intent. A worm copies itself from computer to computer by using the fact that almost all computers access a network. Using a network, a worm can expand from a single copy incredibly quickly. In July 2001 the 'Code Red' worm replicated itself over 250 000 times in approximately 9 hours. A worm usually exploits some sort of security hole in a piece of software or the operating system.

WYSIWIG 'What you see is what you get.' Used to describe the display of graphical-based applications such as word processors. The display on the screen is the same as will appear on the printed page. In the days before graphical applications, the screen display bore no resemblance to the printed output.

Index

Page numbers in **bold** indicate main discussion; numbers in *italic* refer to figures and tables.